from Charleston
11/99

CHARLESTON RECEIPTS
Repeats

Recipes compiled by
The Junior League of Charleston, Inc.

Additional copies of **_Charleston Receipts Repeats_** may be obtained by sending $16.95 plus $2.00 postage and handling to the address below.

Copies of **_Charleston Receipts_** may also be obtained by sending $14.95 plus $2.00 postage and handling to the address below.

Copies of **_Party Receipts_** may be obtained by sending $12.95 plus $2.00 postage and handling to the address below.

The Junior League of Charleston, Inc.
51 Folly Road
Charleston, South Carolina 29407
(803) 763-5384
FAX: (803) 763-1626

First Printing	October 1986	10,000
Second Printing	December 1986	20,000
Third Printing	November 1987	20,000
Fourth Printing	August 1988	25,000
Fifth Printing	June 1990	25,000
Sixth Printing	June 1992	30,000
Seventh Printing	October 1994	40,000

ISBN 0-9607854-5-0 © 1992 The Junior League of Charleston, Inc.

 The Junior League of Charleston, Inc. has selected a recycled paper for this edition in keeping with its commitment to the protection of our environment.

Paintings and Illustrations by William Jameson
Design by Lee Helmer Design

Printed in the USA by

WIMMER
The Wimmer Companies, Inc.
Memphis • Dallas

INTRODUCTION:

Some things about life in the Charleston area do not change — gracious entertaining, lively arts, and noble history.

In 1950, the Junior League of Charleston first published *Charleston Receipts,* a time-honored favorite among cooks around the world.

With *Charleston Receipts Repeats,* a new dimension is added to Lowcountry cookbooks — a collection of recipes that celebrates an abundance of fresh seafood and game, garden-grown vegetables and succulent fruits while keeping efficiency in mind.

This tempting assortment of recipes reflects the sophisticated elegance that has marked Charleston through its 300-year history as well as the casual elegance that is just as much a part of this area's heritage.

In 1994, *Charleston Receipts Repeats* was inducted into the Walter S. McIlhenny Tabasco Community Cookbook Award Hall of Fame.

The Junior League of Charleston, Inc.

The Junior League of Charleston, Inc. is an organization of women committed to promoting voluntarism and to improving the community through effective action and leadership of trained volunteers. Its purpose is exclusively educational and charitable. The Junior League of Charleston, Inc. reaches out to women of all races, religions and national origins who demonstrate an interest in and commitment to voluntarism.

Proceeds from the sale of **Charleston Receipts** and **Charleston Receipts Repeats** have been used to support the following community projects:

Arts in Education
Ashley Hall Women in Leadership
Base
Beginnings
Business Education Partnership
Carolina Youth Development Center
Charleston Museum "Discover Me" Room
Charleston Museum Library Restoration
Charleston Nursery and Day Care Center
Charleston Speech and Hearing Center
Comprehensive Emergency Service
Child Guidance Bureau
Children at Risk
Environmental School of the Year
Famous Artist Series
Guardian Ad Litem Special Project
Hands On
Heritage Mini Conference
Homework Helpers
Horizon House
Hospice
Housewise-Streetwise

I'm Special
Kids on the Block
"Lively Arts" Brochure and Calendar
Low Vision Book Fair
Lowcountry Children's Center
Middleton Gardens Tearoom
Mother's and Company
Music in the Schools
National Trust Conference
Our Charleston
Parent Youth Association
Pennsylvania Ballet
Roper Hospital Rolling Library
Safety Village
Sage Day
Saturday Soup Kitchen
Swamp
Teen Outreach
V.I.E. Project
Voluntary Action Center
Woman to Woman

TABLE OF CONTENTS

About the Artist

William Jameson was born in Honea Path, South Carolina. He grew up in Anderson, South Carolina, and moved to Charleston in 1962. He majored in Fine Art at the Ringling School of Art in Sarasota, Florida.

After serving with the US Army in Viet Nam, he studied graphics, sculpture, and jewelry design at the Instituto Allende, San Miguel de Allende, Mexico. There he also taught figure drawing and watercolor. He later returned to Charleston where he taught, painted, and exhibited until moving to New York City in 1974.

While living in New York, he had traveling group and one-man shows. His paintings were also used in Woody Allen's films, *Interiors* and *Manhattan*.

Mr. Jameson continues to paint and teach in Mt. Pleasant, S.C.

The Original *Charleston Receipts Repeats* Committee of The Junior League of Charleston, Inc.

Co-Chairmen:

Eunice S. Logan
Elizabeth L. Speights

Committe Members:

Patricia C. Alexander	Elizabeth W. Grimball	Hope H. Parker
Susan C. Burns	Virginia C. Good	Gaylord B. Paul
Molly Chilsolm	Beverly B. Gumb	Pamela Mc. Pearce
Cynthia D. Collins	Gray W. Hurt	Polly S. Player
Ann W. Dibble	Deborah F. Knowlton	Ann B. Smith
Nora Mc. Fowles	Barbara D. Lyles	Gayle R. Spears
Melissa T. Fox	Linda L. Martschink	Sally B. Wallace
Ann W. Gideon	Emma A. McLain	Janice D. Waring

6

APPETIZERS, SOUPS AND SANDWICHES

Behind the formal doors of many a side porch, you will find Charlestonians doing what they like best — enjoying good food and drink with good friends.

In spring, they enjoy the casual elegance of outside entertaining beneath drooping wisteria and overlooking gardens filled with azaleas in full bloom.

It becomes very clear why Charleston single houses were so designed. The long porches catch the prevailing breeze and carry garden scents up to the house. And the spacious proportions of the porches lend themselves to a grand gathering with silver trays, white-coated butlers and sumptuous hors d'oeuvres; or an intimate twosome sipping lemonade on the joggling board.

APPETIZERS

Lavington Plantation Venison Pâté
"Well worth the time and effort."

Complicated
Prepare Ahead

Makes: 7 cups
Bake: 1½ hours at 350°
Chill: 6 hours

1	pound bacon	1½	teaspoons salt
1¼	pounds venison	⅛	teaspoon pepper
¾	pound fresh (unsalted) pork fat	½	teaspoon thyme
2	tablespoons of butter	¼	teaspoon allspice
½	cup onion, chopped	¼	teaspoon tabasco
2	eggs	3	juniper berries, crushed
2	cloves garlic, crushed		(optional)
¼	cup cognac	3	tablespoons flour
¼	cup heavy cream	½	pound cooked ham, diced

- Preheat oven to 350° and set rack ⅓ from bottom of oven.
- Blanch bacon in simmering water for 5 minutes to remove salty flavor. Drain. Line bottom and sides of an 8 cup loaf pan or mold with a single layer of bacon strips so that strips overhang the sides (remove any extra pieces of bacon for later use). Set aside.
- Grind venison and fresh pork fat together in meat grinder or food processor. Set aside.
- Sauté onion in butter until tender. Set aside.
- In large bowl or food processor, combine eggs, garlic, cognac and cream. Add the meat mixture slowly.
- Add remaining ingredients and sautéed onions. Mix well.
- Pack meat mixture into lined mold and fold overhanging strips to cover top of pâté. Use reserved bacon slices to make sure pâté is completely covered. Seal the pâté with a double layer of aluminum foil.
- Place mold in pan of boiling water. Bake for 1½ hours in lower third of oven. During last 20 minutes, remove foil so top will brown.
- Pâté is done when internal temperature is 170° - 175° or juices are yellow (not pink).
- To assure firmness of pâté, place weight equal to 3 pounds on top of pâté (still in loaf pan) until cool.
- Wrap and refrigerate. Pâté will keep for 10 days or more tightly wrapped in refrigerator.

Mrs. John F. Maybank (Kay McCracken)

Chicken Curry Cheese Pie
"Elegant cocktail fare."

Average
Prepare Ahead

Serves: 35
Cook: 5 minutes
Chill: 6 hours

2 envelopes unflavored gelatin
1 cup milk
2 chicken bouillon cubes
2 eggs, separated
½ teaspoon Accent
2 teaspoons curry powder
3 cups creamed cottage cheese

2 tablespoons lemon juice
2 cups finely chopped cooked chicken
¼ cup chutney
2 tablespoons minced onion
1 cup whipping cream, whipped

◆ Sprinkle gelatin over milk in saucepan.
◆ Add bouillon cubes and egg yolks. Mix well.
◆ Place mixture over low heat and stir constantly until gelatin and bouillon cubes dissolve and mixture thickens slightly (about 5 minutes).
◆ Remove from heat; stir in Accent, curry powder, cottage cheese, lemon juice, chicken, chutney, and onion.
◆ Chill until mixture mounds slightly when dropped from a spoon.
◆ Beat egg whites until stiff, but not dry. Fold into gelatin mixture. Fold in whipped cream.
◆ Spoon into 8-inch spring-form pan or mold.
◆ Chill until set.
◆ Serve with melba rounds.

Mrs. G. Simms McDowell, III (Elsa Freeman)

Sausage Stuffed Mushrooms

Easy
Partial Prepare Ahead

Serves: 6-8
Bake: 15 minutes at 325°

1 pound hot sausage (bulk)
1 pound fresh mushrooms, cleaned and stems removed

1 8-ounce package cream cheese (softened)

◆ Brown sausage and drain well.
◆ Mix cream cheese and sausage.
◆ Stuff each mushroom with a teaspoon of sausage mixture.
◆ Bake for 15 minutes or until mushrooms are cooked through.

Margaret Meynardie

Ham Roll Ups
"No last minute fuss."

Average
Prepare Ahead
Freezes Well

Serves: 6
Freeze: 10 minutes

1   16-ounce package boiled ham in rectangular slices
1   package Roman Meal bread, square top, not round top
2   8-ounce packages cream cheese, softened
½   stick butter

1   tablespoon Worcestershire sauce
¼   teaspoon garlic salt
¼   cup green onions and tops, sliced
1   dash celery salt

- Trim crusts off bread.
- Mix cream cheese, butter, Worcestershire, garlic salt, green onions and celery salt.
- Spread small amount of cream cheese mixture on ham slice.
- Top with slice bread.
- Spread more mixture on this.
- Roll and place in freezer for 10 minutes until firm.
- Slice in ½ inch slices.
- Top with touch of parsley.
- Will keep in refrigerator for several days.

Mrs. D. William Wallace (Sally Benson)

English Muffin Yummies

Easy
Partial Prepare Ahead

Makes: 48-72 wedges

1   cup chopped black olives
½   cup chopped green onions
½   cup mayonnaise

1½ cups parmesan cheese
6   English muffins, split

- Mix first four ingredients.
- Spread on muffin halves.
- Cut halves into four to six wedges.
- Put under broiler until bubbly.
- Serve warm.

Mrs. Henry Lide DuRant (Kay Ravenel)

Ham-Asparagus Rolls
"Wonderful for lunch"

Easy
Partial Prepare Ahead
Serve Immediately

Serves: 4
Broil: 3 minutes

16 fresh or frozen asparagus spears, cooked
4 thin slices cooked ham

toast points
creamy cheese sauce

- Place 4 stalks of asparagus on each slice of ham and roll up.
- Secure with a wooden toothpick.
- Broil 3 minutes.
- Place ham on toast points and remove toothpick.
- Pour sauce over each roll.

Creamy Cheese Sauce

2 tablespoons margarine
2 tablespoons all-purpose flour
1 cup milk
½ teaspoon salt

⅛ teaspoon pepper
½ cup sharp cheddar cheese, grated

- Melt margarine in a heavy saucepan over low heat.
- Add flour, stirring until smooth. Cook one minute, stirring constantly.
- Gradually stir in milk and cook over medium heat, stirring until thick.
- Add salt, pepper, and cheese.
- Stir until cheese melts.

Mrs. Charles Talmadge Cole, Jr. (Joanne Gilmer)

Chutney-Cheese Pâté

Easy
May Prepare Ahead

Quantity: 1 cup
Chill: 2 hours

1 3-ounce package cream cheese, softened
½ cup (2 ounces) shredded sharp cheddar cheese
2 teaspoons dry sherry

¼ teaspoon curry powder
⅛ teaspoon salt
½ cup chutney
green onions, finely chopped (optional)

- Combine first five ingredients.
- Beat until smooth.
- Shape mixture into a ½ inch thick circle.
- Chill until firm.
- Spread chutney on top.
- Sprinkle with green onions if desired.
- Serve pâté with crackers.

Mrs. J. Stanley Claypoole, III (Barbara Pringle)

Garlic Chicken Rollups

Complicated
May Prepare Ahead
Freezes Well

Serves: 8
Bake: 15 minutes at 400°

2 chicken breasts, skinned and boned	½ teaspoon oregano
2½ tablespoons lemon juice	½ teaspoon dill weed
2½ tablespoons olive oil	½ teaspoon salt
1 teaspoon finely chopped garlic	1 stick butter
	½ pound phyllo pastry

- Cut chicken into one inch cubes.
- Combine lemon juice, olive oil, garlic, oregano, dill weed and salt in a small bowl.
- Mix well.
- Add chicken and cover to marinate overnight.
- Melt butter over low heat.
- Unwrap phyllo and cover with wax paper to keep from drying out.
- Halve phyllo lengthwise, forming 2 strips, about 6 inches wide.
- Take one strip, fold in half crosswise and brush with butter.
- Place 2 pieces of chicken at the short end and roll up to the midpoint.
- Fold both sides toward the center over the filling and continue rolling.
- Brush all over with butter and place seam down on cookie sheet.
- Repeat with remaining chicken and phyllo.
- Bake at 400° for 15 minutes.
- Roll ups can be frozen on a cookie sheet then transferred to a plastic bag before cooked.
- To cook, brush with additional butter and bake 400° for 20 minutes.

Mrs. Gregory A. Jones (Betsy Fant)

Butter Cheese Wafers

Easy
May Prepare Ahead

Yields: 4 to 5 dozen
Bake: 15 to 18 minutes at 350°

1 cup rice crispies	1 cup grated cheddar cheese
1 stick butter, room temperature	pinch salt
1 cup flour	dash tabasco

- Preheat oven.
- Blend butter and cheese. Mix in other ingredients.
- Pinch off marble-sized pieces.
- Place on ungreased cookie sheet.
- Mash balls flat with fork.
- Bake for 15-18 minutes at 350°.

Mrs. William A. Boyle, III (Grace Dibble)

Marinated Tenderloin In Cognac Sauce

Average
Prepare Ahead

Serves: 50
Bake: 4-5 minutes per lb. at 500°
Marinate: 12 hours

1 beef tenderloin, 5-7 pounds

- Preheat oven to 500°.
- Trim excess fat from tenderloin.
- Place trimmed tenderloin in an uncovered pyrex dish and cook 4-5 minutes per pound.
- When halfway through cooking time, remove tenderloin from oven and pour off excess grease.
- Return to oven for remainder of cooking time or until medium rare.
- When cool enough to handle, cut into ¾-inch cubes.

Marinade

1 cup red wine	1½ teaspoons fresh black pepper
1 tablespoon Worcestershire sauce	3 tablespoons lemon juice

- Mix together all ingredients.
- Add cubed tenderloin to this marinade and refrigerate at least 12 hours.

Cognac Sauce

½ cup chopped shallots	¼ teaspoon salt
3 tablespoons butter	1 teaspoon black pepper
⅔ cup cognac	2 teaspoons Worcestershire
¼ cup red wine	¾ cup beef bouillon

- Sauté shallots in butter over medium heat until tender.
- Add remaining ingredients and simmer for 10 minutes.
- To serve, drain the marinated tenderloin cubes and place in chafing dish.
- Pour heated sauce over them and serve with small rolls.

Mrs. W. John Langley (Hibernia "Mac" Cuthbert)

Savory Steak Slices

Easy
Prepare Ahead

Serves: 15
Marinate: 24 hours
Broil: 12 minutes

1½ pound flank steak
⅓ cup soy sauce
⅓ cup dark rum
2 tablespoons salad oil

¼ cup sliced radishes, watercress
sprigs - garnish
Assorted breads, lightly buttered

♦ Trim excess fat from steak and wipe steak with damp towel.
♦ Combine soy sauce and rum in large, shallow dish and place flank steak in mixture.
♦ Refrigerate, covered, turning occasionally for 24 hours.
♦ Remove steak from mixture and brush lightly with oil.
♦ Place steak in broiling pan and broil 6 inches from heat, 1 minute on each side, then 5 more minutes on each side or until medium rare.
♦ Let cool, occasionally brushing with pan juices.
♦ Use immediately or refrigerate, covered, until ready to use.
♦ To serve, cut steak into thin slices, on the diagonal. Arrange on serving board or platter and garnish with watercress sprigs and sliced radishes. Place basket of bread nearby.

Mrs. Robert H. Moore, II (Barbara Black)

Chicken Curry Cream Cheese Ball
"A different cheese ball."

Easy
Prepare Ahead

Yield: 1 cheese ball
Chill: 3 hours

1 8-ounce package cream cheese
1 cup cooked, finely chopped chicken
¾ cup almonds, toasted and finely chopped
⅓ cup mayonnaise

2 tablespoons chutney, chopped
1 tablespoon curry powder
¼ teaspoon salt
chopped parsley or flaked coconut

♦ In large bowl, mix first seven ingredients together.
♦ Chill several hours.
♦ Shape into a ball.
♦ Roll in parsley or coconut.

Mrs. William L. Strunk (Carol Koeller)

13

Won Tons
"All will appreciate the effort."

Average
Partial Prepare Ahead
Freezes Well

Serves: 12
Fry: 2-3 minutes

1 pound Won Ton wrappers	1 teaspoon salt
1 pound ground bulk sausage	2 green onions, chopped
1 egg, slightly beaten	4 teaspoons soy sauce
1 4-ounce can water chestnuts, minced	¼ teaspoon pepper
	½ teaspoon MSG
1 teaspoon minced ginger	oil for frying

♦ Cook sausage and drain.
♦ Mix with egg, water chestnuts, ginger, green onion, salt, soy, MSG & pepper.
♦ Put 1 teaspoon on center of wrapper.
♦ Fold into triangle and pull far points together, wetting the tips to stick.
♦ Keep wrappers moist by spreading out damp paper towels under wrappers.
♦ Fry 5-10 at a time in hot oil for 2-3 minutes in wok or frying pan.
♦ Serve with sweet and sour sauce.

Sweet and Sour Sauce

2 tablespoons corn starch (or) 1 teaspoon thick molasses	1 teaspoon sherry
¾ cup sugar	⅓ cup water
⅓ cup and 1 teaspoon vinegar	2 tablespoons soy sauce

♦ Mix all ingredients.
♦ Boil until thick, stirring constantly.

* May be frozen before or after frying. Red food coloring adds special touch to sauce.

Mrs. Daniel Ravenel (Kathleen Hall)

Asparagus Roll-Ups
"Different and tasty."

Easy
May Prepare Ahead
Freezes Well

Yield: 5 dozen
Bake: 15 minutes at 425°

20 slices white bread, crusts removed	dash tabasco
	dash Worcestershire
1 8-ounce package cream cheese, softened	dash lemon juice
4 ounces bleu cheese, crumbled	20 fresh asparagus spears
1 egg	½ cup butter, melted

♦ Flatten bread with rolling pin.

- Combine cheeses, egg, tabasco, Worcestershire and lemon juice.
- Spread mixture on each slice of bread.
- Place one asparagus spear on each slice of bread and roll up.
- Dip in melted butter and cut into thirds. (Can freeze at this point.)
- Place on ungreased cookie sheet.
- Bake at 425° for 15 minutes.
- Serve hot.

Mrs. G. Simms McDowell, III (Elsa Freeman)

Spinach Puffs
"A long time family secret"

Complicated
Partial Prepare Ahead
Freezes Well

Makes: 7½ dozen
Bake: 20 minutes at 350°

4	10-ounce packages frozen chopped spinach	2	teaspoons chopped dill
1	medium onion, chopped fine	1	teaspoon salt
3	tablespoons olive oil	¼	teaspoon pepper
8	ounces cream cheese, softened	½	teaspoon nutmeg
1	pound Feta cheese, crumbled	¾	cup fresh parsley, chopped
½	cup grated Romano cheese	¾	pound butter, melted
4	eggs, beaten	1	pound filo or strudel leaves

- Allow spinach to stand at room temperature overnight to defrost.
- Squeeze very dry using paper towels. (This is a very important step in making a good filling.)
- Sauté onion about 5 minutes in hot olive oil until golden brown.
- In large bowl, combine spinach, cheeses, eggs, dill, salt and pepper, nutmeg, parsley and onions - mixing very well.
*Note: This mixture may be refrigerated and used the next day. If refrigerated, allow to sit at room temperature for 45 minutes before proceeding.
- Cut filo into 4 x 12 strips.
- For each triangle, brush half the filo lengthwise with melted butter.
- Fold over other half of filo to make a 2-inch strip in width.
- Brush this strip wth melted butter.
- Place 1 teaspoon spinach filling at one end of strip and fold the strip diagonally until a triangle is formed.
- Place triangles on ungreased baking sheet.
- Bake in 350° oven for 20 minutes or until golden brown.
- Serve warm.
*Note: (To freeze) Place triangles in plastic containers, separating layers with wax paper, and place in freezer. When ready to serve, allow to defrost about 20 minutes and bake at 350° for 20 minutes, or until golden brown. May be frozen for at least 2 months.

Mrs. J. Michael Grayson (Hope Gazes)

Melt In Your Mouth Mushrooms
"They will go fast."

Easy
Partial Prepare Ahead

Serves: 8
Bake: 20 minutes at 350°

1 pound fresh mushrooms	1 teaspoon Worcestershire
1 8-ounce package of cream cheese, softened	1 teaspoon dill weed
1 cup grated Parmesan cheese	black pepper to taste

♦ Remove stems and wash mushroom caps in warm salted water. Drain on paper towels.
♦ Mix together remaining ingredients until well blended.
♦ Stuff each cap with approximately 1 teaspoon mixture.
♦ Place on cookie sheet and bake 20 minutes at 350°.
♦ Serve hot.

* May be microwaved for 2-3 minutes, but texture of mushrooms will be closer to a raw mushroom.

Mrs. Barnaby Henderson (Sue Allen)

Cheese Olives

Easy
Partial Prepare Ahead
Freezes Well

Serves: 12 +
Bake: 10-15 minutes at 400°

2 jars stuffed spanish olives	2 cups grated sharp cheddar cheese
1 teaspoon salt	1 stick butter
½ teaspoon paprika	
1 cup all-purpose flour, sifted	

♦ Drain olives well on paper towels.
♦ Blend butter and cheese with paprika and salt.
♦ Add flour.
♦ Wrap about 1 teaspoon dough around each olive.
♦ Place on cookie sheet.
♦ Refrigerate at least 4-5 hours before baking.
♦ Bake in 400° oven for 10 to 15 minutes.
♦ Serve warm.

* Hot dog cubes can be substituted for olives for a hit with kids.

Mrs. Arthur M. Taylor (Sarah Means)

Spinach Stuffed Mushrooms

Easy
May Prepare Ahead

Serves: 4-6
Bake: 20 minutes at 350°

20 medium fresh mushrooms	¼ teaspoon basil
2 tablespoons butter	½ teaspoon Worcestershire sauce
1 medium onion, finely chopped	salt and pepper to taste
1 garlic clove, minced	½ cup grated Swiss cheese
1 tablespoon flour	(optional)
½ cup whipping cream	3 tablespoons Parmesan cheese
1 10-ounce package frozen chopped spinach, cooked and drained	2 tablespoons bread crumbs

- Wash mushrooms in cold water.
- Remove stems from mushrooms, reserving 10 stems.
- Finely chop mushroom stems.
- Melt butter in medium saucepan over medium heat.
- Add chopped mushroom stems, chopped onion and garlic clove. Sauté until tender.
- Blend in flour.
- Stir in whipping cream, spinach, basil, Worcestershire sauce, and salt and pepper. Cook until slightly thickened.
- Salt inside of mushroom caps. Fill mushrooms with sautéed mixture.
- Sprinkle with mixture of Parmesan cheese and bread crumbs.
- Top with grated Swiss cheese (if desired).
- Put a thin layer of water in shallow baking dish.
- Place mushrooms in baking dish and bake 20 minutes.

Mrs. Lawton K. Grimball (Elizabeth Patience Walker)

Cold Artichoke Spread

Easy
May Prepare Ahead

Makes: 2 cups
Chill: 2 hours

1 can artichoke hearts	8 ounces sour cream
1 envelope Hidden Valley original ranch dressing mix	3 tablespoons mayonnaise

- Drain artichokes thoroughly.
- In bowl, break artichoke hearts into bite-size pieces with fork.
- Add package of dry ranch dressing; mix thoroughly.
- Add sour cream and mayonnaise and mix thoroughly.
- Chill and serve with crackers.

Mrs. J. Conrad Zimmerman (Barbara Hubbard)

Myra's Marinated Mushrooms

"Just put them on and let them cook. They are whole, firm and delicious."

Easy
Prepare Ahead

Serves: 25
Cook: 11 hours (yes 11 hours)

1   pound real butter
4   pounds extra large whole fresh mushrooms
1   quart burgundy wine
1½ tablespoons Worcestershire sauce
1   teaspoon dill weed
1   teaspoon ground pepper

1   tablespoon flavor enhancer (Accent)
1   teaspoon garlic powder
2   cups boiling water
4   beef bouillon cubes
4   chicken bouillon cubes
    salt to taste

♦ Combine all ingredients (except salt) in large pot.
♦ Bring to a slow boil on medium heat.
♦ Reduce to simmer and cook 5-6 hours with the pot covered.
♦ Remove top and cook another 3-5 hours until liquid reduces to barely cover mushrooms.
♦ Taste for salt.
♦ Refrigerate.
♦ Serve hot in a chafing dish.

Mrs. Larry J. Collins (Elizabeth Bamberg)

Spinach Dip

"Be creative with the serving bowl, such as a hollowed out red or green cabbage."

Easy
May Prepare Ahead

Serves: 50 +

2   packages frozen chopped spinach, defrosted
1   4-ounce package blue cheese
½   cup celery, chopped
½   cup bell pepper, finely chopped

½   cup spring onion, chopped
½   package Good Seasons garlic dressing
4   eggs, hard-boiled and chopped
1½ pints sour cream

♦ Let spinach thaw and drain well.
♦ Crumble blue cheese in a bowl and mix in spinach.
♦ Stir in celery, bell pepper, onion, garlic dressing and eggs.
♦ Blend sour cream gradually until easily spreadable.
♦ Serve with crackers or thick chips.

Mrs. Joseph L. Johnson, Jr. (Beverly Stoney)

Fresh Stuffed Mushrooms
"Low calorie"

Average
Partial Prepare Ahead

Serves: 8
Bake: 15 minutes at 350°

1 pound fresh mushrooms	½ teaspoon thyme
1 tablespoon lemon juice	2 ounces Monterey Jack cheese,
½ teaspoon herb season salt	grated
2 tablespoons chopped onions	½ tablespoon ground nutmeg
1 garlic clove	3 tablespoons chopped chives

- Wash mushrooms and break stems from caps.
- Put caps in a large skillet and season inside and out with herb salt.
- Add water to fill skillet ¼ inch.
- Add lemon juice.
- Cover and cook slowly - about 5 minutes. Cool.
- Grate or chop mushroom stems, onions and garlic.
- Put in small skillet. Add thyme and herb salt.
- Cover and cook on low heat until water has yielded from mushrooms about 5 minutes.
- Remove lid and cook until all moisture has evaporated, stirring occasionally.
- Add cheese and let cook until cheese is creamy.
- Add nutmeg and chives and stir until blended.
- Fill mushroom caps with stuffing mixture and reheat.
- Serve hot.

Mrs. Batson L. Hewitt (Ann Turner)

Sullivan's Island Olive Cheese Ball
"Good also as a sandwich spread."

Easy
Prepare Ahead

Serves: 30
Chill: 1 hour

8 ounces cream cheese, softened	12 green olives (with or without
1 stick butter, softened	pimentos), chopped
½ small onion, chopped	1 cup chopped pecans
16 black olives, chopped	

- Combine cream cheese, butter, onions and olives.
- Roll into a ball.
- Roll in pecans.
- Chill for 1 hour.
- Serve at room temperature with crackers.

Mrs. Bachman S. Smith III (Ann Bell)

Cheese and Chilies

Easy
Partial Prepare Ahead
Serve Immediately

Serves: 10
Bake: 30 minutes at 350°

2	eggs	4	ounces Swiss cheese, grated
2	tablespoons milk	4	ounces cheddar cheese, grated
2	4-ounce cans chopped green chilies, drained	4	ounces monterey jack cheese, grated

- Beat eggs and milk together.
- Add green chilies and mix well.
- Add grated Swiss and cheddar cheeses.
- Pour into 8 x 9 square pyrex dish.
- Sprinkle monterey jack cheese on top.
- Bake for 30 minutes or until bubbly and brown on top.
- Serve with crackers.

Kelley Warner

Cheese Bennes
"An old Charleston favorite"

Easy
Prepare Ahead
Freezes Well

Makes: 10-12 dozen
Chill: 3 hours
Bake: 10-15 minutes at 350°

½	pound sharp cheddar cheese, grated		pinch cayenne
¼	pound margarine or butter, softened	1¼	cup sifted flour
½	teaspoon salt	½	cup benne seeds (sesame seeds) roasted

- Cream first four ingredients together.
- Add flour and knead.
- Add seeds and knead.
- Form into four or five long thin rolls.
- Chill in wax paper several hours or freeze.
- Slice rolls into "thin dimes".
- Bake at 350° for 10-15 minutes.
- If desired, sprinkle with salt while hot.
- Keep in tightly covered tin.

Mrs. Hugh Cathcart (Peggy Simons)

Edna's Cheese Puffs

Easy
Partial Prepare Ahead
Freezes Well

Makes: 200
Bake: 5 to 8 minutes at 350°

40 slices white bread	1 cup mayonnaise
2 8-ounce packages cream cheese, softened	4 tablespoons chopped chives
	½ teaspoon cayenne
½ cup grated sharp cheddar cheese	½ cup grated Parmesan cheese

♦ Cut approximately 5 rounds per slice of bread with cookie cutter.
♦ Mix remaining ingredients together in order given.
♦ Spread on bread rounds.
♦ Bake at 350° on cookie sheet for 5-8 minutes or until brown.

* Cook 15 minutes longer if frozen.

Mrs. W. John Langley (Hibernia "Mac" Cuthbert)

Smoked Oyster Cheese Ball

Easy
Prepare Ahead

Yields: 1 cheese ball
Chill: 3 hours

8 ounces cream cheese, softened	½ teaspoon garlic powder
1 3.66 ounce can smoked oysters, drained slightly	1 teaspoon curry powder
	¾ cup chopped pecans
1 tablespoon Worcestershire sauce	

♦ In medium size bowl, combine cream cheese and oysters. (Use fork to mash oysters into cheese.)
♦ Add Worcestershire, garlic powder, and curry powder to oyster mixture. Mix well and form into ball.
♦ Pour pecan pieces onto a piece of wax paper.
♦ Roll oyster cheese ball in pecans.
♦ Refrigerate until hardened.
♦ Serve with crackers.

Mrs. Michael Eugene Piepenbring (Lee Caughman)

Pickled Oysters
"You better make more."

Easy
Prepare Ahead

Yield: 1 pint
Chill: 3 days

3 dozen fresh medium oysters
1 medium or 2 small red onions, thinly sliced and separated into rings
2 red cayenne peppers, halved and seeded

whole peppercorns
1 whole bay leaf
½ cup cider vinegar
½ teaspoon salt
tabasco sauce

♦ Shuck the oysters, reserving juice.
♦ Plunge into 3-4 cups vigorously boiling water. Remove from heat. Let stand for 5 minutes, Drain.
♦ In a pint jar, layer oysters, onions, peppers, and the peppercorns.
♦ Place the bay leaf about halfway up the jar.
♦ Combine vinegar, salt, and a dash or two of tabasco.
♦ Pour into jar.
♦ Refrigerate for at least 3 days.

Ben McC. Moise

Caviar Pie

Easy
Prepare Ahead

Serves: 20

2 teaspoons knox unflavored gelatin
¼ cup cold water
2 cups sour cream
2 cups small curd cottage cheese
¼ cup blue cheese, crumbled
1 package dry Italian salad dressing mix

1 bunch green onions, chopped
1 hard-boiled egg, chopped
1 4-ounce jar black or red caviar (or both)
1 cherry tomato, garnish

♦ In medium saucepan, dissolve gelatin in cold water. Then heat until clear.
♦ Add sour cream, cottage cheese, blue cheese and salad dressing mix. Mix well.
♦ Pour into greased quiche dish and refrigerate overnight.
♦ Prior to serving, flip molded pie onto serving platter.
♦ Top with green onions, boiled egg, and caviar. Garnish with cherry tomato rose in center of pie (if desired).
♦ Serve with crackers.

Mrs. Richard W. Hutson (Anne Smith);
Mrs. Joseph Shisko (Sallie Smith);
Mrs. Joseph Bucknum (Jane Smith)

Clam Dip

Easy
May Prepare Ahead

Serves: 10 +

1   8-ounce package cream cheese, softened
1   6½ can minced clams, drained, reserving 1½ teaspoons juice from can

4   drops tabasco sauce
1   teaspoon minced green onion
½   teaspoon Worcestershire sauce
3   teaspoons lemon juice

♦ Combine all ingredients in small bowl and mix well.
♦ Serve with crackers.

Mrs. Henry L. B. Ravenel (Shannon Wilson)

Salmon Shrimp Delight
"Delicious and elegant"

Average
May Prepare Ahead

Serves: 6

¾   pound smoked salmon (12-14 thinly sliced pieces)
¾   pound peeled, cooked shrimp (coarsely chopped)
¾   cup mayonnaise
3-4   drops tabasco
½   teaspoon paprika
½   teaspoon tomato paste (ketchup or seafood sauce may be substituted)

1   tablespoon heavy cream
12   thin slices buttered whole wheat bread
12- 14 wedges lemon
     lettuce

♦ In a bowl, combine the mayonnaise with tabasco, paprika, tomato paste, and cream.
♦ Stir in the shrimp and spoon some of this mixture in the center of each slice of salmon.
♦ Roll up the slices, encasing the shrimp mixture.
♦ Arrange on individual plates with lettuce, thin slices of buttered whole wheat bread, and 12-14 lemon wedges.

Cynthia B. Newman (by Ann Dibble)

Shrimp Mold Or Paste

*"A favorite from **Charleston Receipts** found at many a cocktail party."*

Easy
Prepare Ahead

Serves: 20-30
Chill: 4 hours

2 pounds shrimp, cooked and peeled
¼ pound butter
3 tablespoons mayonnaise
¼ teaspoon lemon juice

dash of mace
1 teaspoon Worcestershire sauce
2-3 drops hot pepper sauce
1 teaspoon salt
½ teaspoon pepper

◆ Grind shrimp fine.
◆ Rub butter and shrimp together, adding mayonnaise to soften slightly.
◆ Season with remaining ingredients.
◆ Chill mixture and serve with crackers.

* Celery seed may be used instead of mace.

Mrs. C. Stuart Dawson (May Hutson)

Shrimp Mold

Easy
Prepare Ahead

Serves: 25 +
Chill: 6 hours

12 ounces cream cheese
3 tablespoons mayonnaise
½ package unflavored gelatin
1½ tablespoons lemon juice
1 pound shrimp, cooked and finely chopped

½ cup finely diced celery
1 small onion, finely grated
1 tablespoon crushed parsley
1 tablespoon garlic salt
1 teaspoon salt
1 teaspoon pepper

◆ Dissolve gelatin in 2 tablespoons of cold water.
◆ Mix all ingredients together.
◆ Oil mold with 1 teaspoon vegetable oil.
◆ Pour mixture into mold.
◆ Refrigerate.
◆ To serve, garnish mold with fresh parsley, cherry tomatoes and fresh boiled shrimp.

* Crabmeat or clams may be substituted for shrimp.

Mrs. Earl Clayton (Janie May)

Marinated Lemon Shrimp

Average
Prepare Ahead

Serves: 15 +
Marinate: 8 hours

2 pounds shrimp	1½ teaspoons salt
3 cups beer	½ teaspoon pepper
1 cup water	dash tabasco
1 teaspoon salt	2 onions, sliced very thin
⅔ cup oil	2 lemons, sliced very thin
½ cup white tarragon vinegar	2 tablespoons capers with liquid
¼ cup fresh chopped parsley	

♦ Boil shrimp in beer, water, and salt.
♦ Drain shrimp and peel.
♦ In a small jar with lid, combine oil, vinegar, parsley, salt, pepper, and tabasco.
♦ Cover and shake well.
♦ In a large bowl, alternate layers of shrimp, onion slices, lemon slices and capers.
♦ Pour oil and vinegar mixture over all and marinate in refrigerator at least eight hours.
♦ Serve with toothpicks.

Mrs. Robert M. Hollings, Jr. (Marie Ferrara)

Marinated Shrimp

Easy
Prepare Ahead

Serves: 20 +
Marinate: 8 hours

3 pounds shrimp, cooked and peeled	2 tablespoons prepared mustard
1 large onion, sliced thin	2 tablespoons Worcestershire sauce
1 green pepper, cut into thin strips	1 teaspoon salt
1 cup vegetable oil	½ teaspoon pepper
2 cups ketchup	2 dashes tabasco sauce
1 cup cider vinegar	garlic powder to taste
2 tablespoons sugar	

♦ Combine all ingredients in a large bowl and mix well.
♦ Marinate for at least 8 hours in regrigerator.
♦ Serve in bowl with toothpicks and crackers on the side.

Mrs. C. Capers Smith (Anne Thomas)

Stuffed Shrimp

"This will make you popular with your guests"

Average
Partial Prepare Ahead

Makes: 25-35 shrimp
Broil: 3-5 minutes

1   1½ pounds large shrimp (25 count)

1   pound very thin sliced bacon

Crabmeat Stuffing:

1   pound crabmeat, picked for shells
3   teaspoons Worcestershire sauce
2   teaspoons dry mustard
2   tablespoons sherry

1   tablespoon mayonnaise
⅛   pound butter, melted
¼   cup lemon juice
10 saltines, mashed
   salt and pepper to taste

- Peel shrimp down to last joint above tail.
- Butterfly shrimp by cutting along vein without cutting all the way through.
- Wash and allow to drain.
- Combine all ingredients of stuffing, mixing well.
- Stuff shrimp with a moderate amount of crab mixture.
- Wrap in bacon and secure with toothpicks.
- Place shrimp on broiler pan and broil until bacon is crispy.
- Serve plain or with lemon juice squeezed over them.

Mrs. Michael T. Watson (Mary "Rusty" Thomas)

Smoked Fish Paté

Easy
May Prepare Ahead

Serves: 6

6   ounce piece of smoked fish (marlin preferred)
   juice of one lemon
1   cup mayonnaise, may need more if fish is dry

   dash of Worcestershire sauce
½   teaspoon tabasco sauce

- Grate fish in a bowl.
- Add lemon juice.
- Add mayonnaise.
- After thoroughly mixed, add Worcestershire and tabasco.
- Serve with crackers.

Mrs. Frank P. Rhett (Frances Cheshire)

Legaré Street Canapés

Easy
Serve Immediately

Serves: 15-20

1 8-ounce package cream cheese, softened
1 12-ounce jar cocktail sauce
½ pound fresh shrimp, cooked and peeled
1 4-ounce package Monterey Jack cheese, grated

6 green onions (tops included), chopped
½ bell pepper, chopped
½ cup chopped ripe olives
1 tomato, chopped and seeded

- Spread cream cheese on bottom of serving platter.
- Layer ingredients on top as follows: cocktail sauce, shrimp, cheese, green onions, bell pepper, olives, tomatoes.
- Serve with Melba rounds or crackers.

* ½ pound of crab can be substituted for shrimp.
* Cheddar or mozzarella cheese may be substituted for Monterey Jack.

Mrs. Felix Chisolm Pelzer (Carol Cole)

Pickled "Swimpee"
"Simple, delicious and attractive!"

Easy
Prepare Ahead

Serves: 8
Marinate: 24 hours

1 pound shrimp, boiled and peeled
3 large bermuda onions, cut in rings

3 green peppers, cut in rings
1 16-ounce bottle Catalina French Dressing
1 16-ounce bottle vinegar

- Alternately layer shrimp, onion rings, and pepper rings in a jar or container with tight seal.
- Pour equal amounts of dressing and vinegar over shrimp and vegetables.
- Seal container and marinate for 24 hours.
- Shake container occasionally to mix.
- To serve, drain off liquid and serve in large bowl with toothpicks.

* Mushrooms, artichoke hearts or cauliflower can be added.

Mrs. Isaac A. Speights, III (Elizabeth "Betsy" Lesesne)

Hot Shrimp Dip

Easy
Partial Prepare Ahead

Serves: 6-8
Bake: 30 minutes at 325°

1	8-ounce package cream cheese	½	pound fresh shrimp cooked,
¼	cup mayonnaise		cleaned and chopped
1	teaspoon grated onion		(or 1 4½ ounce can of shrimp,
1	teaspoon prepared mustard		drained)
1	teaspoon sugar		dash salt and garlic powder
3	tablespoons sherry	½	cup sliced almonds

♦ Melt cream cheese in double boiler.
♦ Blend remaining ingredients, except almonds, in blender or with mixer.
♦ Pour in soufflé dish.
♦ Add almonds on top.
♦ Bake 30 minutes at 325°.

Mrs. Frank Brumley (Blanche Cauthen)

Shrimp Paste

Easy
May Prepare Ahead
Freezes Well

Serves: 10 +
Bake: 30 minutes at 250°

1	pound shrimp, boiled	½	cup milk
	and peeled	1	teaspoon prepared mustard
¼	cup softened butter	1	tablespoon Worcestershire sauce
8	Ritz crackers		salt and pepper to taste
1	egg		

♦ Using a meat grinder, grind shrimp, butter, and crackers together.
♦ Add remaining ingredients and mix well.
♦ Pat into a loaf pan and place on a cookie sheet.
♦ Bake for 30 minutes.
♦ Serve cold or warm with crackers.

Mr. Eugene Frost Lesesne

Crab Dip

Easy
Prepare Ahead

Makes: 3½ cups
Chill: 2 hours

½ pound crabmeat
1 8-ounce package cream cheese, softened
½- ¾ cup mayonnaise
1 cup shredded cheddar cheese

1 small onion, grated
dash Worcestershire sauce
dash tabasco sauce
salt and pepper to taste

♦ In medium size bowl, combine all ingredients until well mixed.
♦ Cover and refrigerate at least 2 hours before serving.
♦ Serve with assorted crackers or make into small party sandwiches.

Ann Robbins Brackett

Hot Crab Dip

Easy
May Prepare Ahead

Serves: 15 +
Cook: 40 minutes

2 8-ounce packages cream cheese
½ cup milk
¼ cup chopped green onions
1½ tablespoons horseradish
2 teaspoons Worcestershire sauce

dash white pepper
dash salt
12 ounces crabmeat
2 tablespoons wine or sherry

♦ Combine all ingredients except crabmeat and wine in top of double boiler.
♦ Cook for 30 minutes.
♦ Add crabmeat and wine and cook for 10 more minutes.
♦ Serve with crackers or in pastry shells.

Mrs. Daniel Ravenel (Linda Compton)

Hot Crab Meat Canapé

Easy
Partial Prepare Ahead

Serves: 10 +
Bake: 30 minutes at 350°

1	can Alaskan crab meat
1	8-ounce package cream cheese
2	tablespoons mayonnaise
½	teaspoon curry powder

1	tablespoon Worcestershire
½	small onion, finely chopped
	juice of ½ lemon
	grated Parmesan cheese

♦ Mix together all ingredients except Parmesan cheese.
♦ Place in shallow baking dish and top with Parmesan cheese. Bake at 350° for 30 minutes.
♦ Serve hot with crackers.

Longitude Lane Crab Mold With Caviar
"A beautiful dish."

Average
Prepare Ahead

Serves: 20 +
Refrigerate: 4 hours or more

1	cup cottage cheese
1	cup sour cream
1	teaspoon lemon juice
1	teaspoon Worcestershire sauce
¼	teaspoon salt
2	envelopes unflavored gelatin
⅓	cup dry white wine, chilled

2	cups crab meat
3	eggs, hard-boiled
3	green onions, finely chopped
2	ounces black caviar
	lemon slices
	parsley

♦ In food processor, blend first 5 ingredients until smooth.
♦ In small saucepan, sprinkle gelatin over wine and let stand to soften.
♦ Over low heat, stir until gelatin dissolves.
♦ Stir into cottage cheese mixture.
♦ Gently add crabmeat.
♦ Pour into 10-inch quiche pan.
♦ Cover with wax paper and refrigerate until firm (at least 4 hours).
♦ Invert on serving platter.
♦ Grate eggs and sprinkle on top.
♦ Top with onions and then caviar.
♦ Surround with lemon and parsley.
♦ Serve with melba rounds or thinly sliced rye bread.

Mrs. Keating L. Simons, Jr. (Julianne Bell)

Crab Corners

*"Great and very elegant hors d'oeuvre to keep on hand
for unexpected company."*

Average

Prepare Ahead

Freezes Well

Serves: 8

Bake: 10 minutes at 425°

4	English muffins, split
7	ounces white or claw crab meat
1	jar Old English cheese
2	tablespoons mayonnaise
1	teaspoon garlic salt

½ cup butter or margarine,
softened
dash of tabasco or cayenne
pepper

♦ Lightly toast split muffins and set aside.
♦ Mix together well the crabmeat, cheese, mayonnaise, butter, garlic salt, and tabasco.
♦ Evenly divide mixture on 8 muffin halves and spread.
♦ Score each muffin half into fourths.
♦ Place on cookie sheet in freezer.
♦ When frozen, break into fourths and store in baggies in freezer until ready to use.
♦ Place frozen pieces on cookie sheet and bake 10 minutes in 425° oven.
♦ Serve hot.

* Use garlic powder instead of garlic salt for less salty taste.

Mrs. H. Brown Hamrick (Elizabeth Crawford)

Creamed Beef Dip

Easy
May Prepare Ahead

Serves: 10 +

1   2¼-ounce jar dried beef
½   cup boiling water
1   tablespoon margarine
¼   cup chopped onion
1   cup milk

1   8-ounce package cream cheese, softened
¼   cup Parmesan cheese
2   tablespoons chopped parsley
    French bread chunks

- Cut beef into small pieces and place in medium size bowl.
- Cover with boiling water and then drain immediately.
- In medium saucepan, melt margarine and sauté onion. Add drained beef, milk, cream cheese, Parmesan cheese, and parsley. Mix well.
- Serve hot with French bread chunks.

Mrs. Eugene Gaillard Johnson, III (Elizabeth Burns)

Hot Taco Dip
"Ole!"

Easy
Partial Prepare Ahead

Serves: a crowd
Bake: 30 minutes at 350°

1   pound ground beef
1   package taco seasoning mix
1-2 16-ounce cans refried beans
1   8-ounce carton sour cream
2   ounces Jalapeno peppers, puréed

4   ounces grated Monterey Jack cheese
4   ounces grated cheddar cheese
    taco chips

- Brown ground beef and drain.
- Add taco seasoning mix and refried beans and mix thoroughly.
- Spread mixture in deep 3 quart casserole.
- Layer remaining ingredients (omitting taco chips) in order listed.
- Bake until hot and bubbly.
- Serve with taco chips.
* Great on a very cold day.

Mrs. David Mc. Smythe (Ruth Conway)

Cold Mexican Dip
"Many layers of goodness"

Easy
May Prepare Ahead

Serves: a crowd

2 10½ ounce cans jalapeno bean dip
3 medium ripe avocados, peeled and mashed
2 tablespoons lemon juice
½ teaspoon salt
¼ teaspoon pepper
1 8 ounce container sour cream

½ cup mayonnaise
1 package taco seasoning
1 bunch green onions, chopped
2 medium tomatoes, peeled and chopped
1 can pitted ripe olives, chopped
8 ounces sharp cheddar cheese, grated

♦ In 9 x 12 dish, spread bean dip.
♦ Mix avocados, lemon juice, salt and pepper. Spread on top of bean dip.
♦ Mix sour cream and mayonnaise. Spread over avocado mixture.
♦ Sprinkle taco seasoning over sour cream mixture.
♦ Layer remaining ingredients in listed order over dip.
♦ Serve with tortilla chips.

Mrs. William McG. Morrison, Jr. (Felicia Howell)

Vegetable Dip
"Simple And Good"

Easy
May Prepare Ahead

Serves: 12 +

½ cup sour cream
½ cup Hellmann's mayonnaise
juice from 1 lemon

1 teaspoon Dijon mustard
¼ teaspoon white pepper
1 tablespoon dill weed (not seed)

♦ Mix all ingredients together.
♦ Cover and refrigerate until ready to serve.
♦ Top with a sprinkling of dill weed.

* This also makes an interesting cole slaw dressing.

Mr. Ben McC. Moise

Embassy Dip
"The scotch makes it!"

Easy
May Prepare Ahead

Serves: 12 +

1 cup mayonnaise
4 tablespoons ketchup
⅛ teaspoon cayenne pepper

dash Worcestershire sauce
½ ounce scotch

♦ Mix as listed above, adding scotch last.
♦ Serve with fresh vegetables or taco chips.
♦ Can be made ahead if kept chilled.

Mrs. William C. Prewett (Karen Padgett)

Upcountry Party Spread

Easy
May Prepare Ahead

Serves: 15

6 slices bacon
1 cup grated sharp cheddar cheese
1 cup Parmesan cheese

1 cup mayonnaise
¼ cup finely chopped onion
dash garlic powder
small bag slivered almonds

♦ Fry bacon until crisp. Crumble.
♦ Mix bacon and all remaining ingredients.
♦ Spread on crackers or Pepperidge Farm round party bread and toast, or not, as desired.

Mrs. Charles E. Montgomery (Louisa Miles)

Bombay Dip
"Easy and delicious with raw vegetables."

Easy
Prepare Ahead

Makes: 1 cup
Chill: 2 hours

½ cup sour cream
½ cup mayonnaise (or salad dressing)
2 tablespoons lemon juice

2 teaspoons grated onion
2 teaspoons sugar
1 teaspoon curry powder

♦ In a small bowl, combine all ingredients until well mixed.
♦ Cover and refrigerate at least 2 hours before serving.
♦ Serve with raw vegetables.
* May substitute plain yogurt for sour cream.

Kathleen Anderson

BEVERAGES

Fruit Parfait Punch
"Beverage or light dessert"

Easy
May Prepare Ahead
Freezes Well

Serves: 12
Freeze: 8 hours

4 ripe bananas
½ cup lemon juice
1 16-ounce can peeled apricots
3 cups sugar
1 16-ounce can crushed pineapple

1 small can frozen orange juice
  with 2 cans water
1 8-ounce bottle maraschino
  cherries, drained and chopped
  ginger ale

- Mash bananas.
- Add lemon juice.
- Mash apricots and add to bananas.
- Boil sugar and water.
- Add pineapple, orange juice, sugar water, and cherries.
- Mix well.
- Pour into plastic container with lid and freeze.
- Spoon into parfait glasses and pour ginger ale on top.

Mrs. F. Strait Fairey, Jr. (Charlotte Davis)

Fruit Punch

Easy
May Prepare Ahead

Serves: 20

1 10-ounce package frozen
  strawberry halves
1 ripe banana
2 6-ounce cans frozen orange
  juice concentrate

1 6-ounce can frozen lemonade
  concentrate
6 cups cold water
2½ cups chilled ginger ale

- Thaw strawberries.
- Place bananas and strawberries in blender on medium speed and process
  until smooth.
- Add to concentrated juices and water.
- Chill until ready to serve.
- Pour into punch bowl.
- Add ginger ale and ice.

Mrs. William J. Bates (Cheryl Dangerfield)

Orange Street Punch

"Refreshing party punch or delightful for breakfast."

Easy   **Serves:** 50
Freezes Well   **Freeze:** 6 hours

8   cups water   6   orange juice cans of water
2   cups sugar   ½   cup lemon juice
5   large bananas   2   quarts ginger ale
1   46-ounce can pineapple juice
2   12-ounce cans frozen orange
    juice

♦ Combine 8 cups water and 2 cups sugar in large boiler.
♦ Boil for 10 minutes, then let cool.
♦ Purée bananas in blender.
♦ Add pineapple juice, orange juice, water, lemon juice and bananas to the
  sugar syrup.
♦ Mix thoroughly and freeze in plastic containers.
♦ Add ginger ale at serving time. Garnish with fresh fruit.

* Orange juice mixture should be slushly when you serve it.
* Freeze in ½ gallon containers then microwave for 3 minutes before serving.

Mrs. William H. Johnson (Rebecca Cashwell)

Orange Julie

"Delicious and Nutritious"

Easy   **Serves:** 4
May Prepare Ahead
Freezes Well

1   6-ounce can orange concentrate   ½   cup sugar
1   cup milk   1   teaspoon vanilla
1   cup water   1   tray ice cubes

♦ Combine all ingredients and place in blender.
♦ Blend until smooth.

* May add orange liquor.

Mrs. Joseph Pepper (Linda Akin)

Spiced Tea

Easy
May Prepare Ahead

Yields: 45 cups

2 cups powdered orange drink (Tang)
1½ cups sugar
½ cup instant tea

1 small envelope unsweetened lemonade mix
1 teaspoon cinnamon
1 teaspoon cloves

♦ Combine all ingredients together and store in air tight jar.
♦ When ready to serve, add 2-2¼ teaspoons of tea in a cup and add boiling water.

Mrs. Dennis Lamson-Scribner (Julia Moseley)

Sherry Cooler
"Refreshing"

Easy
Serve Immediately

Serves: 1

⅓ cup white grape juice
⅓ cup cream sherry

⅔ cup ginger ale (chilled)

♦ Combine ingredients and pour over ice.

Elizabeth L. Cannon

Whispers
"Dessert, coffee and liqueur—all in one"

Easy
Serve Immediately

Serves: 6

2 ounces crème de cocao
2 ounces brandy

½ gallon coffee ice cream

♦ Place liqueurs in blender. Fill with as much coffee ice cream as blender will hold.
♦ Blend well.
♦ Serve in short glasses after dinner.

Mr. George C. Evans

Sewanee Rum Tea Punch
"Watch out!"

Easy   **Serves:** 100-150
Serve Immediately

1 20-gallon trash can (clean)	10 pounds sugar
3 gallons tea, brewed strongly	30 pounds ice
3 gallons dark rum	4 dozen lemons
9 16-ounce bottles real lemon	

For smaller quantities:

1 quart tea	1 cup sugar
1 quart rum	12 lemons

- Fill trash can half full.
- Pour in warm tea and dark rum.
- Blend together.
- In large bowl, combine sugar and real lemon and add to mixture.
- Slice lemon and add to mixture.
- Stir ingredients well.
- Keep plenty of ice on hand to add.

Mr. Edward Drummond Izard (Bru)

Windward Islands Rum Drink
"This is served throughout the West Indies"

Easy   **Serves:** 1
Serve Immediately

2 ounces light rum	3 teaspoons of sugar syrup (can
2 ounces grapefruit juice	be bought or made by heating
nutmeg	equal parts of sugar and water)
1/8 lime	

- In a short glass, combine rum, juice and sugar syrup.
- Fill glass with ice. Add lime and grate fresh nutmeg over top.

* Any type of juice can be substituted.

Mrs. J. Walker Coleman, Jr. (Anne Frizelle)

Walker's Rum Daiquiri

Easy
May Prepare Ahead
Freezes Well

Serves: 4-6

4 ounces concentrated limeade
1 ounce grenadine syrup

8 ounces light rum
  ice

◆ Place all ingredients except ice into 5-cup blender.
◆ Fill blender to the top with ice.
◆ Blend until smooth.

Mr. J. Walker Coleman, Jr.

My Father's Egg Nog

Average
Prepare Ahead

Yields: 5 pints
Chill: 1-3 days

6 fresh eggs, separated
¾ cup sugar, divided
1 pint cream
1 pint whole milk

1 pint mild blended whiskey
1½ ounces dark Jamaican Rum
  nutmeg

◆ Beat separately yolks and whites of 6 eggs.
◆ Add ½ cup sugar to yolks while beating.
◆ Add ¼ cup sugar to whites after they have been beaten very stiff.
◆ Fold whites into yolks.
◆ Add cream and whole milk. (For more stiffness, cream can be partially whipped.)
◆ Add whiskey and dark rum.
◆ Refrigerate using a glass container if possible.
◆ The flavor is best when aged for 3 days (will keep longer covered).
◆ Stir well before serving.
◆ Grate nutmeg in each cup.

Mrs. Edgar S. Jaycocks, Jr. (Lucia Harrison)

Wild Cocktail
"Rich and potent, a delicious dessert drink"

Easy   **Serves:** 1
Serve Immediately

1 shot crème de cacao   1½ shots half and half cream
1 shot crème de menthe   cracked ice
1 shot Kahlua

♦ Combine all ingredients in cocktail shaker.
♦ Shake thoroughly and enjoy.

Mrs. Joanna M. Millis (Jody Morgan)

Powerful Punch

Easy   **Serves:** 24
May Prepare Ahead
Freezes Well

½ cup benedictine   1 cup unsweetened pineapple
1 cup grenadine liqueur   juice
1 6-ounce can frozen pink   2 bottles champagne, chilled
  lemonade   cherries and pineapple slices for
2 cups orange juice   garnish

♦ Mix benedictine and grenadine in 4 quart punch bowl.
♦ Add champagne just before serving.
♦ Mix lemonade, pineapple juice and orange juice together.
♦ Pour into mold, garnish, and freeze to make ice mold.

Mr. James J. Ravenel, III

Fireside Amaretto

Easy   **Serves:** 1
Serve Immediately

1 cup almond Amaretto coffee whipping cream
1 scoop vanilla ice cream   toasted almonds
1 tablespoon Amaretto

♦ Put scoop of ice cream in a large mug.
♦ Pour hot coffee in, and then add Amaretto to mug.
♦ Top with whipped cream and almonds.

Ann W. Dibble

Jo Vincent's Wedding Punch

Easy
May Prepare Ahead

Yields: 2 gallons

½ gallon bourbon (or vodka)
½ gallon white port
2 large cans frozen lemonade,
(undiluted)

5 bottles soda water
ice ring–optional

♦ Combine first 3 ingredients and chill.
♦ Add chilled soda water just before serving.
♦ May serve from punch bowl with floating ice ring or from a pitcher.

Mrs. James Alden Huggins (Marsha Hemphill)

Peach Cooler
"Have plenty on hand."

Easy
May prepare ahead
Freezes well

Serves: 4

5 medium peaches (unpeeled),
quartered

1 6-ounce can frozen lemonade
concentrate
6 ounces vodka or gin

♦ Combine all ingredients in blender and fill with ice cubes.
♦ Blend and serve.
♦ Garnish with fresh mint.

Mrs. Harris Thaxton (Lavinia Mikell)

SOUPS

Vegetable Soup
"A Good Basic."

Easy
May Prepare Ahead

Serves: 8
Cook: 1½ hours

7   cups chicken or beef or
    vegetable stock
5   cups diced or sliced vegetables
    Can use any combination of the
    following: potatoes, carrots,
    corn, green beans, lima beans,
    broccoli, celery, cauliflower,
    cabbage, squash.

½   cup uncooked pasta or rice
1   bay leaf
½   teaspoon basil (dried)
⅛   teaspoon thyme (dried)
    salt and pepper to taste

♦ In large saucepan or stockpot, bring stock to a boil.
♦ Add vegetables, herbs, salt and pepper to stock.
♦ Simmer 30 minutes to 1 hour or longer.
♦ Serve steaming hot.

Emma A. McLain

Vegetable Beef Soup
"Great for a Crowd or Your Freezer"

Average
May Prepare Ahead
Freezes Well

Yields: 12 quarts
Cook: 2½ hours

1   18-ounce can tomato paste
1   12-ounce can tomato paste
4   pounds rump roast, cut in
    ½" cubes
1   large bunch celery with leaves,
    diced fine
1   1-pound bag carrots, diced fine
4-5 large green peppers, diced fine
6   small new potatoes, unpeeled,
    diced

1   large bunch fresh parsley,
    minced
4   large yellow onions, diced fine
    handful fresh basil, minced
2   2¼-pound bags frozen mixed
    vegetables
3   tablespoons imported paprika
    salt
    pepper
1   quart water

♦ Whisk 2 cans tomato paste in large soup pot with one quart water until
smooth. Add remaining ingredients. Bring to a boil. Allow soup to simmer 2½
hours stirring often.
♦ Add water to desired consistency.

Mrs. Glen O'Grady (Janie Bruckbauer)

Crab Stew

Easy
May Prepare Ahead
Freezes Well

Serves: 8
Cook: 30 minutes

1	medium onion, grated	1	tablespoon prepared mustard
¼	pound butter	1	tablespoon Worcestershire sauce
1	pound crab claw meat		dash tabasco sauce
10	cups milk		garlic salt to taste
½	cup flour		sherry to taste

- Sauté onion in butter until clear. Add crab meat and continue sautéing for 3 additional minutes.
- In separate bowl combine milk, flour, mustard, Worcestershire sauce, tabasco sauce, and garlic salt.
- Combine all ingredients and cook over medium heat.
- Stir constantly until mixture begins to boil.
- Re-heat in double boiler or microwave. Add sherry to taste.

Mrs. James Walker Coleman, Jr. (Anne Frizelle)

Tom Chason's Easy Italian Fish Stew
"A family favorite of the Lowcountry"

Easy
Serve Immediately

Serves: 6-8
Cook: 1 hour

3	pounds of fish, chopped	1	cup white wine
4	bell peppers, chopped	6	tomatoes, chopped
3	cloves garlic, crushed	¼	cup olive oil
2	pounds new potatoes, sliced	1	bunch parsley, chopped

- Place all ingredients in large pot and cook on medium high for about 20-30 minutes. Reduce heat to simmer and cook for 30 minutes.

Mrs. William Tamsberg (Merle Sparkman)

Chili

Easy
May Prepare Ahead

Serves: 10
Cook: 2½ hours

2	pounds hamburger meat		dash cayenne
3	bell peppers		salt and pepper to taste
3	onions, chopped	3	cans red kidney beans
1	clove garlic, crushed		dash tabasco
4	cans tomatoes, chopped	2	bay leaves
3	tablespoons chili powder		

♦ Brown hamburger meat in skillet and drain.
♦ Add remaining ingredients (except kidney beans) and simmer uncovered 2-3 hours.
♦ Add kidney beans.
♦ Cook another 10 minutes to allow beans to heat through.

Mrs. Robert M. Hollings, Jr. (Marie Ferrara)

Corn Chowder

Easy
May Prepare Ahead
Freezes Well

Serves: 8
Cook: 20 minutes

5	slices of bacon, chopped	3	cups milk
1	large onion, diced	2	teaspoons sugar
4	potatoes, diced	¼	cup margarine
1	cup water	2½	teaspoons salt
2	10-ounce packages frozen corn	¼	teaspoon pepper

♦ Cook bacon and remove from pan.
♦ Sauté onions in bacon grease.
♦ Drain grease.
♦ Add potatoes and water. Cook 10 minutes.
♦ Add remaining ingredients. Cook over low heat for 10 minutes.
♦ Serve in bowls with bacon crumbled over top.

Mrs. Joseph Pepper (Linda Akin)

Broccoli Bisque
"Can be served hot or cold"

Easy
May Prepare Ahead

Serves: 4
Cook: 20 minutes

1- 1½ pounds fresh broccoli, trim and cut or 2 packages of frozen
2 10-ounce cans Campbells chicken broth
1 can water

1 medium onion, quartered
1 teaspoon salt
1 teaspoon curry powder
2 tablespoons lemon or lime juice
10 ounces lowfat milk

- Cook broccoli until tender.
- Mix with broth, water, onion, salt and curry powder.
- Put mixture into blender in two batches and blend until smooth.
- Pour mixture back into pot and stir in lemon or lime juice and milk.
- Garnish with lemon slice.

Mrs. E.B. Rogers (Jean Richards)

Cream Of Broccoli Soup

Easy
May Prepare Ahead

Serves: 4
Cook: 30 minutes

1 bunch fresh broccoli or 2 (10 ounce) packages frozen broccoli onion
3 cups chicken stock
½ onion, chopped
4 tablespoons butter

5 tablespoons flour
1 pint half and half cream
salt and white pepper to taste
garnish: paprika, croutons, and parsley

- Cook broccoli and onion in stock until soft.
- Place in blender and blend quickly. Leave small pieces of broccoli.
- Using butter and flour, make a roux. Stir constantly until thickened.
- Add broccoli mixture to the roux, stirring constantly to prevent lumps.
- Thin with cream until desired consistency. Add salt and pepper.
- Garnish.

Mrs. Robert W. Pearce, Jr. (Pam McCain)

Cucumber Soup
"A Summer Hit."

Easy
May Prepare Ahead

Serves: 4
Cook: 30 minutes

4 cucumbers, seeded, chopped, and peeled
1 large onion
2 tablespoons butter
3 cups chicken broth

2 tablespoons lemon juice
1 cup yogurt
salt and pepper
dill

♦ Sauté cucumbers and onion in butter over low heat until soft.
♦ Add broth, bringing to a boil and simmer.
♦ Pureé soup in blender and add lemon juice.
♦ Cool slightly and add yogurt.
♦ Salt and pepper to taste.
♦ Chill and add dill just before serving.

* Float a slice of cucumber to identify the soup.

Mrs. Henry L. B. Ravenel (Shannon Wilson)

Strawberry Soup
"A beautiful first course."

Easy
Prepare Ahead

Serves: 6
Cook: 25 minutes
Chill: 2 hours

1½ cups water
¾ cup light red wine
½ cup sugar
2 tablespoons lemon juice

1 quart strawberries, hulled and pureéd
½ cup heavy cream, whipped
¼ cup sour cream

♦ Combine water, wine, sugar and lemon juice.
♦ Boil 15 minutes, stirring occasionally.
♦ Add strawberries and boil 10 minutes more, stirring frequently.
♦ Cool to lukewarm.
♦ Combine whipped cream and sour cream and fold into strawberry mixture.
♦ Chill well.

Mrs. Lloyd Arthur Pearson (Margaret Ann Boyd)

Gazpacho

"This may be served in glasses as a first course, before your guests are seated."

Easy
Prepare Ahead

Serves: 6
Chill: 2 hours

1½ cups chopped fresh tomatoes
½ cup chopped green pepper
¼ cup canned sliced beets, drained
¼ cup chopped celery
½ cup chopped cucumber
2 tablespoons chopped onion
1 chopped garlic clove

1 teaspoon salt
⅛ teaspoon tabasco
1 tablespoon paprika
½ teaspoon basil
½ cup beef consomme
½ cup red wine vinegar
½ cup reputable olive oil

♦ Place tomatoes into blender and mix. Add other ingredients in order slowly. Mix well. Chill until very cold.

Mrs. J. Addison Ingle (Helen Garvin)

Cold Fresh Tomato Soup
"Refreshing"

Easy
May Prepare Ahead

Serves: 8
Chill: 2 hours

12 ripe tomatoes
2 onions
1½ teaspoons salt
1 teaspoon black pepper

1 tablespoon sugar
1 teaspoon basil
1 carton sour cream, for garnish

♦ Peel tomatoes after dropping into boiling water for 1 minute.
♦ Place tomatoes into food processor.
♦ Add onion, salt, pepper, sugar and basil.
♦ Chill thoroughly.
♦ Garnish with spoonful of sour cream.

Mrs. R. Edward L. Holt, III (Kitty Trask)

Vichyssoise
"Great for weekend guests for lunch or dinner"

Average
May Prepare Ahead
Freezes Well

Serves: 6

5 leeks, white part sliced
¼ cup butter
5 medium sized potatoes (Idaho) peeled and sliced
1 carrot, sliced
1 quart chicken stock

1 teaspoon salt
2 cups milk
3 cups cream (half and half)
¼ teaspoon cayenne
½ teaspoon nutmeg

- Sauté leeks in butter.
- Add potatoes, carrot, stock, and salt. Bring to a rapid boil.
- Cover and reduce heat. Simmer until potatoes and carrots are soft.
- Pureé above mixture well.
- Return to heat and add milk.
- Season to taste with salt, cayenne, and nutmeg.
- Cool.
- Stir in 1 cup cream.
- Refrigerate or freeze at this point.
- Before serving stir in 2 cups of cream.
- Serve chilled in cups with chives.

Mrs. Geoffrey S. Parker (Kearby Bon)

Pank's Cold Avocado Soup
"Rich Taste"

Easy
May Prepare Ahead

Serves: 6 to 8
Chill: 4 hours

1   large avocado
1   10-ounce can consomme
    several dashes hot sauce

3   tablespoons lemon juice
1   pint sour cream
    chopped parsley or chives

- Peel and pit avocado.
- Cut into small pieces and place in blender along with consomme, hot sauce, and lemon juice.
- Blend well and add sour cream and blend in with first mixture.
- Chill in refrigerator, several hours.
- Serve cold with chopped parsley or chives.

Mrs. Thomas A. Huguenin (Mary Vereen)

Zucchini Soup

Easy
May Prepare Ahead

Yields: 1 quart
Cook: 30 minutes

1   pound zucchini, thinly sliced
1   onion, chopped
1   tablespoon margarine
2   cups chicken stock

½   teaspoon curry
½   teaspoon lemon juice
    salt
    chives

- Cook zucchini and onion in margarine, in covered frying pan for 10 minutes or until tender.
- Combine with stock, curry and lemon juice and blend in blender. (May need to divide in half to blend.)
- Add salt and chives to taste.
- Chill 2 hours before serving. Stir well.

Elizabeth Cleveland

SANDWICHES

Louise's Spinach Sandwich

Easy
Partial Prepare Ahead

Yields: 10 sandwiches
Chill: overnight

2   packages chopped spinach
    (frozen)
1   package Knorr vegetable
    soup mix
½   cup mayonnaise

1   carton (6 or 8 ounce)
    plain yogurt or sour cream
1   can water chestnuts, chopped
1   loaf thin sliced wheatbread

♦ Combine spinach, soup mix, mayonnaise, yogurt, and chestnuts. Let set over-
  night in refrigerator.
♦ Prior to serving, spread thin sliced bread with mayonnaise, lightly.
♦ Place one tablespoon spinach mixture on slice of bread.
♦ Serve cut in squares or triangles.

Mrs. Edward Wilson Riggs (Becky Turner)

Crunchy Cheese Sandwiches
"For party fare, serve open face"

Easy
May Prepare Ahead

Yield: 1½ cups

1   cup (4 ounces) cheddar cheese,
    shredded
1   (3-ounce) package
    cream cheese, softened
2   tablespoons Parmesan cheese
2   tablespoons milk
2   tablespoons sour cream
2   tablespoons fresh lemon juice

½   teaspoon prepared horseradish
½   teaspoon seasoned salt
⅓   cup celery, chopped
⅓   cup pecans, chopped
    lettuce
    whole wheat bread, buttered
    (or party rounds)

♦ Place cheese, milk, sour cream, lemon juice, horseradish and seasoned salt in
  blender container.
♦ Cover and mix until smooth and well blended.
♦ By hand, stir in celery and nuts.
♦ Store, covered, in refrigerator for up to one month.

Mrs. H. Parker Jones (Josephine Neil)

Vegetable Sandwich Spread
"Also an excellent spread for crackers"

Easy
Prepare Ahead

Yield: 3 cups
Chill: 3 hours

1	envelope gelatin	1	small onion
¼	cup water	1	teaspoon salt
1	cup celery	1	teaspoon lemon juice
2	cucumbers peeled and seeded	2	cups mayonnaise
2	carrots		

♦ Dissolve gelatin in water. Warm to activate.
♦ Pureé all vegetables in food processor.
♦ Add all other ingredients.
♦ Chill for approximately 3 hours or until mixture is well set.

Mrs. Thomas E. Myers (Elizabeth Norcross)

Janice's Beach Sandwich

Average
Partial Prepare Ahead

Serves: 4

6	medium ripe tomatoes, sliced		mayonnaise
⅓	cup olive oil		Alfalfa sprouts, washed
2	tablespoons dried dill weed or		and drained
	⅓ cup fresh dill	4	six inch pita bread pockets
1	teaspoon salt	8	slices honey baked ham,
3	medium avocados, sliced		spiral cut

♦ Slice tomatoes and marinate in mixture of olive oil, dill weed, and salt a day ahead.
♦ Slice each bread round in half and spread evenly with mayonnaise.
♦ Toast until brown.
♦ Fill pockets with ham, avocados, tomatoes, and alfalfa.

Mrs. Thomas Waring (Janice Duffie)

Ham Delights
"Perfect for those who plan ahead"

Easy
May Prepare Ahead
Freezes Well

Yield: 72 rolls
Bake: 10 minutes at 400°

2½ cups margarine, softened	¾ pound boiled ham, shredded
3 tablespoons mustard	⅔ pound Swiss cheese, grated
3 tablespoons poppy seeds	4 packages Pepperidge Farm
1 medium onion, chopped finely	party rolls
1 teaspoon Worcestershire sauce	

♦ Combine margarine, mustard, poppy seeds, onion and Worcestershire sauce.
♦ Combine ham and cheese seperately.
♦ Slice open party rolls. Spread both sides of rolls with mixture.
♦ Add ham and cheese.
♦ Wrap stuffed rolls in foil. Store in refrigerator until ready to heat.
♦ Bake 10 minutes at 400°

Judy Still Brasel

Cheese Dreams

Easy
Serve Immediately

Serves: 1
Bake: 30 minutes at 350°

1 slice bread	1 strip bacon
1 slice cheese	dry mustard
1 slice onion (thin)	

♦ Place cheese on bread.
♦ Sprinkle dry mustard of mild flavor over the cheese.
♦ Add onion and bacon.
♦ Bake in oven slowly at 350° for 30 minutes.
♦ Just before serving, turn oven to broil and let bacon get crisp.

Mrs. W. Hampton Logan, Jr. (Virginia Watson)

Delicious Hot Sandwich
"May be used for brunch or hors d'oeuvre."

Easy
Prepare Ahead

Yield: 1 loaf
Bake: 15 minutes at 350°

1 small jar sharp Ole English Cheese spread	¼ pound margarine
1 egg	¼ pound butter
	1 loaf bread, thin sliced white

- Combine first 4 ingredients.
- Beat until fluffy and spread between 2 slices of bread.
- Press slices together and trim bread crusts.
- Cover all sides with mixture.
- Cut bread to make 4 small squares.
- Cover edges with mixture.
- Place in refrigerator for 8 to 12 hours.
- When ready to serve, bake on greased cookie sheet for 15 minutes at 350°.

Mrs. Charles B. Anderson (Emee Marjenhoff)

Chicken Pita Sandwich

Average
Partial Prepare Ahead

Serves: 8
Bake: 4 minutes at 400°

1	whole chicken, boiled and chopped		pepper
			dillweed
¼	pound Swiss cheese, grated		lemon juice
3	stalks celery, chopped		mayonnaise
1	can water chestnuts, sliced	8	pita bread pockets
	salt		

- Combine chicken, cheese, celery, chestnuts, salt, pepper, dill, and lemon juice.
- Add mayonnaise to desired consistency.
- Stuff mixture into pita bread pockets.
- Heat at 400° for 4 minutes.

Mrs. John H. Warren (Helen Smith)

Monte Cristo Sandwich
"A delicious hot sandwich"

Average
Serve Immediately

Serves: 1
Fry: 2 minutes
Bake: 7 to 8 minutes at 350°

2	slices ham	2	slices white bread
2	slices American cheese	2	tablespoons butter
1	slice turkey (chicken optional)	1	egg, beaten

- Place ham, cheese and turkey on bread.
- Slightly butter each half (mayonnaise optional).
- Press together, trim and cut in half.
- Melt butter in electric fry pan at 300°, dip the sandwich in beaten egg.
- Put halves together and fry in hot butter for 2 minutes only, on each side.
- Place on baking sheet and put in pre-heated oven for 7 or 8 minutes.

Mrs. Charles B. Anderson (Emee Marjenhoff)

Pizza

"Not hard, but takes time and well worth it."

Complicated
Serve Immediately

Yield: 4 10-inch pizzas
Bake: 10-15 minutes at 500°

Dough

2	tablespoons yeast	2½ cups whole wheat flour
1¼	cups warm water	1 cup soy flour (or whole wheat flour)
1	teaspoon honey	
¼	cup olive oil	1-2 tablespoons corn meal (for dusting pans)
1	teaspoon salt	

♦ Dissolve yeast in water with honey.
♦ Mix oil, salt and flour.
♦ Combine two mixtures.
♦ Knead and let rise 1½ hours.
♦ Punch down.
♦ Dust pans with corn meal.
♦ Make crusts ⅛-inch thick, pinching rims.

Sauce

3	tablespoons olive oil	1 tablespoon basil
1	cup onions, chopped	1 bay leaf
1	tablespoon garlic, minced	2 teaspoons honey
4	cups tomatoes	1 tablespoon salt
1	small can tomato paste	pepper to taste
1	tablespoon oregano	

♦ Sauté onion and garlic in oil.
♦ Add remaining ingredients and simmer uncovered 1 hour.
♦ Use ½ cup sauce for each pizza.

Topping

2	cups mozzarella cheese
2	tablespoons Parmesan cheese

other garnishes

♦ Add ½ cup sauce to each pizza crust.
♦ Layer with ½ cup mozzarella cheese then 2 tablespoons Parmesan cheese per pizza.
♦ Add topping(s) of your choosing.
♦ Bake 10-15 minutes at 500°.

Mrs. Robert M. Hollings, Jr. (Marie Ferrara)

Nowhere is the living easier than at Sullivan's Island in the summer.

Families lock up their city houses, spread white sheets on the furniture and retreat across the bridges to a life of sandy beaches, salty breezes, daily strolls and informal gatherings.

It's time for crabbing, swimming and sunning. It's time for sitting on the porch and watching the tensions disappear. And it's time for casual picnics and barbeques.

It's overhead fans instead of air-conditioning; Bermuda shorts instead of suits; and rocking chairs that wet bathing suits can't stain. It's not a resort, and Sullivan's Islanders wouldn't have it any other way.

CHEESE

Cheese Soufflé

Easy
Prepare Ahead

Serves: 8
Chill: overnight
Bake: 1½ hours at 325°

4   slices white bread, broken
½   pound sharp cheddar cheese, grated
4   eggs, separated and beaten
1   teaspoon salt

½   teaspoon dry mustard
⅛   teaspoon red pepper
½   teaspoon minced onion
2½ cups milk

- In greased two-quart casserole dish, alternate layer of bread and layer of cheese (four layers in all).
- Combine eggs, salt, mustard, pepper and onion with milk.
- Pour mixture over the bread and cheese layers.
- Let stand in refrigerator at least 5 hours or overnight.
- Bake in pan of hot water at 325° for one and a half hours.
- Hot water should cover the bottom of the pan.
- Serve immediately after baking.

Mrs. Raymond L. Murphy (Nancy Jane Dennis)

Tomato Topped Cheese Pudding

Easy
May Prepare Ahead
Freezes

Serves: 6
Bake: 60 minutes at 300°

3   cups bread crumbs, freshly made with untoasted bread
2   small onions, finely chopped salt and pepper
12 ounces sharp cheddar cheese, grated

1½ cups milk
4   eggs, beaten
¼   teaspoon Worcestershire sauce
2   teaspoons prepared mustard
3   tomatoes, sliced
2   tablespoons butter

- Combine bread crumbs, which should be coarse not fine, with onions, salt, pepper, and 8 ounces of cheese.
- Spread in bottom of an 8½ x 11 greased baking dish.
- Add milk, Worcestershire sauce and mustard to the beaten eggs and mix together.
- Pour over the bread crumb mixture.
- Sprinkle the rest of the cheese on top.
- Cover with sliced tomatoes.
- Sprinkle with pepper.
- Add butter.
- Bake until firm, about 1 hour at 300°.

Mrs. Keating Lewis Simons, Jr. (Julianne Bell)

Cheese And White Wine Casserole

Average
Serve Immediately

Serves: 6
Bake: 40 minutes at 350°

½ pound gruyére cheese, grated	½ cup heavy cream
6 slices bread (white)	½ cup dry white wine
6 tablespoons butter	1½ cups chicken bouillon
1 garlic clove, crushed	1 teaspoon paprika
6 eggs	¼ teaspoon dry mustard

- Grate cheese.
- Trim crust from bread.
- Cream butter and garlic together, spread on bread.
- Arrange bread in casserole, buttered side down.
- Beat eggs until foamy then beat in cream.
- Add all other ingredients, stirring only enough to mix.
- Pour over bread and bake in 350° oven for 40 minutes or until puffed and brown.

Mrs. James B. Jackson (Carol Adams)

Vidalia Onion-Bacon Quiche
"Everybody's Favorite"

Easy
May Prepare Ahead
Freezes

Serves: 6
Bake: 20 minutes at 350°

1 unbaked 9-inch deep dish pastry shell (homemade or frozen)	1 cup light cream
3 tablespoons butter	1 cup sour cream
4 cups Vidalia onions, chopped	4 eggs, lightly beaten
½ teaspoon salt	2 cups Swiss cheese grated
¼ teaspoon pepper	2 tablespoons grated Parmesan cheese
6 slices of bacon, cooked and crumbled	

- Bake frozen pie shell according to directions on package.
- In large skillet, sauté onions in butter until translucent.
- Add salt and pepper.
- In large bowl beat eggs.
- Stir in cream, sour cream and cheese.
- Add onions and bacon and pour into pie shell.
- Bake in preheated oven at 350° for 20 minutes.

Mrs. Bissell Jenkins Witte (Linda Burton)

Broccoli Quiche

Average
May Prepare Ahead
Freezes

Serves: 3
Yields: 6 slices
Bake: 40 minutes at 350°

1	pastry for 9-inch pie
4	slices bacon, cooked, and crumbled, (reserving one tablespoon of drippings)
1	medium onion, chopped
1	4-ounce can sliced mushrooms, drained
6	broccoli spears, cooked

1	cup (4 ounces) cheddar cheese
3	large eggs, beaten
1¾	cup half-and-half
¼	cup Parmesan cheese, grated
½	teaspoon salt
½	teaspoon pepper
¼	teaspoon ground nutmeg

- Line a 9-inch quiche dish with pastry.
- Trim edges and prick bottom and sides of pastry with a fork.
- Bake at 400° for 3 minutes.
- Remove from oven and gently prick with a fork.
- Bake 5 minutes longer.
- Crumble bacon and set aside.
- Sauté onion in bacon drippings until tender.
- Sprinkle bacon, onion, mushroom, broccoli and cheddar cheese into pastry shell.
- Combine next 6 ingredients, mixing well.
- Pour into pastry shell.
- Bake at 350° for 40 minutes or until filling is set.

Mrs. Donald F. Parker (Elizabeth Guerard)

Sausage Quiche

Easy
May Prepare Ahead
Freezes

Serves: 6
Bake: 35 to 40 minutes at 350°

1	frozen deep dish pie crust
½	pound sausage, cooked and drained
½	cup mayonnaise
½	cup milk

2	eggs, beaten
1	tablespoon cornstarch
1½	cups sharp cheddar cheese, grated
⅓	cup onion, chopped

- Bake pie crust for 8 minutes.
- Mix all ingredients and pour into pie crust.
- Bake in oven at 350° for 35 to 40 minutes.

Mrs. Edward B. Lockwood (Dorothy McAlister)

EGGS

Kugel

"Delicious for breakfast buffet or with coffee."

Easy
Serve Immediately

Serves: 8
Bake: 40 minutes at 350°

12 ounces fine noodles
4 large eggs, beaten
1½ cups sour cream
½ pound cream cheese, softened

⅔ cup sugar (put aside 2 tablespoons)
⅔ cup melted butter or margarine

Topping

2 cups crushed corn flakes
1 tablespoon butter or margarine

2 tablespoons sugar
dash cinnamon

◆ Prepare noodles following directions on box.
◆ Drain and set aside.
◆ Combine next 5 ingredients in bowl and beat with electric mixer on high for about 10 minutes or until foamy.
◆ Fold in noodles.
◆ Place in greased casserole dish (9 x 9).
◆ Blend topping and sprinkle over noodles.
◆ Bake at 350° for 40 minutes.

Mrs. Charles Fox (Melissa Tuttle)

Apple Omelette

"Try this with pork or as a side dish for breakfast."

Easy
Serve Immediately

Serves: 4
Bake: 350°

5 tart apples, chopped
½ tablespoon butter, melted
½ cup sugar

¼ teaspoon cinnamon
¼ teaspoon nutmeg
2 eggs, beaten

◆ Peel and chop apples.
◆ Cook apples until very soft, then mash them.
◆ Add butter, sugar, eggs and spices.
◆ Bake 350° in a shallow pudding dish until brown.

Mrs. Bissell Jenkins Witte (Linda Burton)

Scots Eggs
"Very British – a picnic favorite."

Average
Serve Immediately

Serves: 6
Fry: 4 to 5 minutes

6   eggs, hard-boiled
1   pound sausage
2   tablespoons parsley,
    finely chopped
½   teaspoon ground sage

¼   teaspoon pepper
2   eggs, beaten
¼   cup flour
½ to ¾ cup bread crumbs
    vegetable oil for frying

♦ Peel hard-boiled eggs and chill well
♦ Combine meat, parsley, sage and pepper in a large bowl; mix well.
♦ Divide meat into 6 equal parts.
♦ Press meat around eggs with hands, keeping the oval shape.
♦ Coat eggs with flour on all sides.
♦ Dip into beaten eggs and roll in bread crumbs.
♦ Heat oil in deep fryer or heavy sauce pan to 350°.
♦ Fry eggs until well browned, about 4-5 minutes.
♦ Drain. Can be served hot or cold.

Mrs. Henry Lide DuRant (Kay Ravenel)

Golden Stuffed Eggs
"Different Brunch Dish"

Average
May Prepare Ahead

Serves: 6

½   pint whipping cream
½   teaspoon dry mustard
1   tablespoon water
1   teaspoon curry

1   tablespoon mango chutney
    dash tabasco
½   teaspoon honey
12 eggs, hard-boiled

♦ Whip cream lightly.
♦ Mix dry mustard with water to make a paste. Add curry.
♦ Combine mustard and curry paste with whipped cream, then add chutney, tabasco, and honey.
♦ Split eggs lengthwise. Remove yolks and mash them in a bowl.
♦ Take half the cream mixture and add to the yolks. Stuff the whites with the yolk and cream combination.
♦ With the remaining cream mixture, make a bed in the bottom of a flat platter. Perch stuffed egg whites on top.
♦ Chill well.

* Serve with slices of lemon and brown bread and butter.
* Serve with melon salad and perhaps steamed asparagus wrapped with proscuitto.

Mr. Charles L. Dibble

BREAD

Bread Lover's Loaves
"Yum........."

Complicated
May Prepare Ahead
Freezes Well

Yields: 4 loaves
Bake: 20 to 30 minutes at 350°

2 packages active dry yeast
½ cup very warm water
¼ cup sugar
1 teaspoon salt
1 cup milk

¼ cup butter or margarine, softened
1 egg, well beaten
4½ to 5 cups flour
butter or margarine, melted

Filling

¼ cup butter or margarine
1 cup onion, finely chopped
2 tablespoons Parmesan cheese, grated

2 tablespoons poppy seed
1 teaspoon garlic salt
1 teaspoon paprika

- Soften yeast in water in large mixer bowl.
- Add sugar, salt, milk, ¼ cup butter or margarine, egg and 2 cups flour.
- Blend at low speed until moistened.
- Beat 2 minutes at medium speed.
- Stir in enough remaining flour by hand to make a soft dough.
- Let rise until double, about 30 minutes.
- Prepare filling by mixing all ingredients and blending well.
- Set aside.
- Stir down dough and knead on floured surface until no longer sticky - until smooth and elastic.
- Roll into a large ¼-inch thick circle.
- Cut into 4 wedges.
- Spread with filling, spreading lighter toward points and edges.
- Roll each wedge tightly beginning at wide end.
- Seal points, ends and wedges.
- Brush with melted butter or margarine and place on greased baking sheets.
- Cover and let rise until double, 30-35 minutes.
- Bake at 350° for 20-30 minutes.
- Brush again with melted butter after removing from oven.

Mrs. Philip W. Cotton (Ann Copenhaver)

Pullapart Loaves

"Worth the time and effort"

Complicated
May Prepare Ahead
Freezes Well

Serves: 10
Bake: 30 minutes at 400°

5½ -6½ cups unsifted plain flour
3 tablespoons sugar
2 teaspoons salt
1 package yeast

1½ cups water
½ cup milk
3 tablespoons margarine
melted butter

- Mix 2 cups flour, sugar, salt and yeast in a bowl.
- Combine water, milk and margarine in a saucepan.
- Heat mixture over low heat, until very warm. (Margarine does not have to melt.)
- Gradually add heated mixture to dry mixture.
- Beat 2 minutes with electric mixer.
- Add ¾ cup flour.
- Beat at high speed 2 minutes.
- Stir in enough additional flour to make a stiff dough.
- Turn out onto lightly floured board.
- Knead until smooth and elastic (8 to 10 minutes).
- Place in greased bowl, turning until top is greased.
- Let rise in a warm place until doubled (about 1 hour).
- Punch down dough and divide in half.
- Cover and let rest on board 15 minutes.
- Roll ½ of dough to a 8 x 12 rectangle.
- Brush with melted butter.
- Cut into 4 equal strips; 8 inches long.
- Stack strips and cut into 4 equal pieces 2 inches wide.
- Place around edge in greased loaf pan.
- Repeat with remaining half of dough.
- Cover pan and let rise until double (about 1 hour).
- Bake at 400° about 30 minutes, or until done.

Mrs. William W. Boles, III (Elizabeth Brown)

Light Bread (No Knead)

Average
May Prepare Ahead

Yields: 2 loaves
Bake: 30 minutes at 350°

1 tablespoon yeast
¼ cup sugar
½ cup warm water
1 stick butter or margarine, softened

1 tablespoon salt
6-8 large eggs, beaten
4 cups flour

- Combine yeast, sugar and water in large bowl and allow to "work".
- Beat in butter, salt and eggs with electric mixer.
- Beat in flour with large spoon.
- Cover bowl and let rise for 30 minutes.
- Stir down and pour into two greased 9 inch tube pans.
- Let rise for 30 minutes.
- Bake at 350° for about 30 minutes.

Mrs. John Chrisman Hawk, III (Fran Solley)

Tyebrook Batter Bread

Average
May Prepare Ahead

Serves: 6
Bake: approx. 20 minutes at 350-400°

3 eggs
4 tablespoons lard (Crisco), melted
2 cups buttermilk

2 cups yellow corn meal
¾ teaspoon salt
½ teaspoon baking soda
½ teaspoon baking powder

- Break eggs into a bowl.
- Pour in melted lard and 1 cup buttermilk.
- Sift in corn meal and stir thoroughly
- Sift in salt, soda and baking powder and mix well.
- Add 1 cup buttermilk until batter is soft enough to pour.
- Pour into oblong aluminum baking pan that is 10½ x 7½ x 1½.
- Bake in moderate oven starting at 350° and then turn up to 400° until medium brown on top.

Mrs. Thomas Waring (Janice Duffie)
Mrs. Robert Berretta (Randolph Waring)

Dilly Bread

Average
May Prepare Ahead
Freezes Well

Yields: one loaf
Bake: 45 minutes at 350°

¼	cup warm water		2	teaspoons dill seed
1	package yeast		1	egg, beaten
1	cup cottage cheese		1	teaspoon salt
1	tablespoon butter, softened		¼	teaspoon baking soda
2	tablespoons sugar		2¼	cups flour, sifted
1	tablespoon minced onion			

- In small bowl, dissolve yeast in water.
- In large bowl, stir until just blended, cottage cheese and butter.
- Add the sugar, onion, dill seed, egg, salt, soda and yeast mixture.
- Stir until well blended.
- Add the flour and stir well.
- Cover with damp cloth and let rise until doubled in size—1 to 1½ hours.
- Stir the dough down and put in a greased loaf pan.
- Cover and let rise 40 to 50 minutes.
- Bake at 350° for 45 minutes.
- Remove from oven and brush the top with melted butter.

Mrs. Milon C. Smith (Mary Lou Hodges)

English Muffin Bread I
"Excellent-tastes just like English Muffins"

Average
May Prepare Ahead

Yields: 2 loaves
Bake: 25 minutes at 400°

¼ -½	cup cornmeal		2	tablespoons salt
2	tablespoons yeast		¼	teaspoon baking soda
6	cups flour		2	cups milk
1	tablespoon sugar		½	cup water

- Grease two loaf pans and sprinkle them with cornmeal.
- Combine yeast, flour, sugar, salt and baking soda in a bowl or in processor using dough blade.
- Heat the milk and water to 120-130°.
- Add liquids to dry ingredients and beat well (about 30 seconds in processor).
- Spoon mixture into loaf pans.
- Sprinkle more cornmeal on top.
- Cover pans with a towel or foil and let rise in a warm spot for 45 minutes.
- Bake at 400° for 25 minutes.
- Remove from pans immediately and cool on a rack.

Mrs. Darryl Lamar Forrester (Catherine Huffman)

English Muffin Bread II
"Delicious eaten as toast"

Average
Prepare Ahead
Freezes Well

Yields: 2 loaves
Standing Time: 6 hours or overnight
Bake: 60 minutes at 350°

5 cups flour, plain and unsifted
1 package active dry yeast
1 tablespoon salt
1 tablespoon sugar

1½ teaspoons corn oil
2 cups very warm water
 butter for pans

- Mix dry ingredients and corn oil.
- Pour in water and mix thoroughly.
- Cover bowl with plastic wrap and towel.
- Let stand at room temperature overnight, or at least 6 hours.
(Dough may more than double and may fall somewhat, which is normal.)
- Generougly butter 2 bread pans.
- Divide dough, without kneading, into 2 portions.
- Place in pans and shape.
- Cover and let rise until double.
- Pre-heat oven to 350°
- Bake for l hour at 350°
- Cool in pans or rack.

Carolyn Weatherford Hutson

Olive Cheese Bread
"Perfect for watercress sandwiches."

Average
Prepare Ahead
Freezes Well

Yield: 1 loaf
Bake: 1 hour at 350°

3 cups self-rising flour
 (spoon this in)
2 tablespoons sugar
3 eggs, beaten
¾ cup milk

3 tablespoons olive oil
1½ cups (6 ounces) shredded cheddar cheese
2½ cups stuffed green olives

- Stir together flour and sugar.
- Combine eggs, milk and oil.
- Fold in cheese and olives.
- Add to flour mixture. Stir only until moistened.
- Line pans with waxed paper and spray with non-stick coating.
- If top browns too quickly, loosely cover with foil.
* Makes 1 large loaf or 2 small loaves. Small loaves bake 30-45 minutes.

Mrs. William Haywood Mapp, Jr. (Mary Lou Owen)

Spoon Bread I
"A real southern treat"

Easy **Serves:** 4
Serve Immediately **Bake:** 60 minutes at 350°

¾	cup corn meal mix	1	teaspoon salt
3	cups milk	1	teaspoon baking powder
2	tablespoons butter	3	eggs, separated

- Mix 1 cup cold milk and corn meal mix.
- Scald 2 cups milk and add to mix.
- Cook over medium heat until thickened.
- Remove from heat and add butter, salt, baking powder and egg yolks.
- Beat egg whites until stiff and fold into mix.
- Pour into buttered baking dish and bake at 350 for 1 hour.

Mrs. Barry Gumb (Beverly Brooks)

Spoon Bread II
"Outstanding served with fried fish."

Easy **Serves:** 6
May Prepare Ahead **Bake:** 40 minutes at 350°

1	8½ ounce box corn bread mix	1	17 ounce can niblet corn, drained
1	stick butter, melted		
1	large egg, beaten	1	8 ounce carton sour cream

- Mix all ingredients together and pour into greased 8-inch square pan.
- Bake at 350° for 40 minutes.

Martha J. Lott

Onion Corn Bread

Average
May Prepare Ahead

Serves: 6
Bake: 30-35 minutes at 425°

¼ cup butter, melted
1½ cups onions, chopped
1 cup sour cream
¼ teaspoon salt
1 cup sharp cheddar cheese, shredded and divided

1 egg, beaten
½ cup milk
1 8½ ounce package corn muffin mix
1 8 ounce can cream corn
2 drops red pepper sauce

- Sauté onions in butter for 10 minutes.
- Cool slightly.
- Add the sour cream, salt and ½ cup cheese to onion mixture and set aside.
- Mix together the egg, milk, muffin mix, corn and red pepper sauce.
- Spread muffin mix in an 8-inch square greased pan.
- Put the sour cream mixture on top.
- Sprinkle the rest of the cheese on top.
- Bake at 425° for 30-35 minutes.
- Let set before cutting.

Mrs. Lloyd Arthur Pearson (Margaret Ann Boyd)

Angel Biscuits
"Dough keeps refrigerated for one week."

Average
May Prepare Ahead

Yields: 20 to 30
Bake: 12 to 14 minutes at 450°

2¾ cups flour (regular) plain
1½ teaspoons baking powder
½ teaspoon soda
1 teaspoon salt
2 tablespoons sugar

1¼ teaspoons yeast (½ pkg.), dissolved in 2 tablespoons of warm water
½ cup shortening
1 cup buttermilk (at room temperature)

- Combine and sift dry ingredients (flour, sugar, soda, baking powder and salt). Cut in shortening.
- In separate bowl, stir yeast and water into buttermilk.
- Add dry ingredients a little at a time to the liquid, until a dough is formed.
- Roll out dough on floured surface and cut as desired (can cut in squares then fold over to form a triangle).
- Bake at 450° for 12 to 14 minutes or until brown.
- Dough may be covered and refrigerated for as long as a week — using as needed.

*Makes beautiful ham biscuits or cloverleaf rolls.

Mrs. William C. Prewitt (Karen Padgett)

Baking Powder Biscuits

Average
May Prepare Ahead

Yields: 30 biscuits
Bake: 12 to 15 minutes at 450°

2	cups flour	4	tablespoons shortening
4	teaspoons baking powder	¾-1 cup milk	
1	teaspoon salt		

- Sift together flour, baking powder, and salt. Add the shortening.
- Work it in well with a pastry blender.
- Add the milk slowly. Work in with a spoon until slightly sticky.
- Toss the mixture onto a well floured surface. Knead well.
- Roll out to ¾ inch thickness. Cut with floured biscuit cutter.
- Place on ungreased cookie sheet about ¼ inch apart.
- Bake 12-15 minutes at 450°.

Mrs. Robert Oliver Maguire (Lucie Hall)

Cheese Biscuits

Average
May Prepare Ahead
Freezes Well

Yields: 20
Bake: 10 to 15 minutes at 425°

2	cups all purpose flour	⅔	cup sharp cheddar cheese, coarsely grated
1	tablespoon baking powder		
½	teaspoon salt	½	cup milk mixed with ¼ cup water
8	tablespoons Crisco shortening		

- Preheat oven to 425°.
- In large mixing bowl, put flour, baking powder and salt.
- Add shortening and cut in with pastry cutter until crumbly.
- Add cheese and mix until cheese is covered with flour.
- Add ⅔ cup milk and water mixture and stir lightly with a fork until mixed.
- Add more liquid if necessary to have dough form a ball.
- Roll dough out gently on floured board. Do not knead.
- Cut out biscuits with a biscuit cutter and place on ungreased cookie sheet.
- Bake at 425° for 10-15 minutes.

*If making ahead to freeze, bake only 5 minutes, then later place partially thawed in oven for 5 to 10 minutes.

Mrs. John H. Warren (Helen Smith)

Benne Cheese Biscuits
"EASY AS 1, 2, 3"

Easy
Serve Immediately

Yields: 8 biscuits
Bake: 8 minutes at 500°

1   package refrigerator baking powder biscuits

¼   cup melted butter
¾   cup grated cheddar cheese
3   tablespoons benne seeds (sesame)

- Dip biscuits in melted butter.
- Mix cheese and benne seeds in shallow dish.
- Roll each biscuit in mixture coating both sides well.
- Place on well greased cookie sheet and bake 8 minutes.

Margaret Meynardie

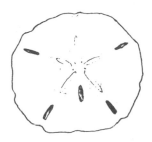

Cream Cheese Biscuits
"Perfect for a buffet — no butter needed."

Easy
Prepare Ahead

Yields: 40 biscuits
Chill: 1 hour
Bake: 20 minutes at 350°

1   3-ounce package cream cheese.
1   cup all-purpose flour

1   stick butter
½   teaspoon salt

- Soften cream cheese and butter.
- Mix all ingredients together.
- Shape into a log (1½ inch diameter) and refrigerate.
- When dough is hardened, slice into ¼ inch wafers.
- Bake on ungreased baking sheet for 20 minutes at 350° or 10 minutes at 400°.
- Biscuits will be light brown around the edges.

Martha J. Lott

69

Biscuits Supreme

Average
May Prepare Ahead
Freezes Well

Yields: 12 biscuits
Bake: 12-15 minutes at 450°

2 cups flour	½ teaspoon cream of tartar
½ teaspoon salt	½ cup shortening
4 teaspoons baking powder	⅔ cup cold milk

- Sift together first 5 ingredients.
- Cut shortening into flour mixture.
- Add milk and knead mixture gently for ½ minute.
- Roll out to ½ inch thickness. Cut with biscuit cutter.
- Bake on ungreased cookie sheet in 450° oven for 12-15 minutes.

Mrs. William Russell Tyler (Linda Cochron)

Debbie's Biscuits

Easy
May Prepare Ahead
Freezes Well

Yields: 6 dozen
Bake: 12-15 minutes at 350°

3 cups self-rising flour	1 cup ice water
¾ cup shortening - Crisco	

- Preheat oven to 350°.
- Put flour in bowl.
- Add shortening and cut up with pastry cutter.
- Add cold water.
- Stir into ball.
- Roll out on floured surface ½ inch thick.
- Cut with cookie cutter.
- Place on ungreased cookie sheet and cook in 350° oven for 12-15 minutes.

Mrs. Daniel Ravenel (Kathleen Hall)

Cranberry Bread
"Wonderful"

Average
May Prepare Ahead
Freezes Well

Yields: 1 loaf
Bake: 60 minutes at 350°

2 cups flour, sifted	¼ cup shortening
1 cup sugar	1 egg, beaten
1½ teaspoons baking powder	¾ cup orange juice
½ teaspoon baking soda	1 tablespoon grated orange rind
½ teaspoon salt	2 cups chopped cranberries
	¾ cup pecan pieces

- Sift flour, sugar, baking powder, baking soda and salt together in a large mixing bowl.
- Add shortening and cut in with a fork until the consistency of coarse meal.
- Stir egg, orange juice and rind together.
- Add juice mixture to dry ingredients.
- Stir well.
- Fold in cranberries and pecans.
- Pour into greased and floured 9 x 5 pan.
- Bake at 350° for 1 hour.

Mrs. F. Strait Fairey, Jr. (Charlotte Davis)

Banana Wheat Bread

Average
May Prepare Ahead
Freezes Well

Yields: 1 loaf
Bake: 60 minutes at 350°

2 cups whole wheat flour	½ cup honey
¼ cup wheat germ	¼ cup vegetable oil
1 teaspoon salt	2 eggs
1 teaspoon soda	1 teaspoon vanilla extract
1½ cups mashed ripe bananas	½ cup chopped nuts

- In a large bowl, stir together well, flour, wheat germ, salt and soda.
- In another bowl, mix bananas, oil, honey, eggs, and vanilla, stirring well.
- Make a well in the center of the dry ingredients, add the banana mixture, and stir until moistened.
- Spoon the batter into a greased and floured 9 x 5 x 3 loaf pan.
- Bake at 350° for 1 hour or until done.

Mrs. Samuel Edward Parker (Diane Prosser)

Orange Bread

Average
Partial Prepare Ahead

Yields: 1 loaf
Simmer: 1 hour
Rise: 30 minutes
Bake: 60 minutes at 300°

2	cups orange peel	4	tablespoons melted butter
2	cups water	½	teaspoon salt
2	cups sugar	1	egg
	pinch of salt	½	cup milk
4	cups flour	4	teaspoons baking powder

♦ Cut up orange peel and cook covered with sugar, water and pinch of salt slowly for 1 hour or until like a rather thick marmalade.
♦ Mix flour, butter, ½ teaspoon salt, egg, milk and baking powder together.
♦ Add orange mixture to flour mixture, stirring well.
♦ Put in greased loaf pan.
♦ Let rise 30 minutes.
♦ Bake at 300° for one hour or until done.

Pumpkin Bread

Average
May Prepare Ahead
Freezes Well

Yields: 2 loaves
Bake: 1 hour and 5 minutes at 350°

3	cups sugar	½	teaspoon cloves
1	cup corn oil	1	teaspoon cinnamon
4	eggs	1	teaspoon allspice
2	cups pumpkin (1 lb. can size)	1	teaspoon nutmeg
3½	cups flour	1	cup water
1	teaspoon baking powder	⅔	cup pecans
2	teaspoons soda	1	cup light raisins (optional)
2	teaspoons salt		

♦ Combine sugar, oil and eggs.
♦ Add pumpkin.
♦ Sift together dry ingredients.
♦ Add to pumpkin mixture.
♦ Add water, stir well.
♦ Add pecans.
♦ Pour into two 9 x 5 greased and floured pans.
♦ Bake at 350° for 1 hour and 5 minutes or until done.
♦ Let set 10 minutes.
♦ Turn out to cool.

Mrs. John M. Hart (Brenda Weaver)

Pear Bread

Average
May Prepare Ahead
Freezes Well

Yields: 1 loaf
Bake: 55 minutes at 375°

1 cup sugar	1 teaspoon cinnamon
¾ cup salad oil	1 teaspoon soda
2 eggs	1 teaspoon baking powder
1½ cups plain flour	1 cup grated pears
¼ teaspoon salt	½ cup chopped nuts

♦ Cream sugar, oil and eggs together.
♦ Add dry ingredients.
♦ Mix in pears and nuts.
♦ Pour into greased loaf pan.
♦ Bake at 375° for 55 minutes.

Mrs. Floyd I. Dovell, III (Elizabeth Simons)

Betty Bullard's Poppy Seed Loaf

Average
May Prepare Ahead
Freezes Well

Yields: 1 large loaf or 4 small loaves
Bake: 1 hour at 350° or 45 minutes
for 4 small loaves

3 cups flour (plain)	2¼ cups sugar
1½ teaspoons salt	1½ tablespoons poppy seeds
1½ teaspoons baking powder	1½ teaspoons vanilla
3 eggs	1½ teaspoons almond flavoring
1½ cups milk	1½ teaspoons butter flavoring
1⅛ cups cooking oil	

Glaze

¼ cup orange juice	½ teaspoon almond flavoring
¾ cup sugar	½ teaspoon vanilla flavoring
½ teaspoon butter flavoring	

♦ Put all ingredients into a mixing bowl and beat for 2 minutes.
♦ Pour mixture into greased and floured loaf pan.
♦ Bake at 350° for 1 hour or until toothpick inserted into center is clean and top is cracked.

Glaze

♦ Stir (don't cook) all glaze ingredients together.
♦ About 5 minutes out of the oven, take the loaf out of its pan.
♦ Pour glaze over loaf.

Mrs. Lloyd Arthur Pearson (Margaret Ann Boyd)

Bridget Latimer's Strawberry Coffee Cake

Average
May Prepare Ahead

Yields: 1 cake
Bake: 40 minutes at 350°

8	ounces softened cream cheese	1	teaspoon baking powder
1	stick margarine	½	teaspoon baking soda
¾	cup sugar	¼	teaspoon salt
1	cup milk	18	ounces strawberry preserves
2	eggs, beaten	1	tablespoon lemon juice
1	teaspoon vanilla	¼	cup brown sugar
2	cups plain flour	½	cup chopped pecans

- Combine cream cheese, margarine and sugar.
- Stir the milk, eggs and vanilla into the cream cheese mixture.
- Sift together flour, baking powder, baking soda and salt.
- Add sifted dry ingredients to cream cheese mixture.
- Pour ½ of cream cheese batter into 13 x 9 x 2 casserole.
- Stir the strawberry preserves and lemon juice together.
- Spread the strawberry preserve mixture over the batter. (Dab small spoonfuls over the batter and gently spread around - don't stir.)
- Add the remainder of the cream cheese batter on top of the preserves.
- Sprinkle top with brown sugar and pecans.
- Bake at 350° for 40 minutes.

Mrs. Lloyd Arthur Pearson (Margaret Ann Boyd)

Breakfast Coffee Cake

Average
May Prepare Ahead

Yields: 1 coffee cake
Bake: 30 minutes at 325° and 10 minutes at 375°

2	eggs	1½	teaspoons baking powder
1	teaspoon vanilla	¼	teaspoon salt
1	cup sugar	½	cup heavy cream
1	cup flour plus 1 tablespoon	½	cup melted butter

Topping

3	tablespoons sugar	½	cup almonds (sliced)
¼	cup butter		

- Mix eggs, vanilla and sugar.
- Sift together flour, baking powder, salt.
- Add dry ingredients to egg mixture.
- Stir in cream and melted butter.
- Pour into a greased and floured pie plate.
- Bake at 325° for 30 minutes.

- Combine butter, sugar and almonds in pan on top of stove.
- Cook slowly until butter has melted.
- Spoon topping on top of baked cake and return to a 375° oven for 10 minutes.
- Cut cake in wedges to serve.

Mrs. E.L. Query (Carolyn Rivers)

Cinnamon Meringue Coffee Cake
"Wonderful holiday fare"

Complicated	**Yields:** 2 coffee cakes
Prepare Ahead	**Rise:** overnight
Freezes Well	**Bake:** 20 to 25 minutes at 325°

¼	cup milk, warmed	1	package yeast
2	tablespoons sugar	3	egg yolks
1	cup margarine, softened	2	cups flour

Meringue Filling

3	egg whites	1	cup coarsely chopped nuts
¾	cup sugar	2	teaspoons cinnamon

Icing

1	cup confectioners sugar	1	tablespoon milk

- Combine warmed milk, sugar and yeast - set aside.
- Mix together margarine, egg yolks, and flour - stir into yeast mixture until well blended.
- Cover and refrigerate overnight.
- To make meringue: beat egg whites until stiff but not dry. Then add sugar and mix well. Set aside.
- Divide dough into 2 parts.
- Roll ½ of the dough on a floured surface into a 16 x 18 rectangle.
- Spread ½ of the meringue over surface of dough.
- Sprinkle with 1 teaspoon cinnamon and ½ cup nuts.
- Roll the rectangle as if rolling a jelly roll.
- Place coffee cake in a greased 9-inch cake pan and shape into a semi-circle.
- Repeat same procedure with remaining dough and ingredients.
- Bake 20-25 minutes in a 325° oven.
- Let cool and drizzle with confectioner sugar icing.

* Can be shaped into a circle and decorated with red and green cherries to look like a Christmas wreath.

Mrs. Gregory A. Jones (Betsy Fant)

Elizabeth's Coffee Cake
"Out of this world"

Complicated
May Prepare Ahead
Freezes Well

Yields: 2 coffee cakes
Rise: overnight
Bake: 20 minutes at 350°

½ cup milk	1 stick butter, melted
½ cup oil	⅔ cup dark brown sugar
½ cup sugar	2 teaspoons cinnamon
½ teaspoon salt	1 cup nuts, chopped
2 eggs, beaten	1 cup powdered sugar
1 package yeast (¼ oz.)	2 tablespoons warm milk
¼ cup warm water	½ teaspoon vanilla
3½ to 4½ cups flour	

- Scald milk.
- In blender, combine milk, oil, sugar, eggs and salt. Blend until mixed.
- Add yeast which has been combined with warm water.
- Add flour until you get a stiff dough.
- Place in greased bowl - cover until doubled (overnight).
- Punch down and knead dough. Divide dough in half.
- Roll out ½ dough into 8 x 12 rectangle.
- Brush with ½ stick melted butter.
- Cover with ½ brown sugar, cinnamon and nuts mixture.
- Starting with long side, roll up jelly-roll fashion.
- Place roll in pie pan to form a circle and pinch ends together. Fill empty center of pie pan by pulling dough at the seam, filling side down.
- Cut at 1-inch intervals with scissors ¾ of the way through.
- Repeat with other half of dough.
- Allow to rise until doubled.
- Bake at 350° for 20 minutes.
- Glaze each cake with powdered sugar icing when hot from oven.

Mrs. J. David Hawkins (Louisa Pritchard)

Skufful Farm Coffee Cake
"Wonderful"

Average
May Prepare Ahead
Freezes Well

Yields: 1 bundt size cake
Bake: 1½ hours at 325°

2 sticks butter or margarine	¼ teaspoon salt
2 cups sugar	1 teaspoon baking powder
2 eggs	1 tablespoon sugar
½ teaspoon vanilla extract	1 teaspoon cinnamon
½ pint sour cream	powdered sugar
2 cups sifted all-purpose flour	

- Cream butter and sugar.
- Add eggs, one at a time.
- Add vanilla.
- Add sour cream, mix well.
- Sift together flour, salt and baking powder.
- Add to sour cream mixture.
- Pour ½ cake batter into a greased and floured bundt pan.
- Sprinkle 1 tablespoon sugar and 1 teaspoon cinnamon over the batter layer.
- Add second layer of batter.
- Bake at 325° for 1½ hours or until done.
- After cake has cooled thoroughly, turn out and sprinkle with powdered sugar.

Mrs. Thomas A. Huguenin (Mary Vereen)

Emma's Sweet Potato Rolls

Average
Partial Prepare Ahead

Yields: 2 dozen
Bake: 20 minutes at 375°

1 package of yeast	1 teaspoon salt
1 teaspoon sugar	2 cups cooked, mashed sweet
¼ cup warm water	potato
½ cup sugar	1 egg
½ cup shortening	4 cups (more or less) plain flour

- Dissolve yeast and sugar in warm water. Let stand.
- Mix sugar, shortening and salt into hot potatoes. (Cook earlier in boiling water about one hour, remove skins.)
- When potato mixture is cool, stir in yeast and egg.
- Add flour a little at a time. Dough should be slightly stiff and cover.
- Let rise in a warm place, as the oven with its light on.
- Mash down and roll out as for thick biscuit or hand shape into rolls.
- Place in a well greased pan with sides almost touching. Let rise until double in bulk.
- Bake at 375° about 20 minutes. Bottoms burn easily.
- Dough will keep 3 or 4 days in refrigerator.
- Good served with a cheddar cheese sauce, especially when leftovers are split open and warmed for breakfast.
- * Canned sweet potatoes can be drained and used.

Mrs. Edgar S. Jaycocks (Lucia Harrison)

French Rolls

"Great for afternoon coffee."

Average
May Prepare Ahead
Freezes Well

Yields: 24 rolls
Bake: 25 minutes at 350°

⅓ cup shortening	¼ teaspoon nutmeg
½ cup sugar	½ cup water
1½ cups flour	6 tablespoons melted butter
1½ teaspoons baking powder	½ cup sugar
2 tablespoons dry milk	1 tablespoon cinnamon
½ teaspoon salt	

- Cream shortening and sugar until creamy.
- Sift together flour, baking powder, dry milk, salt, nutmeg.
- Add dry mixture to creamed mixture slowly, alternating with ½ cup of water.
- Fill greased muffin cups ⅔ full and bake at 350° until golden.
- Roll each roll, while still hot, in melted butter and cinnamon sugar.

Mrs. Robert Oliver Maguire (Lucie Hall)

Pat Holman's Buttermilk Whole Wheat Rolls

Complicated
May Prepare Ahead
Freezes Well

Yields: 2 dozen
Rising: 2 hours
Bake: 20 to 25 minutes at 400°

¼ cup warm water (100°-115°)
1 package dry yeast
1 tablespoon sugar
¾ cup buttermilk, room
   temperature
1 egg
¼ cup cooking oil

1 teaspoon salt
¼ cup sugar
1¼ cups bread flour (or
   unbleached flour)
1½ cups whole wheat flour
1 teaspoon baking powder

- "Proof" the yeast in the warm water until bubbly and let stand.
- Mix yeast, sugar and water together. Let it stand 10 minutes, until bubbly.
- Add buttermilk, egg, oil, salt and sugar to yeast mixture.
- Combine bread flour, whole wheat flour and baking powder, and add to yeast mixture.
- Dough will be sticky, but easy to handle.
- Flour a board with ½ cup of bread flour to knead. Knead about 5 minutes, return to bowl.
- Let rise until double in size, appoximately 1 hour.
- Punch down and shape into rolls.
- Let rise second time, approximately 1 hour.
- Bake at 400° for 20 to 25 minutes.

Mrs. Lloyd Arthur Pearson (Margaret Ann Boyd)

Ladson Street Rolls

*"Dough may be refrigerated for several days
or partially cooked and frozen."*

Complicated
May Prepare Ahead
Freezes Well

Yields: 6 dozen
Rising: 3 hours
Bake: 8 minutes at 400°

1 cup milk, scalded	¼ cup warm water
½ cup butter (no substitute)	3 eggs
½ cup sugar	5-6 cups bread flour
1 teaspoon salt	melted butter
1 package dry yeast	

- Add butter, sugar, and salt to milk, and cool slightly.
- Dissolve yeast in warm water.
- Beat eggs with mixer, add milk mixture and yeast mixture.
- Mix well. Add 2 cups flour and beat on medium speed.
- Add remaining flour, mixing gradually.
- Cover with damp cloth and allow to rise for approximately 2 hours or until doubled in size.
- Punch down dough.
- Pinch off about ⅓ of the dough at a time.
- Roll out on a floured surface.
- Cut with biscuit cutter and score in the center.
- Dip in melted butter and fold over (as for Parker House Rolls).
- Let rise 1 hour.
- Bake at 400° for 8 minutes.

* Secret to the lightness and fine texture is in the bread flour.

Mrs. Thomas A. Kirkland, Jr. (Patricia Trotter)

Ice Box Rolls

Average
Prepare Ahead
Freezes Well

Yields: 12 rolls
Rising: 12 hours
Bake: 7 minutes at 400°

⅓ cup sugar	1 package yeast
½ tablespoon salt	½ teaspoon sugar
1 big (size of an egg) tablespoon Crisco	¼ cup warm water
	1 egg
1 cup water	4 cups plain flour

- In a pot, put sugar, salt and Crisco.
- Add 1 cup of water and cook over low heat stirring constantly until everything dissolves.
- Set to cool until lukewarm.
- Dissolve 1 package of yeast in ¼ cup warm water and ½ teaspoon sugar. Add to above mixture.

- Beat egg slightly and add.
- Add flour and stir until moist.
- Let rise in refrigerator for at least 12 hours.
- Roll out dough, cut and butter and let rise for 1½ hours.
- Bake at 400° until brown (approximately 7 minutes).

Mrs. Stanley R. Hurt (Gray Webb)

Rich Egg and Whole Wheat Rolls

Complicated
May Prepare Ahead
Freezes Well

Yields: 5 dozen rolls
Rising: 1½ hours approximately
Bake: 10 to 20 minutes at 375°

2½ cups all purpose white flour
2 packages instant dry yeast
⅓ cup sugar
1 tablespoon salt
¾ cup water

1 cup milk
¼ cup oil
3 eggs
3 cups whole wheat flour
¾ cup to 1¼ cups white flour

- Combine 2½ cups flour, yeast, sugar and salt in a large mixing bowl and blend. (Lightly spoon flour into measuring cup and level off.)
- In saucepan combine ¾ cup water, milk and oil and heat over low heat until very warm - 120°-130°.
- Add eggs and warm liquid to flour mixture and mix at low speed until moistened, then beat 3 minutes on medium speed.
- Stir in 3 cups whole wheat flour to form a sticky dough.
- In bowl or on a board add ¾ to 1¼ cups white flour, kneading with hands until dough is smooth and pliable and no longer sticky.
- Place dough in greased bowl; cover. Let rise in warm place until light and doubled in size, about 45 minutes.
- Punch fist into dough to remove all air bubbles; divide into 2 long logs. Cut dough into 1-inch pieces and shape into balls.
- Place in greased pans. Cover; let rise in warm place until light and doubled in size, about 30 minutes.
- Bake 375° 10 to 20 minutes.

Bread Glazes

Crisp, shiny crust - Brush rolls with a mixture of 1 egg and 1 tablespoon water just before baking. Sprinkle with sesame or poppy seeds. (Our favorite.)
Soft, buttery crust - Brush rolls with melted butter after baking.
Slightly crisp, shiny, sweet crust - Brush rolls with a mixture of 1 tablespoon each sugar and water after baking.

Mrs. Isaac A. Speights, III (Elizabeth (Betsy) Lesesne)

Applesauce Muffin
"Batter will keep up to 1½ weeks in refrigerator"

Average
May Prepare Ahead

Yields: 4 dozen
Bake: 15 minutes at 450°

2	sticks soft margarine	1	teaspoon cloves
2	cups white sugar	2	teaspoons allspice
2	eggs	1	cup chopped nuts (optional)
1	teaspoon vanilla	1	16 ounce can applesauce
4	cups plain flour	2	teaspoons baking soda
3	teaspoons cinnamon		

- Cream margarine and sugar.
- Add eggs and vanilla. Blend well.
- Sift flour and 3 spices together, add to butter mixture.
- Add nuts if desired.
- Mix applesauce and soda together, add last. Mix well.
- (Before adding applesauce batter will be very stiff).
- Keep batter refrigerated and bake as needed.
- Bake in muffin cups at 450°.

Mrs. Jeff Chisolm (Molly Martin)

Bran Muffins
"Batter will keep several days in refrigerator"

Average
May Prepare Ahead
Freezes Well

Yields: 2 dozen
Bake: 20 minutes at 375°

2	cups buttermilk	½ teaspoon salt
¾	cup oil	1¼ cups sugar
¼	cup molasses	1 cup all-bran cereal
2	eggs, beaten	1½ cups bran flakes
4	teaspoons soda	½ cup walnuts
2¾ cups whole wheat flour		

- Mix together buttermilk, oil, molasses and eggs.
- Mix together flour, salt, sugar, cereals and nuts.
- Blend together the dry and wet ingredients.
- Grease muffin tin. Fill ½ full.
- Bake 375° for 20 minutes.

Sarah Turpin

Linda's Banana Muffins

Easy
May Prepare Ahead

Yields: 18 to 20 large muffins
Bake: 15 to 20 minutes at 350°

5 large bananas, mashed	1 teaspoon vanilla
1 egg	¼ cup butter, softened
1 teaspoon soda	1 cup walnuts, chopped
1 teaspoon baking powder	1½ cups flour
1 cup sugar	

- Mix all ingredients together in large bowl.
- Pour into greased muffin tins.
- Bake 15-20 minutes at 350°.

* Best served right out of the oven.

Mrs. Telfair H. Parker (Hope Haselden)

Blueberry Cake Muffins
"A delicious accompaniment to a summer salad luncheon"

Average
May Prepare Ahead
Freezes Well

Yields: 15 muffins
Bake: 15 to 20 minutes at 375°

2 cups cake flour	2 eggs, unbeaten
1½ teaspoons baking powder	1 teaspoon vanilla
½ teaspoon salt	½ cup milk
½ cup butter, softened	1 cup fresh blueberries (frozen
1 cup sugar	may be used)

- Combine flour, baking powder and salt. Set aside.
- Beat butter, eggs, sugar and vanilla, until smooth.
- Add flour mixture.
- Stir in milk gradually.
- Wash and drain blueberries, fold into batter.
- Fill greased muffin tins ½ full.

Mrs. Hugh Michael Doherty (Mary Pierce)

Easy Blueberry Muffins

Easy
May Prepare Ahead
Freezes Well

Serves: 4 to 6
Bake: 22 minutes at 425°

1 cup self-rising flour	⅔ cup milk
2 tablespoons mayonnaise	¼ cup blueberries

- Cut mayonnaise into flour.
- Mix with milk.
- Add blueberries.
- Pour into greased muffin tin.
- Bake 425° for 22 minutes.

* Do not use muffin papers—muffin sticks to papers.

Mrs. Thomas Hunter McEaddy (Kitty Tilghman)

Blueberry Muffins

Average
May Prepare Ahead

Yields: 1 dozen
Bake: 25 minutes at 425°

⅓ cup butter (6 oz.)	1½ cups flour
⅓ cup sugar	¼ teaspoon salt
1 egg, well beaten	3 teaspoons baking powder
½ cup milk	1 can blueberries (drained)

- Cream butter and sugar until light.
- Add egg.
- Sift together flour, baking powder and salt. Add to above and mix alternately with milk.
- Fold in drained blueberries.
- Bake 25 minutes in greased muffin pan at 425°.

Carolyn Weatherford Hutson

Blueberry Oatmeal Muffins

Easy
May Prepare Ahead
Freezes Well

Yields: 1 dozen
Bake: 20 to 25 minutes at 400°

2 cups blueberries	2 teaspoons baking powder
2 tablespoons flour	1 stick butter
¾ cup oatmeal	⅔ cup milk
1½ cups flour (all-purpose)	1 egg
¾ cup sugar	

- Fold together blueberries and flour. Set aside.
- Mix remaining ingredients well and fold into floured berries.
- Pour into muffin cups.
- Bake at 400°, 20 to 25 minutes.

Mrs. Richard W. Hutson, Jr. (Anne Smith)

Orange Muffins
"So good"

Easy
May Prepare Ahead
Freezes Well

Yields: 2 dozen
Bake: 15 minutes at 350°

1 cup whole wheat flour	3 eggs, beaten
1½ cups plain flour	1 teaspoon vanilla
2 teaspoons baking powder	1 teaspoon orange extract
½ teaspoon salt	⅔ cup orange juice
1½ sticks butter, melted	½ cup walnuts or pecans
1⅔ cups sugar	1 tablespoon orange marmalade

- Mix together flour, baking powder, salt and sugar.
- Add butter, eggs, vanilla, orange extract, orange juice, marmalade and nuts.
- Stir until moist. (May be lumpy.)
- Grease muffin tin, fill ½ full.
- Bake 15 minutes at 350°.

Sarah Turpin

Refrigerator Muffins
"Batter keeps 1 to 2 months in refrigerator!"

Average
May Prepare Ahead

Yields: 4 dozen
Bake: 20 minutes at 400°

2 cups All-Bran cereal	2 teaspoons salt
2 cups shredded wheat cereal	4½ teaspoons soda
½ cup boiling water	½ teaspoon baking powder
1 cup shortening	1 quart buttermilk
3 cups sugar	1 cup chopped dates
4 eggs	1 cup chopped raisins
5 cups flour	

- ◆ Pour boiling water over all-bran and shredded wheat, in medium bowl.
- ◆ Cream shortening, sugar and eggs in large bowl and beat well.
- ◆ Add cereal mixture and stir well.
- ◆ Mix with dry ingredients and add to egg mixture, alternating with buttermilk.
- ◆ Add chopped dates and raisins.
- ◆ Covered, batter will keep in refrigerator 1 to 2 months.
- ◆ Grease muffin tins well.
- ◆ Bake 20 minutes at 400°.
- ◆ Muffin mixture improves with age.

Mrs. John Ball Howard (Eleanor Vest)

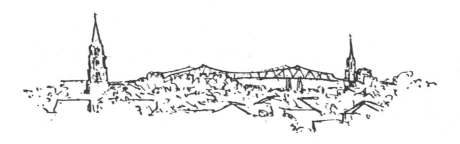

Buttermilk Pancakes

"These are like eating peanuts—once you start eating them, it's hard to stop!"

Average
Serve Immediately

Serves: 4
Cook: on hot griddle

3	eggs, separated	1	cup flour
2½	cups buttermilk	½	teaspoon salt
2	teaspoons baking powder	2	tablespoons sugar
1	teaspoon soda	6	tablespoons butter, melted

- Beat egg whites, set aside.
- Beat egg yolks and add buttermilk.
- Sift dry ingredients into the milk mixture. Stir well.
- Add melted butter.
- Fold in egg whites.
- Cook on hot greased skillet until golden brown, turning once.

* Waffles—add ½ cup more flour.

Mrs. Robert H. Hood (Bernie Burnham)

Dot's German Pancake

"Makes one wonderful giant pancake!"

Easy
Serve Immediately

Serves: 6 to 8
Bake: 40 to 45 minutes at 375°

4	eggs	2	cups unsifted all purpose flour
2	cups milk	1	teaspoon vanilla extract
1	teaspoon salt		butter
⅓	cup sugar		

- Beat eggs until fluffy.
- Add remaining ingredients.
- Beat until smooth.
- Butter, thickly, a 12 inch heavy skillet.
- Bake 375° for 40 to 45 minutes.

Topping:

¼	cup powdered sugar	½	to 1 cup fresh fruit
½	teaspoon lemon juice		

- Sprinkle baked pancake with powdered sugar, lemon juice and fresh fruit of your choice. (May use heated syrup also.)

Mrs. John Palmer Gaillard, III (Henrietta Freeman)

Lorell's Blender Pancakes

Easy
Serve Immediately

Serves: 3 to 4
Cook: on hot griddle

2 eggs
½ cup small curd cottage cheese
¾ cup sour cream

½ cup flour
½ teaspoon salt
¼ teaspoon soda

♦ Combine eggs, cottage cheese, and sour cream in blender. Blend.
♦ Combine flour, salt, and soda and add to blender. Blend well.
♦ Pour in hot greased griddle in desired size.

* Can sprinkle blueberries on pancake before flipping. Top with sour cream and/or strawberry or blueberry jam or fresh fruit.

Mrs. Thomas J. Parsell (Susan Poston)

Sourdough Pancakes Or Waffles

Average
Serve Immediately

Serves: 4
Cook: on hot griddle

1 cup flour, sifted
2 tablespoons sugar
1½ teaspoons baking powder
½ teaspoon salt
½ teaspoon baking soda

1 egg, beaten
1 cup sourdough starter
½ cup milk
2 tablespoons vegetable oil

♦ Combine flour, sugar, baking powder, salt and soda, in large bowl.
♦ Combine egg, starter, milk, and oil; stir in flour mixture until completely moistened. Do not worry about lumps.
♦ Spoon batter, 2 tablespoons per pancake, onto lightly greased hot griddle or frying pan.
♦ Cook, turning once until golden.
♦ Makes about 2 dozen silver-dollar pancakes.

* For WAFFLES, prepare batter as for pancakes, but increase oil to ¼ cup.

Mrs. Stanley M. Wilson (Penny Hawk)

Crepes
"If you haven't tried these, you're missing out."

Average
May Prepare Ahead
Freezes Well

Serves: 4
Cook: until crepe no longer
bubbles or steams!

1¼ cups flour
    pinch salt
3 eggs, beaten

1½ cups milk
2 tablespoons butter, melted

+ Place all ingredients in blender and mix well.
+ Let batter stand 1 hour.
+ Dip crepe pan into batter.
+ Lift up and turn over, placing pan back on burner.
+ When crepe no longer steams or bubbles, it is done.

Mrs. Joseph P. Bucknum (Jane Smith)

Best Breakfast Waffles
"Batter will keep refrigerated for several days."

Average
May Prepare Ahead
Freezes Well

Serves: 4
Cook: waffle iron

4 eggs
1 cup unbleached flour
1 cup whole wheat flour
1 teaspoon salt
1 teaspoon baking soda
1 teaspoon baking powder

1 cup butter, melted
½ cup bran (optional)
2 cups buttermilk or 1 cup milk
    plus 1 cup either yogurt
    or sour cream

+ Preheat waffle iron.
+ Beat eggs until light.
+ Mix together dry ingredients.
+ Add dry mixture and milk alternately to beaten eggs, beating well after each addition. Begin and end with dry mixture.
+ Add melted butter.
+ Blend thoroughly.
+ Stir in bran.
+ Pour in waffle iron. Serve hot.

Mrs. Horry Heriot Kerrison (Dorothy Barnwell)

My Mother's Waffles

Easy
Serve Immediately

Serves: 3-4

2 eggs, separated
1 cup flour
¾ teaspoon salt
1 cup milk

4 tablespoons butter
2 heaping teaspoons baking powder

- Sift flour and salt together.
- Beat egg yolks. Add milk and flour alternately.
- Beat in melted butter. Add baking powder.
- Fold in beaten egg whites.

Mrs. G. MacFarlane Mood, Jr. (Martha Beverly Wayt)

Orange French Toast
"Wonderful Sunday breakfast tradition"

Easy
Serve Immediately

Yields: 8 slices
Fry

2 eggs
1 teaspoon grated orange rind
juice of one orange
1 tablespoon sugar (or more, depending on sweetness of orange)

½ teaspoon vanilla
8 slices of French bread

- Beat together all ingredients except bread.
- Dip bread into mixture.
- Fry bread in butter.
- Top with powdered sugar.

* Serve with sliced country ham.·

Mrs. James Mitchell Stelling (Kathleen Hubbard)

SALAD, SALAD DRESSINGS

It's as though city planners intended Charleston to be seen from above. The view from the top of the Calhoun Mansion is a mosaic of colors and textures so vivid and varied that it cries out to be put on canvas.

The rooftops reflect the intimacy of a European city and the stout independent feeling that marks Charleston. The different architectural forms blend into a kaleidescope of beauty. The houses are close to each other but, at the same time, seem to keep a respectful distance.

And the vista is crowned with the cooling blue of Charleston Harbor.

SALADS

Pink Cranberry Freeze

Easy
Prepare Ahead

Serves: 6 to 8
Freeze: overnight

2   (3 ounce) packages
    cream cheese
½   cup mayonnaise
2   tablespoons sugar
1   (16 ounce) can whole berry
    cranberry sauce

½   cup chopped nuts
1   cup whipping cream
    (Coolwhip may be substituted)

- Soften cheese.
- Mix in mayonnaise and sugar.
- Add cranberries and nuts.
- Fold in whipped cream.
- Pour into square casserole and freeze.

Mrs. Lillian Green Yarborough

Fresh Cranberry Salad

Easy
Prepare Ahead

Serves: 15
Chill: overnight

1   3-ounce package cherry Jello
½   envelope unflavored gelatin
1   cup hot water
1   cup sugar
1   tablespoon lemon juice
    (fresh or frozen)
1   15½-ounce can crushed
    pineapple, reserve juice

2   cups fresh whole cranberries,
    chopped to equal 1 cup
    chopped berries
1   orange, chopped
1   cup chopped celery
1   to 1½ cup chopped , pecans

- Dissolve jello and gelatin in hot water.
- Add sugar and lemon juice.
- Drain juice from pineapple and add pineapple.
- Stir well to dissolve sugar.
- Coarsely chop cranberries in a food processor.
- Cut orange in sections.
- Remove center membrane and seeds before chopping finely in the food processor.
- Chop celery and nuts.
- Add all ingredients and pineapple juice to gelatin mixture.
- Spoon into approximately 15 small individual molds.
- Chill until firm.
- Cover top of molds with wax paper before refrigerating.

Mrs. Carlton Simons (Etta Ray Longshore)

Watercress and Orange Salad

Easy
May Prepare Ahead

Serves: 4

Salad

1 bunch watercress	½ medium red onion, thinly sliced
1 medium orange, peeled and sectioned	1 2-ounce package blue cheese, crumbled (optional)

- Wash watercress and drain.
- Remove all tough stems.
- Combine with orange sections and onion.
- Toss with dressing.
- Sprinkle with crumbled blue cheese, if desired.

Dressing

8 tablespoons oil	⅛ teaspoon salt
2 tablespoons red wine vinegar	dash of pepper
1 teaspoon dijon mustard	dash of tarragon

- In small jar, combine dressing ingredients.
- Shake well until blended.

*May substitute different lettuces for watercress and can toss in a few shrimp to change the taste.

Emma A. McLain

Orange Salad Mold
"Very good with a little curry"

Easy
Prepare Ahead

Serves: 8
Chill: overnight

1 package orange jello (3-ounce size)	2 cans mandarin oranges - drained
1 cup boiling water	½ cup slivered almonds
1 cup orange juice	cottage cheese
	mayonnaise

- Pour boiling water over jello.
- Stir until completely dissolved.
- Add orange juice.
- Place bowl containing orange mixture in a bowl containing ice water.
- Stir occasionally.
- When mixture begins to gel, add oranges and almonds.
- Pour into ring mold and refrigerate overnight.
- To serve, turn out on platter with lettuce.
- Fill center with cottage cheese.
- Serve with mayonnaise.

Mrs. Lawrence A. Walker (Phyllis Corson)

Black Bing Cherry Salad

Easy
May Prepare Ahead

Serves: 6
Chill: until set

1   (3 ounce) package cherry Jello
1   cup boiling water
1   cup bing cherry juice
1   (16 ounce) can black bing cherries (pitted)

1   (8 ounce) can pineapples in heavy syrup (cut in small pieces, save juice)
1   (8 ounce) package cream cheese

♦ Dissolve jello in hot water.
♦ Add one cup bing cherry juice, bing cherries and pineapple.
♦ Place in refrigerator until set.
♦ Cream the cream cheese with pineapple juice until consistency of whipped cream, and spread on top of salad.
♦ May add food coloring to topping if so desired.

Mrs. James Mitchell Stelling (Kathleen Hubbard)

Melon Salad Supreme
"Mint makes the difference."

Average
Partial Prepare Ahead

Serves: 6
Chill: 1 to 2 hours

Salad

2   cantaloupes
1   cucumber
1   cup green seedless grapes

3   medium tomatoes
2   tablespoons fresh chopped mint

♦ Cut cantaloupes in half, removing seeds. Use melon baller to make balls. Scrape hull, clean and save for serving salad.
♦ Peel cucumber, cut in half, remove seeds. Cut in strips lengthwise, then across in 1-inch strips.
♦ Peel and seed tomatoes and cut in strips.
♦ Mix cantaloupes, cucumber, grapes, and tomatoes together.
♦ Just before serving, add mint to this combination, and mix dressing in carefully.

Dressing:

2   tablespoons lemon juice
1   tablespoon sugar
2   tablespoons oil

¼   cup half and half
     salt and pepper

♦ Whisk lemon juice with sugar, salt, and pepper until sugar and salt dissolve.
♦ Whisk in oil gradually, and then cream until dressing thickens slightly.
♦ Correct seasoning, if necessary.
♦ Dressing may be made up to 6 hours before serving.

Ann W. Dibble

Ambrosia Salad

Average　　　　　　　　　　　　**Serves:** 10 to 12
Prepare Ahead　　　　　　　　　**Chill:** 24 hours

Dressing

4　egg yolks
½　cup milk

½　teaspoon prepared mustard
1　pint whipped cream

Salad

3　pounds grapes (seedless)
1　20 ounce can pineapple
　　cubes

1　(10½) package mini
　　marshmallows
1　cup nuts

♦ In saucepan, cook dressing until thick over low heat.
♦ When dressing is slightly cooled, add whipped cream.
♦ Stir grapes, pineapple, marshmallows and nuts into dressing and refrigerate
　24 hours.

Kelley Warner

Pistachio Salad

Easy　　　　　　　　　　　　　**Serves:** 8 to 12
Prepare Ahead　　　　　　　　　**Chill:** 4 hours

1　(3½ ounce) box pistachio
　　pudding and pie mix
1　(12 ounce) small curd cottage
　　cheese
1　(15¼ ounce) can crushed
　　pineapple, drained

1　(11 ounce) can mandarin
　　oranges
1　(16 ounce) carton whipped
　　topping (cool whip)

♦ Combine pudding mix with cottage cheese.
♦ Drain pineapple and oranges and add to mixture.
♦ Fold in whipped topping.
♦ Refrigerate for 4 hours or overnight.

* Can be used as dessert.

Mrs. Edward J. Reynolds (May Robertson)

Creamy Cantaloupe Sauce
"Fabulous on fresh fruit"

Easy
Prepare Ahead

Yields: 2½ cups

juice of ½ lemon
1   envelope gelatin
½   cup apricot nectar, heated
⅓   cup sugar

1   cup diced cantaloupe
1   cup half and half
2   tablespoons rum

- Put lemon juice in blender.
- Sprinkle gelatin in lemon juice.
- Add hot nectar and blend for one minute.
- Add sugar and blend.
- While blending, remove cover and add cantaloupe and cream.
- Refrigerate until ready to serve.
- At serving time, stir in rum and pour sauce over fresh fruit compote.

Mrs. Philip W. Cotton (Ann Copenhaver)

Fruit Dip I
"Great with strawberries and melons."

Easy
May Prepare Ahead

Yield: 2 cups

1   pint sour cream
1   tablespoon brown sugar

1   teaspoon vanilla

- Mix all ingredients.
- Serve in side dish for dipping mixed fruit or mixed with fruit for dessert.

Mrs. Joseph L. Johnson, Jr. (Beverly Stoney)

Fruit Dip II

Easy
May Prepare Ahead

Serves: 6 to 8
Chill: 1 hour

1   16-ounce container of
     cottage cheese
¼   cup plain yogurt

¼   cup honey
¼   cup shredded coconut
1   teaspoon orange rind

- Put cottage cheese in blender and mix at low speed until smooth.
- Pour cottage cheese into a bowl and add remaining ingredients. Stir well.
- Cover and refrigerate until chilled, about 1 hour.
- Can be served in a hollowed-out cantaloupe half.

Mrs. Edmund Rhett (Sally Aichele)

Feta Cheese Salad

Average
Partial Prepare Ahead

Serves: 2
Marinate: 2 hours

½ cup olive oil
  thyme
  salt and pepper
  medallions of goat (Feta) cheese

1 cup bread crumbs
  croutons
  butter or garlic butter
  assorted lettuces

- Combine olive oil, salt, pepper and thyme and pour over cheese medallions.
- Marinate for 2 hours.
- Mix 1 teaspoon thyme with 1 cup bread crumbs.
- Coat the cheese medallions with bread crumbs and thyme mixture for a few minutes.
- Put coated cheese medallions on baking dish in 400° oven for 3 to 4 minutes only (just to heat through).
- Brush croutons with butter or garlic butter, and put in oven to dry.
- Arrange lettuces on cold plates, top with warm goat cheese medallions.
- Spoon on vinaigrette salad dressing and garnish with garlic croutons.

Basic Vinaigrette Salad Dressing

1 teaspoon salt
½ teaspoon pepper
  oil
  vinegar

  chopped shallots or garlic
  (optional)
1 teaspoon prepared Dijon mustard
  (optional)

- Combine 1 teaspoon salt, ½ teaspoon pepper, 4-5 parts oil and 1 part vinegar. Can use olive oil or part olive oil and part vegetable oil. Options include a little chopped shallot or garlic. Also, dressing is enhanced with 1 teaspoon of prepared Dijon mustard.

Mr. G. Marshall Mundy

P. A.'s Salad

Easy
Partial Prepare Ahead

Serves: 10
Chill: until serving time

Salad

2 heads Romaine lettuce
1 bag spinach
1 head iceberg lettuce

3 cans mandarin oranges
1 cup bacon bits
1 package sliced almonds

- Wash lettuces and spinach and pat dry.
- Shred lettuces and spinach in large salad bowl.
- Drain oranges and add with bacon bits and almonds to lettuce and spinach.

Dressing: Proportions for one serving. Multiply by # of people serving.

¼	cup oil	2	tablespoons wine vinegar
2	tablespoons sugar	½	teaspoon salt

- In large jar, pour oil, sugar, vinegar, and salt to proportions needed for number of servings.
- Stir well, secure top tightly, and shake well.
- Refrigerate until ready to use.
- Pour on salad and toss well.

Mrs. Edward Drummond Izard (Missy Craver)

Spinach Salad

Easy
Prepare Ahead

Serves: 6 to 8
Chill: overnight

Salad

1	10-ounce package fresh spinach	1	cup chopped scallions
6	slices bacon, cooked and crumbled	8	ounces swiss cheese, grated
6	hard-boiled eggs, sliced	1	10-ounce package frozen peas, thawed

- Tear spinach into bite size pieces.
- Fry bacon until crisp; drain, crumble and set aside.
- In a glass bowl, place 4 cups spinach.
- Line perimeter with egg slices and place remaining ones on top.
- Layer remaining bacon and scallions on spinach and eggs, reserving 1 tablespoon each of bacon and scallions.
- Top with layer of swiss cheese and peas.
- Spread dressing evenly over top, sealing all edges.
- Cover and refrigerate several hours or overnight.
- Sprinkle with remaining bacon and scallions.

Dressing:

1	8-ounce carton sour cream	¼	cup mayonnaise
1	1.4-ounce package buttermilk salad dressing mix	2	tablespoons milk

- In a medium bowl, combine sour cream, mayonnaise, salad dressing mix and milk.
- Stir until well blended, cover and refrigerate.

Barbara Dunbar Lyles

Layered Salad

Easy
Prepare Ahead

Serves: 6
Chill: 24 hours

1	medium head of lettuce
3	small bell peppers (diced)
3	stalks celery
¼	cup onions (diced)
2	cups mayonnaise
1	tablespoon Worcestershire sauce

1	tablespoon sugar
¼	cup bacon bits
¼	cup Parmesan cheese
¼	cup shredded cheddar cheese

♦ Tear lettuce and place in dish as first layer.
♦ Add layer of bell peppers, celery and onions.
♦ Combine mayonnaise and Worcestershire sauce, and pour over layers.
♦ Refrigerate for 24 hours, if possible.
♦ Before serving, top with bacon bits and cheeses.

Mrs. Steven Edward Turner (Legare Hay)

Avocado Shrimp Salad

Easy
May Prepare Ahead

Serves: 6
Chill: until serving time

2	ripe avocados, peeled and halved
	lemon juice
1	pound raw, headless, peeled shrimp
1	small can pineapple rings (drain and mince)
½	cup bell pepper, finely chopped

½	cup celery, destringed and finely chopped
⅔	cup firm sour cream
1	teaspoon onion salt
	Red tip lettuce, picked, washed and drained, for garnish
1	cup swiss cheese, shredded

♦ Coat avocado halves with lemon juice and chill.
♦ Cook shrimp in large quantity salted water for 3 minutes.
♦ Drain and cool in refrigerator.
♦ Combine pineapple, bell pepper, celery, sour cream, onion salt and shrimp.
♦ Refrigerate for 30-45 minutes.
♦ Scoop out hollow of avocado to allow room for mixture.
♦ Mound mixture on halves and cover with shredded cheese.
♦ Refrigerate until ready to serve.
♦ Serve on bed of lettuce.

Mr. Ben McC. Moise

Sea Shells 'N Shrimp Salad
"Wonderful luncheon fare"

Easy
Prepare Same Day

Serves: 6
Chill: until serving time

1   cup sea shell pasta, cooked
    and drained
¾   pound fresh shrimp, cooked,
    peeled and deveined
2   tablespoons pimento, chopped
¼   cup onion, minced
¼   cup green pepper, chopped

¼   cup celery, chopped
4   stuffed olives, sliced
¾   cup ranch dressing
½   teaspoon salt
1   tablespoon lemon juice
    lettuce leaves

♦ Combine first 10 ingredients.
♦ Toss lightly, chill and serve on lettuce leaves with garnish.
COMMENTS: Paprika can be sprinkled lightly over salad for extra color.
Garnish with tomato wedges, boiled eggs (sliced), and green pepper rings.

Mrs. Isaac A. Speights, III (Elizabeth "Betsy" Lesesne)

Shrimp In Grapefruit With Sauce
"Excellent for a light luncheon or a salad course."

Easy
May Prepare Ahead

Serves: 8
Chill: 1 hour

1½ pounds shrimp, cooked,
    deveined, and cut in half
4   grapefruit
1   8 ounce bottle Thousand Island
    dressing

2   tablespoons horseradish
2   tablespoons Hellmann's
    mayonnaise
1   tablespoon lemon juice

♦ Cut grapefruit in half.
♦ Cut out middle and around each section of grapefruit.
♦ Spoon a generous amount of shrimp in middle of grapefruit.
♦ Mix dressing, horseradish, mayonnaise and lemon juice together.
♦ Spoon sauce generously over shrimp.
♦ Chill and serve.

Mrs. C. Deas Gadsden (Lou Kidder)

Curried Turkey Salad

Easy
May Prepare Ahead

Serves: 8
Chill: until serving time

½ turkey breast (3 cups - chopped and cooked)
½ cup celery (chopped)
2 teaspoons onions, grated
1 cup seedless grapes (halved)

½ cup sliced almonds
1 apple, peeled and diced
2 teaspoons curry powder
1½ cups mayonnaise
salt and pepper to taste

♦ In large mixing bowl, mix all ingredients together.
♦ Refrigerate until ready to serve.

Mrs. Robert K. Sadler (Frances Adele Allen)

Fabulous Chicken Salad
"This is great increased for a large crowd."

Easy
Prepare Ahead

Serves: 6

4 cups cubed chicken
1½ cups chopped celery
1 cup mayonnaise
2 tablespoons lemon juice
2½ tablespoons soy sauce

1 tablespoon onion juice
½ cup chutney
½ cup toasted almonds
½ cup water chestnuts
1 cup green grapes

♦ Mix first 7 ingredients a day ahead.
♦ Just before serving add last 3 ingredients.
★ Use any amount of almonds, chestnuts or grapes that you like.

Mrs. Hugh Z. Graham (Mary Ball)

Chicken Salad

Average
May Prepare Ahead

Serves: 6 to 8
Marinate: 3 to 4 hours
Bake: 15 minutes at 325°

3   cups cooked chicken, cubed
1⅓ cups celery
⅓   cup French dressing
1½ cups shredded cheddar cheese
1½ cups seedless grapes
⅓   cup slivered almonds

1½ cups sour cream
1½ teaspoons prepared mustard
½   teaspoon salt
1   cup crushed potato chips
1   cup cheese

♦ Marinate chicken in dressing several hours.
♦ Combine with other ingredients.
♦ Top with chips and grated cheese.
♦ Heat for 15 minutes at 325°.

Mrs. Frank B. Murphy (Amy Bain)

Hot Chicken Salad

Average
Prepare Ahead

Serves: 8
Chill: overnight
Bake: 20 to 25 minutes at 400°

4   cups cooked chicken (cut up)
2   tablespoons lemon juice
¾   cup mayonnaise
1   teaspoon salt
2   cups celery, chopped
4   hard boiled eggs, sliced
¾   cup cream of chicken soup

1   teaspoon onion, finely minced
2   small jars of pimentos, cut fine
1½ cups crushed potato chips
1   cup grated cheese
⅔   cup toasted almonds,
    finely chopped

♦ Combine all ingredients except cheese, potato chips and almonds.
♦ Place in large rectangular baking dish.
♦ Top with cheese, potato chips and almonds.
♦ Let stand overnight in refrigerator.
♦ Bake at 400° for 20-25 minutes.

Mrs. Henry Fishburne (Amy Allston)

Lemon-Vegetable Congealed Salad

Easy
Prepare Ahead

Serves: 8 to 10
Chill: until set

1   (6-ounce) package lemon
    flavored gelatin (reg. or
    unsweetened)
¾ cup boiling water
¼ teaspoon salt
½ cup evaporated milk
¼ cup vinegar
1   (12-ounce) carton small curd
    cottage cheese

1   cup celery, finely chopped
1   cup carrots, shredded
2-3 tablespoons green pepper,
    chopped
1   tablespoon green onion,
    chopped
½ cup mayonnaise

♦ Dissolve gelatin in boiling water.
♦ Add salt, milk, vinegar.
♦ Mix well.
♦ Stir in remaining ingredients.
♦ Pour into lightly oiled 5-cup mold.
♦ Chill until firm.

Mrs. Kevin Fitzgerald (Carole Holeman)

Tomato Aspic
"Just Wonderful"

Easy
Prepare Ahead

Serves: 6 to 8
Chill: until firm

2   packages unflavored gelatin
4   cups tomato cocktail juice
1   cup cottage cheese
½ cup mayonnaise

½ cup pecans, chopped
½ cup green peppers, diced
    salt and pepper to taste

♦ Dissolve gelatin in ½ cup tomato cocktail juice.
♦ Heat rest of juice until it boils and add gelatin.
♦ Pour into mold and refrigerate until almost set (at least 2 hours).
♦ Combine remaining ingredients.
♦ Scoop out center of aspic mold, leaving ½ inch side all around.
♦ Pack cheese and nut mixture into center and spoon remaining aspic back into mold.
♦ Heat the removed gelatin mixture just slightly to melt it, and pour this over the top of the mold.
♦ Return to refrigerator until firm.
♦ Serve on a bed of lettuce.

Ann W. Dibble

Congealed Asparagus Salad
"Great With Turkey"

Average
Prepare Ahead

Serves: 10
Chill: overnight

1 cup sugar	juice one lemon
1 cup water	1 cup chopped celery
½ cup vinegar	1 small can pimentos, chopped
½ teaspoon salt	1 small mild onion, grated
2 envelopes Knox gelatin	½ cup pecans, chopped
½ cup cold water	1 cup asparagus, chopped

- Combine sugar, water, vinegar and salt.
- Let come to a boil, then cool.
- Dissolve 2 envelopes Knox gelatin in ½ cup cold water.
- After gelatin has dissolved, add to warm sugar syrup.
- Add juice of 1 lemon.
- Combine rest of ingredients, mold and refrigerate.

Mrs. Richard H. Lee (Beth Moxley)

Tabbouleh Salad
"Summertime/Lunchtime"

Average
Prepare Ahead

Yields: 1½-2 quarts
Chill: 24 hours

Serve over lettuce or stuff in pita bread.

1 cup uncooked bulghur (or wheat pilaf)	3 tomatoes, finely chopped
½ cup olive oil	3 green peppers, seeded and finely chopped
⅓ -½ cup lemon juice (to taste)	2 large cucumbers, peeled and chopped
1 cup green onions (finely chopped) including green tops	fresh ground pepper to taste
1 cup celery, chopped	2 teaspoons salt
1 cup parsley, chopped	
1 cup fresh mint, or 2 tablespoons dried	

- Use 1½ to 2 quart jar with screw top, if possible.
- Place bulghur in bottom of container.
- Mix oil and lemon juice in small bowl.
- Pour over bulghur.
- Add vegetables in layers in order listed above.
- Sprinkle last layer (cucumbers) with salt and pepper.
- Cover and refrigerate at least 24 hours or until bulghur is light tan in color.
- Just before serving, shake jar well.

Mrs. J. Conrad Zimmerman, Jr. (Barbara Hubbard)

Broccoli Salad Supreme

Easy
May Prepare Ahead

Serves: 8
Chill: 1 to 2 hours

2 heads broccoli
2 medium onions, diced
1 cup Kraft Cracker Barrel cheese, extra sharp

1 pound bacon, fried crisp and crumbled

Dressing:

1 cup mayonnaise
½ cup sugar

6 tablespoons wine vinegar
1 tablespoon bacon drippings

♦ Cut broccoli flowerettes into bite-sized pieces.
♦ Mix together broccoli, onions, cheese, and bacon.
♦ Combine ingredients for dressing.
♦ Top broccoli mixture with dressing and mix well.

Jean C. Bouch

Broccoli Salad

Easy
Prepare Ahead

Serves: 6
Chill: overnight

1 bunch raw broccoli
½ cup green olives, chopped
4 hard boiled eggs, chopped

1 small onion, chopped
1 teaspoon fresh lemon juice
½ cup mayonnaise

♦ Cut clusters of broccoli into bite size pieces.
♦ Combine with all other ingredients.
♦ Place in refrigerator the day before serving to chill.

Sarah Edwards Dargan

Layered Potato Salad
"Different and Delicious"

Easy
Prepare Ahead

Serves: 6 to 8
Chill: 8 hours

8 medium baking potatoes, boiled until just done
2½ cups mayonnaise
2 cups sour cream
1 teaspoon horseradish

1 teaspoon celery seed
½ teaspoon salt
1 medium onion, finely chopped
salt to taste
½ cup fresh parsley

- Peel and slice potatoes in ⅛ inch thick slices.
- Combine mayonnaise, sour cream, horseradish, celery seed and salt, and set aside.
- In another bowl, mix parsley and onion.
- In a large serving bowl, arrange single layer of potato slices.
- Cover with layer of mayonnaise mixture.
- Sprinkle layer with onion and parsley.
- Continue layering ending with parsley and onion.
- Do not stir.
- Cover and refrigerate at least 8 hours before serving.

Mrs. Richard R. Patterson, Jr. (Elizabeth Edmondson)

"New" Potato Salad

Average   **Serves:** 8 to 10
May Prepare Ahead

Serve warm or chilled.

Salad

3	pounds new potatoes	1	teaspoon basil
1	bunch green onions, chopped	¼	cup parsley
1	cup celery, chopped	3	boiled eggs, chopped

- Boil potatoes and drain.
- Do not peel.
- Cut potatoes into fourths.
- Toss potatoes with dressing.
- Combine other ingredients.
- Toss and adjust seasonings.

Dressing:

½	teaspoon salt	3	tablespoons red wine vinegar
¼	teaspoon pepper	½	cup mayonnaise
1	tablespoon dijon	½	cup vegetable or salad oil
2	cloves minced garlic		

- Combine all ingredients.
- Blend well.

Mrs. Ronald B. Shealy (Sharon Amos)

Cold Peas And Cucumber Salad

Easy
May Prepare Ahead

Serves: 6
Chill: until serving time

2   packages frozen peas, thawed, drained, and paper towel dried
6   green onions, coarsely chopped
1   cucumber, seeded

¼   cup mayonnaise
¼   cup sour cream
½   teaspoon dill weed
     touch of garlic salt

♦ Combine all ingredients in mixing bowl.
♦ Stir until well covered with dressing.
♦ Chill and serve.

Pam Edwards

Crunchy Pea Salad

Average
Prepare Ahead

Serves: 4
Chill: overnight

Salad:

1   (10 ounce) package frozen peas, thawed
1   cup chopped celery
¼   cup green onion, chopped
1   cup cashews or macadamia nuts, chopped

¼   cup crisp bacon bits
1   cup sour cream
¼   cup dressing (recipe follows)
½   teaspoon salt

♦ Combine peas, celery, onions, nuts and bacon.
♦ Mix together the sour cream and dressing and fold in gently.
♦ Refrigerate overnight.
♦ Keep several days.

Dressing:

⅓   tablespoon lemon juice
⅓   cup red wine vinegar
½   tablespoon salt
¼   teaspoon pepper
½   tablespoon Worcestershire sauce

½   teaspoon dijon mustard
1   clove garlic, mashed
½   teaspoon sugar
1   cup corn oil

♦ In blender, combine all seasonings, gradually add oil and blend again.
Delicious for all type salads.
Great recipe for summer, but can also be served as a substitute for green salad with dinner entrée.

Mrs. Hugh M. Doherty (Mary Pierce)

Mrs. Roger's Carrot Salad

Easy
Prepare Ahead

Serves: 12
Marinate: 24 hours

1   can condensed tomato soup
¾   cup sugar
¼   cup vinegar
1   teaspoon salt
      dash pepper
¼   teaspoon prepared mustard
1   teaspoon Worcestershire sauce

      dash of tabasco sauce
½   cup corn oil
3   small onions, cut in rings
1   green pepper, chopped
2   pounds carrots, sliced, cooked,
      drained and cooled

♦ Combine all ingredients except carrots to make sauce.
♦ Gently fold in carrots and allow to marinate at least 24 hours in refrigerator.
♦ Drain before serving.

Mrs. John F. Maybank (Kay McCracken)

Green Bean & Mushroom Salad
"Great With Bar-B-Que Chicken"

Average
May Prepare Ahead

Serves: 4 to 6

1½ pounds cooked fresh green
      beans (whole)
2   cups fresh mushrooms
      (chopped)
3   tablespoons shallots, chopped
1½ teaspoons salt
½   teaspoon pepper

½   teaspoon dry mustard
½   teaspoon paprika
2   ounces tarragon vinegar
1   clove garlic, minced
4   ounces olive oil
¼   cup toasted almonds

♦ Combine mushrooms, beans, and shallots.
♦ Combine all other ingredients and pour on top.
♦ Toss with toasted almonds.

Mrs. Kenneth E. Pritchett (Jennifer Boozer)

SALAD DRESSINGS

Aunt Hassie's Salad Dressing

Easy
May Prepare Ahead

Yields: 1 cup

½ cup oil	1 clove garlic, crushed
¼ cup lemon juice	1 teaspoon salt
3 tablespoons tarragon vinegar	½ teaspoon dry mustard
2 tablespoons sugar	pepper
2 tablespoons onion, minced	

- Combine all ingredients together in jar.
- Cucumbers are tasty when marinated in dressing ½ hour before tossed with greens.
- Redwine vinegar may be substituted for tarragon.

Mrs. David Knott (Marian Greely)

Celery Seed Dressing

Easy
May Prepare Ahead

Yields: 1 pint
Chill: Until serving time

a|00
V. g.

⅓ cup sugar	1 teaspoon paprika
1 teaspoon salt	1 teaspoon grated onion
1 teaspoon dry mustard	4 tablespoons vinegar (balsamic)
1 teaspoon celery seed	1 cup salad oil

- Combine all ingredients in a jar and shake well.
- Refrigerate until ready to serve.

Mrs. Telfair H. Parker (Hope Haselden)

Poppy Seed Dressing
"Try this over sandwiches and fruit salads"

Easy
Prepare Ahead

Yields: 2 cups
Chill: overnight

¾ cup sugar	1½ tablespoons onion, grated
1 teaspoon dry mustard	1 cup oil
¼ to ½ teaspoon salt	1½ tablespoons poppy seed
½ cup vinegar	

- Combine first 4 ingredients.
- Add onion and gradually add oil, then add poppy seed.
- Refrigerate overnight.

Mrs. Henry Lide DuRant (Kay Ravenel)

Nancy's Sweet & Sour Dressing

"Great accompaniment for fruit"

Easy
May Prepare Ahead

Yields: 1 quart
Chill

1½ cups sugar
4 teaspoons salt
2 teaspoons dry mustard

1 onion, grated
1½ cups vinegar
2 cups Mazola oil

◆ Combine first 3 ingredients and set aside.
◆ Place vinegar and oil into blender and beat several minutes until well blended.
◆ Add onion to liquid and beat until fine.
◆ Add dry ingredients and beat until well mixed, almost creamy in appearance.
◆ Refrigerate.
◆ Shake well before using.

Mrs. William A. Wier, Jr. (Jean Garrison)

Greek Salad Dressing

Easy
Prepare Ahead

Yields: 1 cup
Chill: until serving time

⅔ cup light oil
2 tablespoons olive oil
1 teaspoon salt
1 teaspoon pepper

1 teaspoon oregano
1 clove fresh garlic, pressed
sugar to taste
⅓ cup wine vinegar

◆ Combine all ingredients in large jar.
◆ Refrigerate until ready to serve.

Mrs. Edward Wilson Riggs (Rebecca Turner)

Sagafjord Cucumber Dressing

Easy
May Prepare Ahead

Yields: 1½ cups
Marinate: overnight

6 small cucumbers (it is important to use small cucumbers with tender seeds)
¾ cup vinegar

1 cup water
6 packets artificial sweetener
1 tablespoon oil

◆ Peel and thinly slice cucumbers.
◆ Marinate overnight in mixture of vinegar, water, sweetener and oil.
◆ Refrigerate until ready to serve.

Mrs. Mac Harley (Nancy Gardner)

Granny's French Dressing

"Excellent marinade for cold peeled shrimp"

Easy
Prepare Ahead

Yields: 1 quart
Marinate: overnight

1 medium onion	1½ cups salad oil
¼ cup catsup	1 cup cider vinegar
¾ cup chili sauce	½ teaspoon Worcestershire sauce
1½ cups olive oil	salt and pepper to taste

♦ Quarter onion and put pieces in bottom of quart jar.
♦ Add remaining ingredients and stir.
♦ Let stand overnight in refrigerator.

Mrs. J. Gilbert Baldwin, Jr. (Constance Montague)

Blue Cheese Dressing

Easy
Prepare Ahead

Yields: 1 cup

3 ounces blue cheese	¼ teaspoon red pepper
½ cup whole milk	4 drops tabasco
½ teaspoon salt	

♦ Allow blue cheese to come to room temperature.
♦ Add ½ cup milk and mix well.
♦ Add salt, pepper, and tabasco.
♦ Let stand a few minutes.
♦ Add additional milk if necessary to attain consistency of cream sauce.
♦ Do not put in refrigerator before use.

Mrs. William Roger Lomax (Nadine Nielsen)

Artichoke Heart Filling

Easy
May Prepare Ahead

Serves: 6
Chill: until serving time

2 cups canned artichoke hearts	¾ cup Hellmann's mayonnaise
½ cup celery, chopped	salt and pepper to taste
½ cup green onions and tops, chopped	6 slices bacon, cooked and crumbled

♦ Combine first 5 ingredients.
♦ Stuff tomato or avocado with mixture.
♦ Line plate with salad greens.
♦ Crumble bacon on top and serve.

Mrs. Harris Thaxton (Lavinia Mikell)

POULTRY, MEAT AND GAME

There's a side of the Lowcountry that is best seen by boat. It's the unspoiled beauty of the tidal islands, the wide expanses of marsh and the tall stands of trees that probably looked the same when Indians inhabited the area.

It's a quietude that wildlife takes for granted. It's a fertile nesting ground for shore birds and marine creatures. It's a haven for deer and racoons.

And it's vast enough to allow abundant hunting and fishing as well as superb nature-watching.

POULTRY

Chicken Asparagus Delight
"An Old Favorite"

Average
May Prepare Ahead

Serves: 6
Bake: 25 minutes at 350°

1 3½-pound cooked chicken or 6 half breasts of chicken
4 tablespoons butter
3 eggs, hard boiled
2 15 ounce cans of asparagus
½ cup mayonnaise

1 10¾-ounce can cream of mushroom soup
1 tablespoon lemon juice
1 cup grated sharp cheese
25 Ritz crackers, crumbled
3 tablespoons butter, melted

◆ Boil and cool chicken, bone, keeping pieces large.
◆ Salt and pepper chicken to taste and sauté for 2-3 minutes in butter.
◆ Slice eggs thinly.
◆ Drain asparagus and spread in bottom of casserole.
◆ Top with layer of eggs, then chicken.
◆ Mix mayonnaise, soup, lemon juice, and cheese and pour over chicken.
◆ Sauté crackers in melted butter and sprinkle on top.
◆ Bake 350° for 25 minutes.

Mrs. Dolph Rodenberg, III (Robin Allen)

Artichoke Chicken & Noodles

Average
May Prepare Ahead
Freezes Well

Serves: 6 to 10
Cook: 1 hour 30 minutes over medium heat

1 whole chicken
½ lb. mushrooms, chopped
1 onion, quartered
1 large can tomatoes with juice
1 small can tomato paste
1 teaspoon sugar
½ cup chicken stock

½ cup red or white wine
1 tablespoon each of oil and butter
1 red or green pepper
1 package frozen artichoke hearts
   capers
   pepper
   noodles

◆ Cook chicken in water for 45 minutes.
◆ Reduce stock and bone chicken.
◆ In large pot, sauté mushrooms and onion in oil until tender.
◆ Add tomatoes, tomato paste, sugar, stock, wine, seasonings, and chicken.
◆ Cook 15 minutes.
◆ Add pepper, capers and artichoke hearts and cook until tender.
◆ Serve over noodles.

Susan Clarkson-Herre

111

Chicken Marengo

Average
May Prepare Ahead
Freezes Well

Serves: 4
Bake: 1 hour 10 minutes at 375°

1	2½ to 3 pound chicken cut up or chicken pieces	1	garlic clove, minced
1	can (16 oz.) tomatoes, broken up	1	teaspoon salt
½	cup frozen small whole onions	½	teaspoon thyme
½	cup dry sherry	½	teaspoon pepper
1	bay leaf	¼	pound mushrooms, sliced
		1	tablespoon cornstarch

- Skin chicken and trim fat.
- Place in uncovered casserole.
- Combine all other ingredients in medium bowl except mushrooms and cornstarch.
- Pour this mixture over chicken.
- Bake uncovered 50 minutes.
- Add mushrooms, cover, and cook 20 more minutes, turning occasionally.
- Remove from oven.
- In small bowl, make a paste with cornstarch and some liquid from casserole.
- Blend into casserole on top of stove.
- Bring to a boil and then turn heat down to simmer for 5 minutes.

Mrs. W. Vaughan Davidson (Sally Barton)

Chicken Wrapped In Bacon

Easy
May Prepare Ahead

Serves: 4
Bake: 1 hour at 350°

4	chicken breasts, boned salt and pepper to taste	4	slices bacon
1	to 2 teaspoons minced onion	1	tablespoon Kitchen Bouquet
		2	teaspoons flour

- Salt and pepper chicken, then sprinkle with onion.
- Wrap each loosely with bacon.
- Mix Kitchen Bouquet and flour into a paste.
- Roll wrapped chicken in paste.
- Place in covered pan and bake 1 hour at 350°.

Mrs. David C. Norton (Florence "Dee" Holmes)

Bullfrog Chicken
"The best way to grill chicken."

Easy
Prepare Ahead

Serves: 4
Refrigerate: overnight
Grill: 45 minutes to 1 hour

1	whole frying chicken	foil
1	jar rosemary	grill
1	cup kosher salt	

♦ The day before serving, clean chicken, removing excess fat.
♦ Cut both sides of the rib cage from tail to shoulder. Open, using the wing joints as pivots.
♦ Pound flat with the side of a knife.
♦ Place on foil, coat with salt and rosemary on both sides.
♦ Seal in the foil and refrigerate overnight.
♦ Cook on the grill.

* This looks just like a giant bullfrog.

Mr. J. Conrad Zimmerman, Jr.

Boursin Chicken

Easy
May Prepare Ahead

Serves: 6
Broil: approx. 20 minutes

1	package Boursin cheese	6	boneless chicken breasts
2	chopped green onions	12	bacon strips
	salt and pepper		toothpicks

♦ Divide Boursin cheese into 6 sections and roll into balls.
♦ Roll each cheese ball in chopped onion.
♦ Salt and pepper chicken.
♦ Wrap each chicken breast around cheese ball.
♦ Wrap 2 bacon strips around chicken breast.
♦ Secure with a toothpick and place on broiler pan.
♦ Broil under high heat until bacon is done.

Mrs. George C. Scarborough (Janet Wells)

DP's Chicken Saltimboca

Average
May Prepare Ahead

Serves: 6
Bake: 40 to 45 minutes at 350°

3   large chicken breasts (skinned, boned and halved)
6   thin slices boiled ham
3   slices mozzarella cheese
1   medium tomato, chopped
½   teaspoon dried sage

⅓   cup fine dry breadcrumbs
2   tablespoons grated Parmesan cheese
2   tablespoons minced parsley
4   tablespoons melted butter

◆ Pound each chicken breast with meat mallet until approximately 5 x 5.
◆ Place slice of ham and ½ slice cheese on each piece.
◆ Top with a teaspoon of tomato and a dash of sage.
◆ Tuck in sides and roll each breast in jelly roll fashion, pressing to seal well and using tooth picks.
◆ Combine breadcrumbs, Parmesan cheese and parsley.
◆ Dip chicken breasts in butter and roll in crumb mixture.
◆ Place in greased shallow baking dish.
◆ Bake at 350° 40-45 minutes.

Mrs. Frederick M. Gunter (Frances Scarborough)

Momma's Chicken Breast With Mushrooms

Easy
May Prepare Ahead

Serves: 8 to 10
Bake: 2½ hours at 325°

8 - 10 chicken breasts
1   stick real butter
    salt, pepper, paprika to taste

2   cans cream of mushroom soup
2   soup cans red port
2   small cans mushrooms

◆ Brown breasts in butter.
◆ Sprinkle with seasonings.
◆ Place chicken in roaster.
◆ Blend soup and port in separate bowl and add mushrooms.
◆ Pour over chicken.
◆ Cover and cook in oven 2½ hours.
◆ Baste occasionally during cooking.

* Serve with wild rice.

Mrs. R.R. Patterson, Jr. (Elizabeth Edmondson)

Lowcountry Cinnamon Chicken

Average
May Prepare Ahead

Serves: 8
Bake: 35-40 minutes at 350°

½ cup raisins
2 medium apples, peeled, cored, and chopped fine
½ cup sliced almonds
1 can water chestnuts, chopped fine
½ - ¾ cup brown sugar

1 stick melted butter
1 teaspoon cinnamon, or more to taste
2 teaspoons curry powder, or more to taste
8 chicken breasts, skinned and boned

- Preheat oven to 350°.
- Mix all ingredients, except chicken in small mixing bowl.
- Place a full tablespoon of apple mixture on each chicken breast.
- Bring up corners and secure with toothpick.
- Turn over and place in medium sized baking dish.
- Place remaining apple mixture on top of each breast.
- Cover tightly with foil and bake for 35-40 minutes, basting at least twice with juices.
- Serve chicken on platter of Cinnamon-Curried Rice: see index.

Mrs. D. William Wallace (Sally Benson)

Overnight Chicken

Easy
Prepare Ahead

Serves: 4
Chill: overnight
Bake: 1 hour and 15 minutes at 350°

½ cup honey
⅓ cup Dijon mustard
1 tablespoon curry powder

2 tablespoons soy sauce
4 chicken breasts

- Mix honey, mustard, curry and soy sauce.
- Place chicken breasts skin side down in baking dish.
- Pour marinade over chicken breasts.
- Cover with foil and refrigerate overnight.
- Turn chicken breasts over when ready to cook.
- Bake at 350° for 1 hour; after 1 hour, remove foil, baste breasts and cook 15 more minutes uncovered.
- Spoon sauce over chicken when serving.

Kathleen McClintic Anderson

Italian Southern Oven Fried Chicken
"1st place winner"

Easy
May Prepare Ahead

Serves: 3 to 4
Bake: 40 to 50 minutes at 375°

9 chicken pieces (3 each - thighs, legs and breasts)	½ cup Parmesan cheese
	1 teaspoon dried basil
¼ pound butter, melted	½ teaspoon dried oregano
olive oil	¼ teaspoon seasoned salt
1 cup dry breadcrumbs	½ teaspoon ground black pepper

- Preheat oven to 375°.
- Coat bottom of baking pan with olive oil.
- In shallow bowl, mix together crumbs, cheese, basil, oregano, salt and pepper.
- Coat chicken pieces with melted butter.
- Roll chicken pieces in crumb mixture and place skin side down in baking pan.
- Bake 20 minutes - turn pieces and bake 20-30 minutes longer.
- Serve on platter, garnished with fresh parsley, lemon wedges and black olives.

Mr. George C. (Bud) Reed

Oven Fried Chicken

Easy
May Prepare Ahead
Doubles Well

Serves: 6
Bake: 45 to 60 minutes at 350°

½ cup sour cream	1-2 cloves of garlic, pressed
1 tablespoon lemon juice	6 chicken breasts or one 2 pound
1 teaspoon Worcestershire sauce	cut up fryer
½ teaspoon paprika	1 cup Waverly wafer crumbs
1 teaspoon salt	3 tablespoons butter, melted
pepper to taste	

- Preheat oven to 350°.
- Combine sour cream, lemon juice and all seasonings.
- Dip chicken pieces in sour cream mixture and then in cracker crumbs.
- Arrange in buttered, shallow baking dish.
- Drizzle melted butter over chicken.
- Bake for 45-60 minutes.

Mrs. John L. Paul (Gaylord Beebe)

Hot Crunchy Chicken

Average
May Prepare Ahead
Freezes Well

Serves: 4 to 6
Bake: 30 minutes at 375°

2 cups diced cooked chicken
1 cup chopped celery
½ cup slivered almonds
½ cup crushed Ritz crackers
½ cup mayonnaise
2 tablespoons chopped onion

1 can cream of chicken soup, undiluted
1 2 ounce can mushroom stems and pieces, drained
½ cup crushed potato chips

- Preheat oven to 375°.
- Combine all ingredients, except potato chips.
- Spoon into a greased 1½ quart casserole dish.
- Bake at 375° for 15 minutes.
- Sprinkle potato chips on top.
- Bake an additional 15 minutes.

Elizabeth Hayden Blackwell

Poulet D'Inde

"Delicious - don't forget the condiments."

Average
May Prepare Ahead

Serves: 4 to 6
Cook: 45 minutes on simmer

1 broiler chicken, cut into parts
¼ cup flour
1½ teaspoons salt
¼ teaspoon pepper
⅓ cup oil
1 onion, sliced

1 clove garlic, crushed
2 8-ounce cans tomato sauce
1 cup water
2 teaspoons curry powder

- Put flour, 1 teaspoon salt and pepper in a bag. Rinse chicken in water, shake off excess water, and put in bag, a piece at a time, shaking well to coat.
- Heat oil in frying pan and fry chicken, turning occasionally, until browned on all sides (about 10 minutes all together). Remove chicken from pan.
- Add onion, celery, and garlic to oil in pan and cook until soft, but not browned.
- Drain off fat, and add tomato sauce, water, curry powder, and ½ tsp. salt. Return chicken to pan, cover and simmer about 45 minutes or until chicken is done.
- Serve on rice with raisins, peanuts, coconut, green onions, and chutney as condiments.

Ann W. Dibble

117

Dot's Chicken Pie

Average
May Prepare Ahead
Freezes Well

Serves: 8 to 10
Bake: 30 to 35 minutes at 425°

Pie

2 small fryers	1 can cream of celery soup
2 cups reserved chicken broth	1 package frozen peas and carrots
3 tablespoons flour	salt and pepper to taste

♦ Boil skinned chickens until meat falls from the bone.
♦ Chop chicken.
♦ Save 2 cups broth.
♦ Mix broth with flour and cook until thickened.
♦ Add soup and blend.
♦ Add chopped chicken, vegetables, salt and pepper.
♦ Place in 13 x 9 casserole.

Topping

1 stick margarine, melted	1 cup self-rising flour
1 cup buttermilk	

♦ Preheat oven to 425°.
♦ Mix margarine and butttermilk.
♦ Blend flour slowly, so as not to lump.
♦ Spread mixture over top of casserole.
♦ Bake for 30-35 minutes.

* Can substitute leftover turkey and use canned chicken broth.

Mrs. Thomas Hunter McEaddy (Kitty Anne Tilghman)

Chicken Poupon

Easy
Serve Immediately

Serves: 4 to 6
Bake: 60 minutes at 350°

6 chicken breasts	parsley
Poupon mustard	4 tablespoons melted butter
bread crumbs	

♦ Coat chicken breasts with mustard - liberally.
♦ Roll in bread crumbs and place in shallow baking dish.
♦ Sprinkle with parsley.
♦ Bake 45 minutes. Remove from oven. Pour melted butter on chicken. Bake 15 minutes longer.

* Serve with salad and wild rice.

Mrs. John Cooper Scarborough (Mary Ann Schiffli)

Chicken Breasts With Dijon Mustard And Tarragon

Average
May Prepare Ahead

Serves: 4
Chill: 2 hours
Sauté: 3 to 5 minutes per side

4   boneless, skinned chicken
    breasts
2   eggs
2   tablespoons water
3   green onions, chopped fine
    (including tops)
2   tablespoons dried tarragon
    leaves

2   tablespoons Dijon style mustard
½   cup flour for dredging, mixed
    with salt and pepper
    (approximately ½ teaspoon
    each)
¾   cup bread crumbs
2   tablespoons butter
2   tablespoons vegetable oil

- Pound chicken breasts between pieces of waxed paper until very thin.
- Beat eggs with 2 tablespoons water.
- Add mustard, tarragon, and chopped onions to egg mixture.
- Dredge chicken breasts lightly in flour and dip in egg mixture, coating well.
- Coat with bread crumbs, pressing crumbs into chicken.
- Refrigerate breasts for 2 hours.
- Sauté chicken in oil and butter approximately 3 to 5 minutes per side or until lightly browned.
- Garnish with lemon wedges and parsley.

Mrs. René Ravenel (Marion Rivers)

Chicken Tarragon

Easy
May Prepare Ahead

Serves: 6
Bake: 45 minutes at 350°

8   boneless chicken breasts or
    1 chicken, cut up
2   sticks margarine, melted
4   tablespoons tarragon leaves
    (or more if needed)

1   cup sour cream
1½ cups grated sharp cheddar
    cheese

- Arrange chicken pieces in a 9 x 12 pan.
- Melt margarine and pour all but 3 tablespoons over chicken.
- Cover well with 3 tablespoons tarragon.
- Put 1 tablespoon tarragon leaves with remaining butter.
- Bake at 350° for 30 minutes.
- Mix sour cream, cheese and remaining butter.
- Pour sauce over chicken.
- Bake 10 to 15 minutes more until cheese is melted.

Mrs. Samuel Richard Clawson (Elizabeth Mapp)

119

Simon And Garfunkle Chicken
"Wonderful luncheon fare"

Average
May Prepare Ahead

Serves: 6
Bake: 50 minutes at 350°

3 chicken breasts, boned, skinned and split in two	1 egg, beaten
1 stick butter, softened	½ cup plain bread crumbs
1 teaspoon salt	2 tablespoons chopped parsley
1 teaspoon pepper	½ teaspoon sage
6 slices mozzarella cheese	½ teaspoon rosemary
½ cup flour	½ teaspoon thyme
	½ cup dry white wine or sherry

- Pound chicken breasts.
- Spread each with softened butter.
- Season with salt and pepper.
- Wrap each piece of chicken with cheese slice and tuck ends under.
- Coat pieces lightly with flour.
- Dip in beaten egg.
- Mix crumbs and herbs together.
- Roll chicken pieces in the herb mixture.
- Place in greased baking dish.
- Melt remaining softened butter and spoon over chicken.
- Bake for 30 minutes.
- Add wine and bake 20 minutes more.

Mrs. Lloyd Arthur Pearson (Margaret Ann Boyd)

Chicken Breasts With Tuna Caper Sauce

Average
May Prepare Ahead

Serves: 6
Poach: 10 to 15 minutes

6 large boneless skinned chicken breasts	juice of 1 lemon or to taste
6 cups chicken stock	¼ cup capers
1 can tuna packed in water	¼ cup chopped parsley
1 cup Hellmann's mayonnaise	salt and pepper to taste

- Poach chicken breasts in chicken stock until done—allow to cool in stock.
- Blend mayonnaise, tuna and lemon (use food processor or blender).
- Fold in capers and parsley—salt and pepper to taste.
- Top each chicken breast with sauce.
- Serve chilled or at room temperature with lemon wedge.

Mrs. Henry C. West (Sally Izard)

120

Chicken Breasts With Shrimp Sauce
"Excellent for company dinner!"

Average
May Prepare Ahead
Freezes Well

Serves: 4
Bake: 1 hour at 350°
Cook: 15 to 20 minutes on medium
heat

Chicken

8	chicken breasts	4	tablespoons butter
½	cup milk		

♦ Preheat oven to 350°.
♦ Wash and pat dry chicken and place in roasting pan.
♦ Pour milk over chicken and place ½ tablespoon butter on each piece.
♦ Cover tightly with foil and bake for 1 hour.

* To freeze at this point, bake for only 45 minutes and cover tightly. Reheat thoroughly, adding a little more milk to prevent dryness.

Shrimp Sauce

4	tablespoons butter	1½	cups cooked shrimp, cut into small pieces
⅓	cup flour		
1	cup milk	1	4-ounce can mushrooms, drained
¼	teaspoon salt		
⅛	teaspoon white pepper	¼	cup dry white wine
⅛	teaspoon seafood seasoning	1	tablespoon Worcestershire sauce
1	teaspoon paprika		

♦ Melt 4 tablespoons butter over low heat.
♦ Stir in flour until well blended.
♦ Add 1 cup milk slowly and stir until thickened.
♦ Add salt, pepper, and seafood seasoning.
♦ Add shrimp, mushrooms, paprika, wine, and Worcestershire sauce.
♦ Stir over low heat for 10 minutes.
♦ To freeze, put in sealed container.
♦ Reheat in top of double boiler or microwave.
♦ Place chicken breast on each plate and spoon sauce over top.
♦ Sprinkle with paprika.
♦ Serve immediately.
* Doubles easily.

Mrs. Gary Graupmann (Lynn Dubois)

Chicken-Shrimp Supreme

Easy
Serve Immediately
Freezes Well

Serves: 8
Cook: 20 minutes

¼ cup butter
½ pound fresh mushrooms, sliced
2 tablespoons green onion, sliced
2 cans cream of chicken soup
¼ cup sherry (or to taste)

½ cup light cream
1 cup cheddar cheese, grated
2 cups cooked chicken, chopped
2 cups shrimp, cooked and peeled
2 tablespoons parsley, chopped

♦ Melt butter in a 3 quart saucepan.
♦ Add mushrooms and sauté.
♦ Add onions and sauté 5 minutes.
♦ Add soup and gradually stir in sherry and light cream.
♦ Add cheese and heat on low, stirring until cheese is melted.
♦ Add chicken and shrimp.
♦ Heat to serving temperature.
♦ Stir in parsley before serving.
♦ Serve over rice.

Mrs. Charles E. Miller, Jr. (Sarah Royall Gregorie)

Curried Chicken Or Shrimp

Average
May Prepare Ahead
Freezes Well

Serves: 4
Cook: 10 to 15 minutes over
medium heat

1 onion, chopped
1 green pepper, chopped
2 tablespoons butter or margarine
4 tablespoons butter
4 tablespoons flour
2 cups hot milk
1 tablespoon curry powder

½ teaspoon salt
   dash red pepper
2 cups cooked, diced chicken or
   1 pound cooked, peeled shrimp
2 sliced, hard-boiled eggs
   hot cooked rice

♦ Sauté onion and pepper in two tablespoons butter until soft.
♦ Melt 4 tablespoons butter in double boiler and stir in flour.
♦ Add milk slowly, curry, salt, red pepper.
♦ Stir in onions, green pepper and either shrimp or chicken.
* May freeze at this point - reheat in top of double boiler.
♦ Add boiled eggs.
♦ Thin with a little more milk, if too thick.
♦ Serve over rice.

* Any of these condiments can be used: chutney, coconut, raisins, crushed
peanuts, crumbled bacon.

Martha J. Lott

Michael's Marvelous Chicken
"Time well spent!"

Complicated
May Prepare Ahead

Serves: 6 to 8
Bake: 25 minutes at 350°
Broil: 10 to 20 minutes

6-8 boned chicken breasts, pounded thin
1 8-ounce carton sweet unsalted whipped butter
3 large scallions, chopped fine
6 mushrooms, chopped fine
½ pound white crab meat
¼ pound shrimp

½ teaspoon ground basil leaves
¼ teaspoon garlic
¼ teaspoon poultry seasoning
½ cup white wine
   paprika and soft butter
4 mushrooms, sliced for sauce
1 scallion, chopped for sauce
½ lemon

- Preheat oven to 350°.
- Mix butter, scallions, mushrooms, crabmeat, and shrimp.
- Add spices, lemon juice, and salt to taste.
- Place 2 tablespoons of mixture on each breast and fold corners to cover.
- Turn over and place in casserole.
- Pour white wine over, then dab each with butter and sprinkle with paprika.
- Bake for 15 minutes covered.
- Uncover and bake additional 10 minutes.
- To prepare sauce, pour liquid from casserole into small sauté pan and bring to boil.
- Add scallions and mushrooms and bring to boil again.
- Lower heat to simmer and reduce liquid to half.
- Deglaze the sauce - stir in one tablespoon butter at a time (3 tablespoons total) with a wisk.
- Allow sauce to cool.
- Sauce can be spooned over each chicken breast.

* Serve with curried rice.

Mr. Michael Norton and Friends

Naked Chicken
"Perfect for a diet - no skin, yet very moist."

Easy
Partial Prepare Ahead

Serves: 4
Bake: 60 minutes at 350°

½ cup soy sauce	½ teaspoon garlic powder
¼ cup oil	½ teaspoon ground ginger
1 tablespoon brown sugar	4 half chicken breasts, skinned

♦ Mix together first five ingredients.
♦ Place chicken in a food storage bag and pour in marinade.
♦ Refrigerate the bag in a bowl for 4-24 hours. The longer the better.
♦ Turn the bag often.
♦ Remove the chicken and place in baking pan.
♦ Bake covered with foil for 40 minutes.
♦ Remove foil and continue baking for 20 minutes.

Mrs. Wade H. Logan, III (Eunice Smith)

Sweet And Sour Chicken
"Delicious served over rice."

Easy
May Prepare Ahead

Serves: 6
Bake: 1 hour at 350°

8 - 10 pieces chicken	2 tablespoons vinegar
10 ounces apricot preserves	1 tablespoon soy sauce
8 ounces tomato sauce	¼ teaspoon nutmeg,
1 envelope dry onion soup	freshly ground
1 teaspoon ground ginger	1 - 2 tablespoons honey (to taste)

♦ Preheat oven to 350°.
♦ Grease 9 x 13 dish.
♦ Wash chicken pieces and put in dish.
♦ Mix together apricot preserves, tomato sauce, onion soup, ginger, vinegar, soy sauce, nutmeg.
♦ Taste and if too sour, add honey.
♦ Pour mixture over chicken.
♦ Bake for 1 hour.

Mrs. Randal M. Robinson (Katherine Shertzer)

Chicken Waikiki Beach

Average
May Prepare Ahead

Serves: 4
Bake: 1 hour at 350°

4 chicken breasts	1 teaspoon salt
½ cup flour	¼ teaspoon pepper
⅓ cup salad oil	

Sauce

1 can (1 lb., 4 oz.) sliced pineapple	1 tablespoon soy sauce
1 cup sugar	¼ teaspoon ginger
2 tablespoons cornstarch	1 chicken bouillon cube
¾ cup cider vinegar	1 large bell pepper, cut in ¼ inch circles

- Preheat oven to 350°.
- Wash chicken, pat dry, coat chicken with flour.
- Heat oil in large skillet. Add chicken a few pieces at a time and brown on all sides.
- Place in shallow baking pan skin side up and sprinkle with salt and pepper.
- Make sauce: Drain pineapple, pouring liquid syrup into 2-cup measuring cup. Add water to make 1¼ cups.
- In medium saucepan, combine sugar, cornstarch, pineapple syrup, vinegar, soy sauce, ginger, bouillon cube and bring to a boil, stirring constantly.
- Boil 2 minutes and pour over chicken.
- Bake uncovered 30 minutes.
- Add pineapple slices and bell pepper.
- Bake 30 minutes longer or until chicken is tender.
- Serve with white rice.

Mrs. James M. Stelling (Kathleen Hubbard)

Easy And Elegant Chicken

Average
Partial Prepare Ahead

Serves: 4
Marinate: 1 hour
Cook: 5 to 10 minutes

1   whole chicken breast, cooked
    (about 1½ pounds)
¼   cup orange juice
1   tablespoon white wine
1   tablespoon Chinese style
    mustard
2   tablespoons soy sauce
½   teaspoon hot sauce
3   tablespoons oil (peanut or
    corn oil)

½   cup onion, chopped
1   can water chestnuts, drained and
    cubed
½   cup cubed green pepper
1   can (11 ounces) mandarin
    orange segments, drained
    hot cooked rice

♦ Cut chicken into ½ inch cubes.
♦ Place cubed chicken in bowl.
♦ Combine orange juice, wine, mustard, soy sauce, hot sauce.
♦ Pour over chicken and marinate for one hour or longer in refrigerator.
♦ Heat oil in large skillet and stir fry onion for one minute.
♦ Remove chicken from marinade with slotted spoon and add to skillet.
♦ Toss for two minutes.
♦ Add water chestnuts, green pepper, and remaining marinade.
♦ Cook together for three minutes.
♦ Add orange segments and toss gently till heated thoroughly.
♦ Serve over rice.

Mrs. Thomas A. Kirkland, Jr. (Patricia Trotter)

Hungarian Chicken Paprika

Average
May Prepare Ahead

Serves: 4
Cook: 30 to 40 minutes over
medium heat

1   medium onion, minced fine
1   tablespoon bacon grease
1   tablespoon paprika
¼   cup water
1   small cut-up chicken (with skin)
    salt and pepper to taste

1   tablespoon flour
¼   cup cold water
1   chicken bouillon cube
¾   cup sour cream
    noodles, rice or dumplings

♦ Sauté onion in bacon grease in large frying pan.
♦ Add paprika and water.
♦ Place chicken in pan, skin side down.
♦ Cook until chicken is tender.
♦ Season with salt and pepper.
♦ Remove from pan when chicken is done.

- Remove skin.
- Mix flour and cold water together and put in pan with drippings.
- Add bouillon cube.
- Cook slowly until thickened.
- Add sour cream and chicken and heat until hot.
- Serve over noodles, rice or dumplings.

Lisa Buzogany

Chicken Breasts Supreme

Average
May Prepare Ahead
Freezes Well

Serves: 12
Bake: 40 minutes at 350°

¼ cup regular all purpose flour	2 teaspoons cornstarch
2½ teaspoons salt	1½ cups half and half
1 teaspoon paprika	¼ cup cooking sherry
6 whole chicken breasts, halved and skinned	1 teaspoon lemon peel
	1 tablespoon lemon juice
¼ cup butter	1 cup grated Swiss cheese

- Preheat oven to 350°.
- Combine flour, salt and paprika on waxed paper.
- Mix well and flour the chicken.
- Melt butter in large skillet and lightly brown the halved chicken breasts on both sides.
- Add ¼ cup of water to skillet and simmer for 30 minutes or until breasts are almost tender.
- Arrange chicken in 13 x 9 x 2 baking dish.
- Mix cornstarch with ¼ cup half and half, stir into skillet and cook over low heat.
- Gradually add remaining 1¼ cups of half and half, sherry, lemon peel and lemon juice to skillet.
- Continue cooking until sauce is thickened.
- Pour mixture over chicken (can freeze at this point).
- Heat chicken, covered, 35 minutes or until sauce is bubbly hot.
- Remove cover and sprinkle with Swiss cheese and bake until cheese is melted.

Mrs. Samuel Edward Parker (Diane Prosser)

Chicken Portuguese

Average
May Prepare Ahead

Serves: 8
Bake: 1 hour at 350°

2   chickens, cut up, or 8 breasts
    flour, salt, and pepper for
    dredging chicken
    oil
2   onions, chopped

1   10-ounce can tomato sauce
6   ounces red wine
6   ounces chicken broth
2   cans water chestnuts
½   pound fresh mushrooms, sliced

♦ Dredge chicken breasts in flour, salt, pepper mixture.
♦ Sauté chicken in oil until nicely browned.
♦ Put chicken in casserole dish.
♦ Sauté onions in same frying pan.
♦ Add tomato sauce, red wine, and chicken broth to onions.
♦ Pour over chicken and bake 45 minutes.
♦ Add water chestnuts and mushrooms and bake 15 minutes longer.

Mrs. William C. Cleveland (Ann Walker)

Chicken Tortilla Casserole

Average
May Prepare Ahead

Serves: 6
Bake: 30 minutes at 350°

4-5 cooked, chopped chicken
    breasts
1   can cream of mushroom soup
1   can cream of chicken soup
1   medium onion, chopped fine
2   3-ounce cans chopped green
    chilies, drained
1   cup sour cream

1   cup black olives, chopped
½   teaspoon garlic salt
    salt and pepper to taste
¾   package (8 ounce size)
    Taco flavored chips, crumbled
12   ounces shredded sharp cheese
4   tablespoons margarine

♦ Preheat oven to 350°.
♦ Mix all ingredients except cheese and margarine, and place in 3 quart casserole.
♦ Sprinkle cheese on top.
♦ Put margarine over cheese.
♦ Bake for 30 minutes.

Mrs. J. Conrad Zimmerman, Jr. (Barbara Hubbard)

Party Chicken And Wild Rice Casserole

Average
May Prepare Ahead
Freezes Well

Serves: 12 to 14
Bake: 45 minutes at 350°

- 1 medium onion, chopped
- 1 cup celery, chopped
- 2 tablespoons butter or oleo
- 2 2½ pound fryers, cooked, boned and cut into large chunks (or 1 fryer and 4 or 5 breast halves)
- 1 6-ounce box long grain and wild rice, cooked per instructions

- 1 4-ounce jar pimentos
- 2 cups Hellmann's mayonnaise
- 1 can cream of celery soup
- 1-2 teaspoons of salt, to taste
- 1 cup toasted, slivered almonds
- 2 16-ounce cans French style green beans, drained
- grated Parmesan cheese
- paprika

- ♦ Sauté onion and celery in butter or oleo in large sauce pan.
- ♦ Add all ingredients except paprika, cheese and 1 tablespoon almonds.
- ♦ Mix thoroughly and pour into greased 3-4 quart baking dish.
- ♦ Sprinkle with Parmesan, almonds and paprika.
- ♦ Bake until bubbly in center, about 45 minutes.

* If any leftovers, add more mayonnaise before reheating.

Mrs. Charles Lowndes Mullally (Pauline "Punch" Slay)

Chicken And Wild Rice Casserole
"Great to serve to a hungry crowd"

Easy
May Prepare Ahead
Freezes Well

Serves: 8 to 10
Simmer: 1 hour
Bake: 1 hour at 350°

- 2 whole chickens
- 1 cup water
- 1½ teaspoons salt
- ½ teaspoon curry powder
- 1 medium onion, sliced
- ½ cup celery, sliced

- 2 6-ounce packages long grain and wild rice with seasonings
- 1 cup sour cream
- 1 10½-ounce can cream of mushroom soup

- ♦ Preheat oven to 350°.
- ♦ Boil chicken in water in large pot with salt, curry, onion, and celery.
- ♦ Once boiling, reduce heat and simmer 1 hour.
- ♦ Remove from heat and save broth.
- ♦ Remove meat from bones in bite size pieces.
- ♦ Cook rice, following package directions, using broth as part of the liquid.
- ♦ Mix together chicken, rice, soup, and sour cream.
- ♦ Bake covered for 1 hour at 350°.

* May add sherry and/or sautéed almonds.

Mrs. James H. Fowles, III (Nora McArthur)

Chicken Breast Lombardy

Average
May Prepare Ahead
Freezes Well

Serves: 4 to 6
Sauté: 8 minutes
Bake: 10 to 12 minutes at 450°

6	chicken breasts, boned and skinned	½	cup fresh mushrooms, sliced
	salt and pepper to taste	¾	cup Marsella wine
½	cup flour	½	cup chicken stock
1¼	cups butter	½	cup shredded mozzarella cheese
		½	cup grated Parmesan cheese

- Flatten chicken to ⅛-inch thick.
- Salt and pepper to taste.
- Dredge in flour.
- Sauté in one cup melted butter 3 or 4 minutes on each side until slightly browned.
- Remove and place in a greased 13 x 9 x 2 baking dish.
- Save drippings in skillet.
- Stir wine and chicken stock into drippings.
- Simmer for 10 minutes.
- Sauté mushrooms in ¼ cup butter and place over chicken.
- Combine cheeses and sprinkle over mushrooms and chicken.
- Pour simmered sauce over chicken.
- Bake for 10-12 minutes.
- Place under broiler for 1-2 minutes.

Mrs. Benjamin Owen Geer, Jr. (Helen Lyles)

Sherry's Chicken Tetrazzini
"A housewarming favorite!"

Average
May Prepare Ahead
Freezes Well

Serves: 6 to 8
Bake: 20 minutes at 350°

6	or 8 large chicken breasts	1	can chopped ripe olives
1	celery stalk	2	small jars pimentos, drained and chopped
1	bouillon cube		
	salt and pepper	1	can mushrooms and liquid
1	medium onion, chopped	1	pound Velveeta cheese, cut into chunks
1	stick butter		
¾	tablespoon flour		salt, pepper to taste
1	can cream of mushroom soup		dash of garlic powder
½	cup milk	1	10-ounce package egg noodles
1	can sliced, drained water chestnuts	1	jigger sherry (optional)

- Boil chicken with celery, salt, pepper, and bouillon cube.
- Bone and cut chicken in bite size pieces.

- Sauté onion in butter.
- Blend in flour.
- Stir in mushroom soup.
- Add milk, water chestnuts, olives, pimentos, and mushrooms and liquid.
- Stir in cheese until it melts.
- Add chicken, salt, pepper, and dash of garlic powder, and heat together.
- Preheat oven to 350°.
- Cook noodles according to directions.
- Drain and add to chicken mixture.
- Pour into large casserole.
- Optional: pour 1 jigger of sherry on top.
- Bake for 20 minutes at 350° or until it bubbles. If mixture seems too thick, add a little milk, particularly when reheating.

Mrs. Thomas J. Parsell (Susan Poston)

Party Chicken Tetrazzini
"Makes two."

Average
May Prepare Ahead
Freezes Well

Serves: 12-14
Bake: 30 minutes at 350°

1 6 pound hen, stewed (reserve 4 cups broth)	1 4-ounce can mushroom slices
¼ pound margarine	1 3-ounce package slivered toasted almonds
8 tablespoons flour (all purpose)	3 tablespoons minced green pepper
1 cup cream	
¾ pound processed yellow cheese, cut into chunks	3 tablespoons minced celery
	1 tablespoon salt
1 pound can ripe olives, pitted and sliced	½ teaspoon pepper
	8 ounces thin noodles, cooked

- Stew hen until tender, reserving 4 cups broth.
- Cut meat into bite-size pieces. Set aside.
- In large saucepan, heat margarine.
- Gradually add flour. Blend.
- Slowly add chicken broth, then cream.
- Stir over low heat until thickened.
- Add cheese. Stir until melted.
- Add chicken and remaining ingredients.
- Turn mixture into 2 buttered 1½ qt. casseroles.
- Refrigerate until ready to bake.
- Bake until bubbly (about 30 min.).

Mrs. Gregory Alan Jones (Elizabeth Fant)

Chicken Jubilee
"Husbands love this"

Average
May Prepare Ahead
Freezes Well
Doubles Well

Serves: 8
Bake: 1 hour at 325°

8 chicken breasts, or any pieces you prefer	1 12-ounce bottle chili sauce
salt and pepper to taste	1 tablespoon Worcestershire sauce
½ cup melted butter	2 medium onions, sliced
½ cup water	½ cup raisins, white
½ cup brown sugar	1 16-ounce can Bing cherries, drained
1 teaspoon garlic salt	1 cup sherry

♦ Place chicken in 13 x 9 glass pyrex, skin side up. Season with salt and pepper.
♦ Dribble with butter. Broil under medium flame until brown.
♦ Combine remaining ingredients, except cherries and sherry. Pour over chicken, cover with foil.
♦ Bake an hour at 325°.
♦ Add cherries soaked in sherry and remove foil for last 15 minutes of roasting time.
♦ To freeze, bake 45 minutes and freeze. Bring to room temperature. Bake 15-20 minutes, add sherry and cherries.
* Doubles easily.

Mrs. Charles S. Way, Jr. (Mary Ellen Long)

Aunt Liz's Chicken Spaghetti Casserole
"Family Fare"

Average
May Prepare Ahead
Freezes Well

Serves: 8 to 10
Bake: 45 minutes at 350°

4 cups boiled chicken, chopped	2 cans cream of mushroom soup
1 cup celery, sliced	1 cup chicken broth
1 cup bell pepper, diced	2 cups spaghetti noodles, broken
1 cup onion, diced	1 cup grated cheddar cheese

♦ Preheat oven to 350°.
♦ Mix together in 2½ quart casserole dish; chicken, celery, pepper, and onion.
♦ Blend soup and broth and add spaghetti.
♦ Pour over chicken and mix together.
♦ Sprinkle with cheese.
♦ Bake uncovered.

Mrs. Charles E. Bennett, Jr. (Fran Seabrook)

Turkey A La Reine

Average
May Prepare Ahead

Serves: 4 to 6
Bake: 25 minutes at 350°

6   tablespoons butter
½   cup chopped onion
¼   pound sliced mushrooms
¼   cup chopped green pepper
2   tablespoons flour
1½   cups hot turkey (or chicken) broth
1½   cups light cream
2   egg yolks

1   teaspoon salt
¼   teaspoon freshly ground black pepper
¼   cup dry sherry
3   cups diced, cooked turkey (or chicken)
½   pound medium noodles, cooked and drained
½   cup Parmesan cheese

♦ Melt 4 tablespoons butter in skillet.
♦ Sauté onion, mushrooms and green pepper for 5 minutes, stirring frequently.
♦ Blend in flour, broth and cream, stirring constantly until sauce reaches boiling point, reduce heat and cook 5 minutes.
♦ Beat egg yolks with salt and pepper and gradually add to hot sauce, stirring steadily to prevent curdling.
♦ Mix in sherry, turkey and noodles.
♦ Turn into 3 quart casserole, sprinkle with cheese and dot with 2 tablespoons butter.
♦ Bake at 350° 25 minutes.

Mrs. Van Noy Thornhill (Jane Lucas)

Company Bar-B-Que Sauce

Easy
May Prepare Ahead

Yields: 4 cups
Cook: 15 to 20 minutes on stovetop

2   6-ounce jars prepared mustard
2   sticks margarine
1   cup apple cider

2   teaspoons salt
2   teaspoons black pepper
2   teaspoons red pepper

♦ Put all ingredients in pot and bring to a boil, reduce heat to simmer and cook 15 to 20 minutes.
♦ Baste on chicken, or other meat if desired, on grill.

Mrs. Milon C. Smith (Mary Lou Hodges)

Bar-B-Que Sauce

Easy
May Prepare Ahead

Yield: 4 cups
Cook: 10 minutes

½ cup butter, melted
1 16-ounce bottle Heinz 57
⅓ cup vinegar

1 tablespoon mustard
3 tablespoons brown sugar

- Combine melted butter and Heinz 57 in saucepan.
- Fill empty Heinz 57 bottle with water and add to mixture.
- Add remaining ingredients.
- Heat until mixed well, approximately 10 minutes.

Mrs. Steven E. Turner (Legare Hay)

Barbecued Chicken Sauce

Easy
Prepare Ahead

Serves: 12
Marinate: 4 to 6 hours
Bake: 10 minutes at 450°,
1 hour at 250°

1 medium onion, chopped
¼ stick margarine
1 cup cider vinegar
3 tablespoons mustard

2 teaspoons black pepper
2 tablespoons sugar
½ cup catsup
1 teaspoon salt

- Sauté onion in margarine.
- Mix with remaining ingredients.
- Pour over chicken pieces and marinate 4-6 hours.
- Bake in uncovered dish at 450° for 10 minutes.
- Bake 1 hour at 250°. Baste several times.

Mrs. Thomas W. Alexander (Patricia Cochrane)

MEATS

Beef Tenderloin
"So very easy"

Easy
Serve Immediately

Serves: 6
Bake: 25 minutes at 500°

1 tablespoon celery salt	1 whole beef tenderloin
1 tablespoon garlic salt	(4-6 pounds)
1 tablespoon onion salt	sturdy aluminum foil boat, large
¾ teaspoon paprika	enough to hold tenderloin, and
¼ teaspoon pepper	turned up about 1 inch all
¼ teaspoon red pepper	around edge
1 egg, well beaten	

- Preheat oven to 500°.
- Mix first 6 ingredients together.
- Roll tenderloin in beaten egg.
- Pat on dry mixture.
- Place in aluminum boat on cookie sheet.
- Cook EXACTLY 25 minutes in 500° oven, without opening door.
- Meat will be medium.

Mrs. Charles M. Fox (Melissa Tuttle)

Whole Tenderloin
"For very special occasions"

Easy
May Prepare Ahead

Serves: 8 to 10
Preheat: 10 minutes at 450°
Bake: 35 to 50 minutes at 350°

1 whole tenderloin,
4 to 6 pounds

salt

- Remove as much fat from roast as possible.
- In shallow baking pan, let the roast come to room temperature.
- Preheat oven to 450° and leave there for 10 minutes before placing meat in oven.
- Immediately turn heat back to 350° and roast for 35 to 50 minutes depending on rareness desired.
- Sprinkle with salt and let stand 15 minutes before carving.

Martha J. Lott

Roast Beef
"Works every time!"

Easy
Serve Immediately

Serves: 12 to 14
Bake: 5 min. per pound at 500°

1 top sirloin butt, approx. 10 pounds slivered garlic clove	salt pepper

- Preheat oven to 500°.
- Have meat at room temperature.
- Cut slits in meat and stuff with slivers of garlic.
- Heavily salt and pepper fat side of beef.
- Place on roasting pan.
- Cook 5 minutes per pound.
- Never open oven.
- Turn oven off and let cool in oven approx. 1½ hours.

Mrs. W. Elliot Hutson, Jr. (Mary B. Means)

Eye Of Round Roast
"Delicious"

Easy
Partial Prepare Ahead
Serve Immediately

Serves: 8
Marinate: 2 to 3 hours or overnight
Bake: 2½ hours at 300°

Marinade

1	clove garlic	3	tablespoons ketchup
1	cup soy sauce		juice of 1 lemon
¾	cup vinegar	2	strips of bacon

1 eye of round roast

- Make a sauce using all ingredients listed above (except bacon).
- Marinate meat several hours ahead of cooking.
- Place strips of bacon on meat.
- Bake.

Mrs. Kenneth M. Shortridge (Linda McPhail)

A Charleston Roast
"Marinade turns chuck to sirloin!"

Average
Partial Prepare Ahead
Serve Immediately

Serves: 6
Marinade: 1 to 2 hours
Grill: approx. 15 minutes per side

1   round bone arm chuck roast or boneless round roast, cut about 2 inches thick (3-4 pounds)

2   teaspoons unseasoned meat tenderizer

Marinade

2   teaspoons thyme
1   teaspoon marjoram
1   bay leaf, crushed
1   cup wine vinegar

½   cup olive or salad oil
3   tablespoons lemon juice
2   tablespoons bottled cracked pepper

- Sprinkle meat evenly on both sides with tenderizer.
- Poke all over with sharp knife and place in shallow pan.
- Mix all marinade ingredients, except pepper, and pour over and around meat.
- Let stand at room temperature 1 to 2 hours, turning every half hour.
- When ready to grill, remove from marinade and pour half the pepper on each side.
- Grill 6 inches above coals about 15 minutes on each side for rare steak.

Mrs. Garrett Tatum (Martha Cronly)

Marinated London Broil
"Excellent on the grill!"

Easy
Prepare Ahead

Serves: 8
Marinade: 24 to 48 hours
Broil/Grill

1 London broil roast, 2 pounds

Marinade

⅓   cup oil
⅓   cup sherry

⅓   cup soy sauce

- Mix ingredients.
- Pour over London broil.
- Marinade for 24-48 hours.
- Broil in oven or cook over charcoal grill.

Mrs. R.D. Mosely, Jr. (Laura Anderson)

Flank Steak Marinade

Easy
Prepare Ahead

Yield: 1 cup

¼ cup soy sauce	1 teaspoon ground ginger
3 tablespoons honey	¾ cup salad oil
2 tablespoons vinegar	1 green onion, chopped
1 teaspoon garlic powder	

♦ Combine all ingredients in jar.
♦ To marinate, pour mixture over meat and marinate all day.
♦ Grill 5 to 10 minutes per side.
♦ Slice diagonally.
* For flank steak or London broil — 2-3 pounds.

Mrs. Wade H. Logan, III (Eunice Smith)

Beef Kabobs
"A summer favorite"

Easy
Partial Prepare Ahead

Serves: 12
Grill: 15 to 20 minutes

½ cup lemon juice	2 large green peppers, cut into
¼ cup Worcestershire sauce	1½ inch pieces
1 cup vegetable oil	½ pound fresh mushrooms
¾ cup soy sauce	12 cherry tomatoes
¼ cup prepared mustard	12 small onions
2 cloves garlic, minced	
3 pounds sirloin tip, cut into	
1½ inch cubes	

♦ Combine first six ingredients to make marinade.
♦ Pour over meat.
♦ Cover and marinade 12 hours in refrigerator.
♦ Remove meat from marinade, reserving marinade.
♦ Alternate meat and vegetables on skewers.
♦ Grill over medium coals 15 to 20 minutes.
♦ Turn every 6 to 7 minutes.
♦ Baste with marinade as grilling.

Mrs. Telfair Parker (Hope Haselden)

Beef Strips-Oriental

Average
Partial Prepare Ahead
Freezes Well

Serves: 8
Cook: 1 hour

Serve with rice or noodles.

2¼ pounds round steak, cut
    1 inch thick
2 tablespoons cooking oil
    water
⅓ cup soy sauce
2 teaspoons sugar
¼ teaspoon pepper
1 clove garlic minced
4 carrots

2 green peppers, cut in 1 inch
    squares
8 green onions, cut in 1½ inch
    pieces
½ pound mushrooms, sliced
1 can water chestnuts, halved
2 tablespoons cornstarch
½ cup water

- Cut round steak into ⅛ inch thick and 3 to 4 inch long strips (easiest when meat is partially frozen).
- Brown in cooking oil.
- Pour off drippings, measure and add water to make 1 cup.
- Combine with soy sauce, sugar, pepper and garlic and add to meat.
- Cover and cook slowly 45 minutes. *It may be frozen at this point.
- Cut carrots lengthwise into thin strips and cut strips in half.
- Add carrots, peppers, onions, mushrooms, and water chestnuts to meat.
- Cover and continue cooking 15 minutes.
- Combine cornstarch and water and use to thicken the liquid for gravy.

Mrs. Gerard Stelling, Jr. (Jane Riley)

139

Brisket Of Beef
"Cocktail Party Brisket"

Easy
May Prepare Ahead

Serves: 8 to 10 for dinner
or 20 for party
Bake: 4 hours at 300°

  1   brisket of beef, 2-3 pounds
  ⅔ jar garlic salt

freshly ground pepper
sliced onions

+ Sprinkle garlic salt and pepper over brisket.
+ Place sliced onions on top.
+ Wrap tightly in foil.
+ Place in tight roasting pan.
+ Cook (300° for 4 hours).
+ Cool and slice thin.

* Serve with sliced bread, mayonnaise and hot mustard.

Mrs. William McG. Morrison (Felicia Howell)

Easy Beef Stew
"Makes a delicious gravy"

Easy
May Prepare Ahead

Serves: 4
Bake: 3 hours at 300°

  1   pound stew beef, cubed
  2   medium onions, thinly sliced

1   can cream of mushroom soup
¼ cup sherry or wine

+ Layer the following in a greased, 1½ quart casserole:
  meat
  onions
  soup and sherry, mixed
+ Cover and bake 3 hours at 300°.

Mrs. Charles Talmadge Cole, Jr. (Joanne Gilmer)

Company Beef Stroganoff
"Double for company"

Average
May Prepare Ahead

Serves: 4
Cook: 25 to 30 minutes on medium low heat

1 pound beef tenderloin, cut into thin strips	2 tablespoons catsup
2 tablespoons butter	1 minced garlic clove
½ pound fresh mushrooms, sliced	1 teaspoon salt
½ cup minced onion	3 tablespoons flour
1 can beef consommé	1 cup sour cream

- Melt butter in pan.
- Add mushrooms and onions.
- Cook until tender (about 5 minutes).
- Remove mushrooms and onions.
- Add beef and brown.
- Reserve ⅓ cup consommé.
- Add to pan remaining consommé together with catsup, garlic, and salt.
- Stir.
- Cover and simmer 15 minutes.
- Add remaining consommé.
- Add flour.
- Stir.
- Add onions and mushrooms. Heat to bubbling, stirring constantly for one minute.
- Reduce heat to low.
- Stir in sour cream.
- Keep on low so sour cream does not bubble.
- Serve over rice or noodles.

Mrs. David H. Maybank (Ann English)

Rosie's Beef Burgundy
"Supper club favorite"

Easy
May Prepare Ahead

Serves: 6
Bake: 3½ hours at 300°

1½ to 2 pounds round steak
3 tablespoons butter or margarine
1 envelope dry onion soup mix
1 envelope dry mushroom beef soup mix
1 can 10¾-ounce golden mushroom soup

½ cup red wine
½ cup sherry
1 ounce good brandy (optional)
2 tablespoons soy sauce
1 tablespoon browning and seasoning sauce (commonly called Kitchen Bouquet)

♦ Slice meat in 2-inch to 3-inch strips.
♦ Brown meat in butter.
♦ Put in a 4-quart casserole.
♦ Add other ingredients.
♦ Cover and cook in oven at 300° for 3½ hours.

* Multiply this times 10 for a crowd of 60.

Mrs. James Allen Lester Glenn (Lucy Robson)

Chili-Cincinnati Style

Easy
May Prepare Ahead
Freezes Well

Serves: 6
Cook: 2 to 3 hours

1 pound ground chuck
1 medium onion, chopped
1½ tablespoons chili powder
2 14½-ounce cans kidney beans

1 28-ounce can whole tomatoes
salt and pepper to taste

♦ Brown meat with onion.
♦ Add remaining ingredients and stir until well mixed.
♦ Simmer very slowly for 2-3 hours.
♦ If it gets too thick too fast, add more tomatoes.
♦ Serve over spaghetti.

* Best if prepared 24 to 48 hours before serving.

Mrs. Claron A. Robertson III (Martha Ann Moore)

Moussaka
"Eggplant"

Complicated
Prepare Ahead

Serves: 10 to 12
Bake: 30 minutes at 350°

4 tablespoons butter	1 teaspoon sugar
2 medium onions, chopped	½ teaspoon oregano
1 clove garlic, minced	½ teaspoon basil
1½ pounds ground beef	¼ teaspoon cinnamon
1 cup tomato sauce	½ teaspoon parsley, chopped
1 cup water	3 medium eggplants, sliced
1½ teaspoons salt	½-inch thick, but not peeled
¼ teaspoon pepper	vegetable oil

Cream Sauce:

6 tablespoons butter	½ teaspoon salt
6 tablespoons flour	¼ teaspoon pepper
3 cups milk	½ teaspoon nutmeg
5 eggs, beaten	½ cup Romano cheese, grated

- Melt 4 tablespoons butter in large, deep pan and sauté onions until transparent.
- Add garlic and sauté.
- Add ground beef and brown well.
- Add tomato sauce, water, salt, pepper, sugar, oregano, basil, cinnamon, and parsley.
- Simmer until thickened for 15 minutes.
- Slice eggplant; soak in deep bowl of salt water for 30 minutes.
- Drain eggplant and squeeze slices with paper towel to absorb excess moisture.
- Brush with vegetable oil.
- Broil 4 minutes on each side, 4 inches from heat.
- Make a cream sauce by melting 6 tablespoons butter in saucepan, then add flour slowly and stir over low heat until well blended. Add milk gradually, stirring constantly until thickened. Remove from heat and slowly add beaten eggs, stirring quickly until well blended. Cook until thick. Add ½ teaspoon each salt and pepper.
- Grease 9 x 13 pan and arrange eggplant slices on bottom of pan, overlapping slices.
- Spread meat mixture over eggplant and arrange rest of the eggplant slices over the meat mixture, again overlapping slices.
- Spread cream sauce over top.
- Sprinkle with nutmeg and Romano cheese. Bake.

Mrs. J. Michael Grayson (Hope Gazes)

Stroganoff
"Fix early in the day, then go play"

Average
May Prepare Ahead

Serves: 4 to 6
Cook: in crock pot 5 to 6 hours or
double boiler 1 to 1½ hours

1½ pounds top round steak
4 medium onions, sliced
¾ pound mushrooms
1 cup sour cream
1 cup water

3 tablespoons flour
½ can cream of mushroom soup
salt, pepper and paprika to taste
butter

- Sauté meat in lots of butter.
- Transfer to double boiler (or crock pot).
- Sauté onions in more butter and add to beef.
- Brown mushrooms slowly in more butter.
- Add to beef and onions.
- Add sour cream to butter in pan.
- Scraping pan well, add to beef mixture.
- Mix flour in water.
- Add to beef mixture.
- Add mushroom soup, salt, pepper and paprika.
* Cook in crock pot for 5 to 6 hours or in double boiler for 1-1½ hours.

Mrs. J. Bruce Weaver (Martha Thompson)

Cheese Noodle Beef Casserole
"A child pleaser"

Easy
May Prepare Ahead
Freezes Well

Serves: 8
Bake: 30 minutes at 350°

2 pounds ground beef
1 onion, chopped
1 can of condensed tomato soup
1 can of cream of mushroom soup
1 8-ounce package of elbow
noodles, cooked per directions

1 8-ounce package of Velveeta
cheese
salt and pepper to taste

- Brown beef and onion and drain off fat.
- Add salt and pepper.
- Mix in tomato and mushroom soups.
- Stir in cooked noodles.
- Grate cheese on top.
- Bake.

Mrs. John A. Stuhr, Jr. (Cameron Webb)

Baked Lasagne
"Perfect for after the game party"

Complicated
Partial Prepare Ahead
Freezes Well

Serves: 10 to 12
Bake: 30 minutes at 375°

1 to 2 tablespoons butter	2 6-ounce cans tomato paste
½ pound hot sausage	1 tablespoon oregano
1 pound ground beef	1 10-ounce package lasagna
1 clove garlic, minced	noodles
3 tablespoons parsley flakes	2 12-ounce cartons cottage cheese
1 tablespoon basil	2 eggs, beaten
3½ teaspoons salt	½ teaspoon pepper
1 tablespoon sugar	½ cup Parmesan cheese
2 cups tomatoes	1 pound mozzarella cheese, grated

♦ Brown meats in butter.
♦ Add garlic, 1 tablespoon parsley flakes, basil, 1½ teaspoons salt, sugar, tomatoes, tomato paste and oregano to mixture.
♦ Simmer uncovered until thick (45-60 min.), stirring occasionally.
♦ Cook noodles according to package directions, then rinse in cold water.
♦ Combine cottage cheese, eggs, 2 tablespoons salt, pepper, 2 tablespoons parsley flakes, and Parmesan cheese.

To assemble:
♦ Place ½ of the noodles in pan.
♦ Spread ½ of cottage cheese mixture over noodles.
♦ Add ½ of meat mixture.
♦ Add ½ mozzarella cheese.
♦ Repeat layers. (May freeze here)
♦ Bake at 375° for 30 minutes.

Mrs. Lloyd Arthur Pearson (Margaret Ann Boyd)

Italian Spaghetti Sauce
"Freeze this and enjoy again and again"

Average
Partial Prepare Ahead
Freezes Well

Serves: 10 to 12
Cook: 8 hours on low

Sauce

3	6-ounce cans tomato paste	4	bay leaves
3	#2 cans tomatoes	½	cup sugar
2	large onions - sliced	1	7-ounce can mushroom bottoms
8	cloves of garlic, chopped fine		and pieces
1	teaspoon dried mint	2	tablespoons Worcestershire
1	teaspoon chopped parsley		sauce
1	teaspoon basil	1	teaspoon hot sauce
1	teaspoon oregano		salt and pepper
½	teaspoon rosemary leaves		

- Put the 3 cans of tomato paste in pot.
- Rinse each can by filling with water 4 times, adding water to tomato paste. (12 cans water)
- Mix all other items in pot.
- Simmer 8 hours.

Meat Balls

2	pounds ground round	1	large cup bread crumbs
1	large onion, chopped fine	3	medium cloves garlic, chopped
½	small green pepper, chopped		fine (or garlic powder to taste)
	fine		salt and pepper
3	whole eggs		flour
3	tablespoons Parmesan cheese		

- Put all ingredients in a bowl and mix.
- Add just enough flour to hold mixture together.
- Shape into balls.
- Fry meat balls in just enough oil to brown.
- Drain.
- Add to the sauce 2 to 3 hours before it is done.

Mrs. Telfair Parker (Hope Haseldon)

Gran's Chipped Beef
"Family breakfast or light supper"

Average
Serve Immediately

Serves: 4 to 6
Cook: 20 to 30 minutes on simmer

3	tablespoons butter	2	tablespoons sherry
3	tablespoons flour	8	slices bread, toasted
2	cups milk		
3	2.5-ounce packages sliced, smoked beef, chopped		

- In medium sauce pan melt butter.
- Stir in flour until blended.
- Add milk, stirring constantly.
- Add chopped beef.
- Simmer until thick.
- Season with sherry.
- Serve on toast.

Mrs. O. Edward Liipfert, Jr. (Susan Simpson)

Veal Provencal
"Wonderful"

Average
Serve Immediately

Serves: 4
Cook: 30 to 35 minutes on medium heat

1	pound veal, cut in small one-inch pieces	8	tablespoons butter
1	cup diced onions	4	tablespoons chopped parsley
2	cups chopped tomatoes (fresh)		fresh thyme, oregano, basil
8	small cloves fresh garlic, minced		salt and pepper to taste

- Sauté onions in butter.
- Add tomatoes and chopped garlic.
- Let simmer for 15 minutes.
- Season to taste with above seasonings.
- In a separate pan, sauté veal in butter until done.
- Serve immediately over pasta with sauce.

Mrs. Joseph Bucknum (Jane Smith)

Roast Loin Of Veal With Lowcountry Sauce

Average   **Serves:** 4
Partial Prepare Ahead   **Bake:** 25 to 30 minutes at 375°

1   veal loin (2½ to 3 pounds)

♦ Brown the loin of veal in oil, in hot, heavy skillet. (Just brown lightly for a
  couple of minutes on both sides.)
♦ Remove loin to rack over roasting pan and season with salt and pepper.
♦ Roast 375° for 25-30 minutes.

Sauce:

2	pounds mushrooms	1	tablespoon flour
½	cup butter	1	teaspoon salt
2	tablespoons chopped shallots	½	teaspoon freshly cracked white
	juice of one-half lemon		pepper
¼	cup dry Madeira wine or	2	cups heavy cream
	dry sherry		

♦ Roughly chop mushrooms.
♦ Heat butter in heavy skillet over medium high heat and cook shallots for 3
  minutes stirring. Do not let them brown.
♦ Add chopped mushrooms and lemon juice. Cook, stirring until mixture
  looks dry.
♦ Add Madeira wine and cook until it evaporates.
♦ Sprinkle flour, salt, and pepper over mushrooms and stir in.
♦ Add heavy cream and continue cooking until sauce is thickened.

To serve:
♦ Slice loin thin and arrange on pretty platter. Generously ladle on mushroom
  sauce. Sprinkle with some chopped fresh parsley.

Mr. G. Marshall Mundy

Veal Scallopini Charleston

Average
Partial Prepare Ahead

Serves: 4
Sauté: 3 to 5 minutes
Heat: briefly

¼ cup clarified butter
8 2 ounces veal scallopini, pounded flat
1 cup crabmeat

2 ounces Proscuitto ham cut into thin, julienne strips
salt
freshly ground pepper

Knead together following ingredients:

¼ cup softened butter
juice from ½ lemon
¼ teaspoon Worcestershire sauce

1 tablespoon chopped parsley
1 tablespoon white wine
½ teaspoon Poupon mustard

◆ Heat oil in sauté pan until it just starts to smoke.
◆ Flour veal.
◆ Season lightly with salt and freshly ground pepper.
◆ Sauté quickly, allowing light brown color to form on veal.
◆ Arrange on platter.
◆ Pour off excess oil from pan.
◆ Add kneaded butter mixture to pan.
◆ When mixture is hot, add ham and crabmeat.
◆ Toss until all is heated.
◆ Serve over scallopinis.

* May be served with Hollandaise or Bernaise Sauce.

Mr. G. Marshall Mundy

Veal With Artichokes And Mushrooms

Average
Serve Immediately

Serves: 4
Sauté: 4 to 5 minutes
Cook: until reduced by a third

12 veal scallops, thinly sliced
½ cup flour
12 artichoke hearts (canned)
10 medium mushrooms, sliced

½ cup white wine
½ cup butter
juice of two lemons
1 cup chicken stock

◆ Dust scallops lightly with flour.
◆ Sauté in butter until done.
◆ Remove veal from pan and set aside.
◆ Add mushrooms to pan and cook until done.
◆ Add artichoke hearts, white wine, lemon juice, and chicken stock.
◆ Cook until reduced by a third.
◆ Return veal and cook 2 to 3 minutes until hot.

Mrs. Thomas J. Parsell (Susan Poston)

149

Veal Goulash

Average
May Prepare Ahead

Serves: 4
Cook: 1 hour on medium low heat

1½ pounds veal cutlet or veal stew meat
1 large onion, chopped
1 clove garlic, minced
3 tablespoons bacon drippings
8 ounces fresh mushrooms

1 tablespoon butter
1½ cups canned chicken broth
1 teaspoon salt
¼ teaspoon pepper
1 tablespoon paprika
1 cup sour cream

♦ Cube veal into bitesize pieces.
♦ In large frying pan, sautè veal, onion, and garlic in bacon drippings until golden.
♦ In smaller pan, sauté mushrooms in melted butter.
♦ Set mushrooms aside until later.
♦ Add chicken broth, salt, pepper and paprika to veal.
♦ Cover and simmer gently for one hour.
♦ Re-season to taste with salt and pepper.
♦ Drain mushrooms and add to veal.
♦ Before serving, stir in sour cream. Do not let it boil.

Mrs. Jules Deas, Jr. (Leigh Tyler)

Pork Loin

Average
Partial Prepare Ahead

Serves: 8 to 10
Bake: 2½ hours at 325°

1 pork loin, 3 to 4 pounds
2 cloves garlic, minced
2 teaspoons salt
1 teaspoon sage
½ teaspoon pepper

½ teaspoon nutmeg
2 onions, sliced
2 carrots, sliced
1 cup water
1 jar currant jelly
1 teaspoon dry mustard

♦ Mix the garlic, salt, sage, pepper, and nutmeg and rub into meat.
♦ Place meat in roasting pan and add onions, carrots, and water.
♦ Bake at 325° for 1½ hours, uncovered.
♦ Take out and cut fat into criss-cross pattern.
♦ Spread top with 1 jar currant jelly mixed with 1 teaspoon dry mustard.
♦ Cook 1 hour more, uncovered.

Mrs. Park Smith (Jeanne deSaussure)

Chikaby Ham
"After serving, all that's left is the bone—so GOOD!"

Easy
May Prepare Ahead

Serves: 50/cocktail party
or 20 dinner party
Bake: 1 hour at 350°

1   ten pound ham
1   brown paper bag, don't laugh-
    grocery bag, not browning bag
    whole cloves and ground cloves

sliced canned pineapple or fresh
sliced oranges
brown sugar

- Wash ham in water.
- Place unseasoned ham in paper bag.
- Place in large roaster with lid.
- Cook for approximately 1 hour at 350°.
- Remove lid and tear away bag.
- Cut off unnecessary fat and score top.
- Place whole cloves in scores.
- Sprinkle with ground cloves.
- Rub brown sugar in.
- Cook without lid for about 15 to 25 minutes.
- Remove from oven and place sliced pineapple on top, or slice oranges.
- Pour any juice from fruit over ham.
- Cook with lid 45 minutes more.
- If not brown enough, take lid off and broil for 5 minutes.

Mrs. Joseph Johnson (Beverly Stoney)

Liver Puddin'
"Wonderful with grits for breakfast."

Average
Prepare Ahead
Freezes Well

Serves: 16-20
Cook: 45 minutes
Chill: 3 hours

3   pounds pork liver
1   pound pork end loin pieces with
    bone and fat
2   teaspoons salt

1   teaspoon pepper
    water to cover
2   tablespoons cornmeal
1   envelope gelatin - dissolved

- Boil pork and liver with salt and pepper in water for 45 minutes.
- Cool. Remove bones and grind.
- Mix ground mixture, stock, cornmeal and gelatin.
- Put in loaf pan or several small containers and chill.

Mrs. Bachman S. Smith, Jr. (Eunice Green)

Smithfield Ham
"Very tender"

Average
Prepare Ahead

Serves: 50/cocktail party
or 20 dinner
Bake: overnight

Soak during the day. Bake during the evening. Take it out of oven the next morning.

10 to 12 pound Smithfield ham
5 cups cold water
   whole cloves

brown sugar
prepared mustard

♦ Scrub ham with a brush to remove any mold on the skin.
♦ Soak ham in cold water for 8 hours.
♦ Place ham in roaster, fatter side down, and add 5 cups cold water.
♦ Cover top of pan with aluminum foil (making it as airtight as possible), before putting on the roaster lid.
♦ Place roaster in a cold oven and set temperature at 500°.
♦ Bake at 500° for 10 minutes.
♦ Turn oven off.
♦ Leave ham in oven for 3 hours, undisturbed.
♦ DO NOT OPEN OVEN.
♦ After 3 hours, set oven for 500° again.
♦ When temperature is reached, bake ham for 15 minutes.
♦ Turn oven off - DO NOT OPEN OVEN.
♦ Leave ham in another 3 hours or until morning.
♦ Skin ham, leaving a thin layer of fat. Coat with brown sugar and mustard.
♦ Dot with cloves.
♦ Run under broiler to brown slightly.

Mrs. J. Gilbert Baldwin, Jr. (Constance Montague)

Fresh Spinach & Ham Lasagna
"Noodles need not be cooked prior to baking"

Average　　　　　　　　　　　　　**Serves:** 12
May Prepare Ahead　　　　　　　**Bake:** 45 to 60 minutes at 350°

Recipe doubles well.

4	cups tomato sauce
¾	cup chopped parsley, basil, and/or oregano
2	pounds noodles, 3 inches wide, uncooked
1½	pounds whole milk ricotta mixed with 1 egg yolk and 1 teaspoon nutmeg
1½	pounds mozzarella cheese, grated

¾	cup grated Parmesan or Pecorino cheese
1	pound ham, thinly sliced
2	pounds fresh spinach leaves, washed, steamed for 1 minute and drained
	salt and pepper

♦ Layer tomato sauce, herbs, pasta, cheeses, ham and spinach in a lasagna pan.
♦ Season lightly as you go.
♦ Top with final sprinkling of mozzarella or Parmesan.
♦ Bake 45-60 minutes.
♦ Cool slightly before cutting.

Mrs. Daniel Ravenel (Kathleen Hall)

Grilled Fresh Ham
"So good and so easy."

Easy　　　　　　　　　　　　　　**Serves:** 20-30
May Prepare Ahead　　　　　　　**Grill:** 8-12 hours

12- 15 pound fresh ham	water
black pepper	tabasco
vinegar	wood chips, soaked

♦ Prepare grill with charcoal and wood chips at one end.
♦ Coat ham with black pepper.
♦ Place ham on opposite end of grill. Not directly over coals.
♦ Mix 1 part vinegar to 2 parts water with a dash of tabasco.
♦ Baste ham periodically.
♦ Add soaked wood chips frequently.
♦ Cook until well done, 180°-190°. Use a thermometer.
♦ Allow to cool 20-30 minutes before slicing.
♦ Serve with a mustard based bar-b-que sauce.

Dr. Daniel Ravenel

153

Chinese Pork Chops
"A sweet and sour taste"

Easy
Serve Immediately

Serves: 4
Cook: 40 minutes

1 tablespoon sherry	4 tablespoons sugar
2 tablespoons soy sauce	5 tablespoons water
3 tablespoons cider vinegar	4 thick cut pork chops

+ Combine first five ingredients.
+ Put pork chops in frying pan.
+ Pour mixture over them.
+ Simmer covered until porkchops are tender (about 40 minutes, turning once).
+ Remove cover.
+ Turn up heat.
+ Boil until sauce reduces to a glaze.
+ Serve immediately.

Mrs. Blaine Ewing, III (Phyllis Walker)

Sausage Rice Casserole
"Great served with game"

Easy
Partial Prepare Ahead

Serves: 6
Bake: 1½ hours at 350°

1 pound ground hot sausage	1 large jar mushrooms, sliced
1 green pepper, chopped	1 cup uncooked rice
1 large onion, chopped	2 cans consommé soup
2 tablespoons butter	

+ Fry sausage until crumbly.
+ Drain throughly on paper towel.
+ Sauté green pepper and onion in butter..
+ Combine all ingredients.
+ Bake in 9 x 13 casserole, uncovered, approximately 1½ hours at 350°.

Martha J. Lott

Leg Of Lamb
"Fabulous!"

Average
Serve Immediately

Serves: 10 to 18
(½ pound per serving)
Bake: 20 minutes per pound at 350°

1 leg of lamb, 5 to 9 pounds
   flour, salt, pepper for dredging
   garlic cloves

½ cup cream
½ cup very strong black coffee
½ to 1 cup red wine

♦ Preheat oven to 450°.
♦ Place leg of lamb in large roasting pan.
♦ Rub entire surface with garlic.
♦ Insert small slivers of garlic in a few slits in the skin surface.
♦ Mix some flour, salt and pepper together.
♦ Dredge lamb in mixture.
♦ Place in 450° oven and sear for 30 minutes.
♦ Mix together cream, coffee, and red wine.
♦ Reduce oven temperature to 350°.
♦ Pour liquid over lamb.
♦ Cook 20 minutes per pound.
♦ Baste frequently.
♦ Add more cream and wine if needed.
♦ Remove to a serving platter.
♦ Make a gravy with remaining liquid.

Mrs. William C. Cleveland (Anne Walker)

Curried Lamb

Easy
May Prepare Ahead
Freezes Well

Serves: 6 to 8
Cook: 25 minutes on low

2 tablespoons margarine
1 small onion, chopped
1 chicken bouillon cube
½ cup boiling water
½ cup tomato juice

½ apple, peeled and cubed
4 cups cooked, cubed lamb
1 teaspoon curry powder
1 teaspoon lemon juice
   cooked rice

♦ Melt margarine in heavy Dutch oven.
♦ Add onions and cook until soft.
♦ Dissolve bouillon in boiling water, add to onion along with all other
  ingredients, except rice.
♦ Bring to a boil, cover and simmer for 25 minutes.
♦ Serve over hot, cooked rice.

Mrs. Charles M. Fox (Melissa Tuttle)

Roasted Leg Of Lamb

Easy
May Prepare Ahead

Serves: 10
Bake: 20 to 30 minutes per pound

leg of lamb
(approximately 7 pounds)
prepared mustard
onion salt
garlic powder
salt

pepper
1   10½-ounce can consommé
juice of 2 lemons
1   or 2 boxes of frozen creamed
onions*

- Cover lamb thick with prepared mustard.
- Sprinkle heavily with onion salt, garlic powder, salt and pepper.
- Put lamb into oven, in uncovered turkey roaster.
- One hour before lamb is done, mix lemon juice with consommé and pour over leg.
- Add creamed onions to the roasting pan.
- Baste often.
- If frozen creamed onions are not available, make white cream sauce and add jar of pearl onions.

* With leftover lamb - slice and put in dish with leftover onions and juice. Reheat and serve over toast.

Mrs. William W. Boles, III (Elizabeth Brown)

Lamb Kebobs

Easy
Partial Prepare Ahead

Serves: 10
Marinate: 8 to 12 hours
Grill

Marinade

1   teaspoon curry powder
1½ tablespoons salt
3   bay leaves
6-8 pepper corns

1-2 garlic cloves, crushed
¼   cup lemon juice
¼   cup red wine
⅓   cup oil

Kebobs

2   pounds lamb, cut into
2 inch cubes
small onions, halved
or quartered

tomato wedges
green pepper, cut into squares
fresh mushrooms

- Mix the ingredients of marinade.

- Place meat and vegetables (except tomatoes) in marinade.
- Marinate 8 to 12 hours.
- Put meat on skewers alternating with vegetables.
- Cook over charcoal, until done, turning and basting often.
- Use left over marinade for basting during cooking.

Mrs. Henry Lide DuRant (Kay Ravenel)

Romanian Lamb Stew
"Quite a colorful array of vegetables."

Average　　　　　　　　　　　**Serves:** 8 to 10
Prepare Ahead　　　　　　　**Simmer:** 1 hour
Freezes Well

¼ cup oil	2 small yellow squash, cut in
3 pounds of stew lamb, cut in	¾-inch cubes
1-inch pieces	1 clove garlic, minced
1 cup sliced onion	1 can tomatoes (1 lb., 12 oz.)
2 green peppers, seeded and cut	2 teaspoon salt
in large dice	1 teaspoon Hungarian paprika
1 small eggplant, peeled and cut	
in ¾-inch cubes	

- Heat oil in Dutch oven over medium heat. Add lamb and brown on all sides. Remove meat and set aside.
- Add vegetables to oil and cook 5 minutes.
- Add garlic and cook 1 minute.
- Return meat to pot and add tomatoes, salt, and paprika.
- Cover and bring to boil.
- Reduce heat and simmer 1 hour or until lamb is tender.
- Skim fat and correct seasoning.
- Serve with egg noodles and salad.
* Prepare at least a day ahead for ultimate flavor.

Ann W. Dibble

MEATS

GAME

Roast Venison
"Well worth the time!"

Average
Prepare Ahead

Serves: 20
Marinate: 3 days
Bake: 2½ hours at 325°

1	haunch of venison, any size	1	teaspoon marjoram
10	cloves garlic, split in half	1	teaspoon sage
¼	cup olive oil	1	tablespoon salt
4	onions, cut into wedges	3	liters dry red wine
4	bay leaves	1	cup brandy
1	tablespoon peppercorns	¼	cup vinegar
2	teaspoons thyme		

- 3 days ahead of serving: Marinate.
- Wash haunch.
- Pierce meat all over with knife point and insert a split garlic clove in each hole.
- Pour oil over meat and rub to cover entire haunch.
- Place in large roaster.
- Sprinkle rest of dry ingredients over meat.
- Pour wine, brandy, and vinegar into bottom of roaster.
- Cover and refrigerate.
- Turn meat twice a day until serving day.

To cook:
- Put covered roaster into 325° oven for 2½ hours, basting often.
- Test for desired degree of doneness. Meat should be pink but not bloody near the bone.
- Allow to rest 10 minutes before carving.
- Garnish with parsley and orange wedges.

* Marinade in which gravy cooks, does not make good gravy.

Mrs. T. Heyward Carter, Jr. (Eleanor Weaver)

Venison Haunch (or Loin)

Average
Partial Prepare Ahead

Serves: 8 to 10
Bake: 3 to 4 hours at 300°-325°

1   venison haunch (or loin)
     vinegar
     garlic powder
2   or 3 onions cut into eighths

1   pound bacon
     garlic salt
1   cup red wine

- Cut 1 inch wide slits in venison all the way through, about 2 inches apart.
- Pour scant capful (off vinegar bottle) vinegar into each slit.
- Shake garlic powder into each slit.
- Stuff slits with cut onion and strip of bacon to the top.
- Shake garlic salt on top of roast.
- Lay strips of bacon across top.
- Pour red wine on top.
- Roast in covered roaster 3-4 hours or until very tender.
- Baste occasionally.
- Remove from roaster and make gravy from drippings.

* Serve with rice, curried fruit, and green beens with almonds.

Mrs. Davies Walker (Patience Davies)

Low Country Fried Venison

"Delicious on a cold winter night"

Easy
Serve Immediately

Serves: 4
Cooks: 2 to 3 minutes

8   venison fillets (4 to 6 oz. each.
     ¾ inch thick cut from saddle)
6   to 8 tablespoons Dijon style
     mustard

½   cup flour
     hot oil

- Coat venison fillets with mustard.
- Dredge in flour.
- Cook 2 to 3 minutes in hot oil until crispy.

Mrs. Joseph S. Shisko (Sallie Smith)

Mustard Fried Venison

Easy
Prepare Ahead

Serves: 4 to 6
Marinate: minimum of 2 hours or overnight
Cook: 3 to 4 minutes

venison ham cut into one inch cubes (1½ to 2 lbs.)
1 cup yellow prepared mustard
1 teaspoon soy sauce
¼ teaspoon black pepper

¼ teaspoon red pepper
½ teaspoon garlic salt
½ teaspoon onion salt
sifted flour

- Marinate venison cubes in mixture of mustard, soy sauce, peppers, and garlic and onion salts.
- Refrigerate a minimum of 2 hours or overnight.
- Heat pot of oil for frying (have deep enough so meat will brown all over).
- Roll cubes in flour.
- Drop in hot oil.
- Cook for 3 to 4 minutes.
- Drain and serve.

Mr. Ben McC. Moise

"In The Bag" Roasted Goose
"Simply Delicious"

Average
May Prepare Ahead

Serves: 4 to 6
Bake: 2 to 2½ hours at 375°

1 wild goose
1 apple, quartered
1 onion, quartered
¼ cup flour
1 cup natural apple juice or cider

1 cup white wine
1 bay leaf
5 peppercorns
cornstarch
currant jelly

- Place apple and onion quarters in cavity of goose.
- Add flour to a large (14 x 20) oven cooking bag and shake.
- Place bag in a 2 inch deep roasting pan.
- Add juice and wine to bag along with bay leaf and peppercorns.
- Stir contents of bag with wooden spoon until blended.
- Place goose in bag and close with tie.
- Make six ½ inch slits in top of bag.
- Roast in 375° oven for 2-2½ hours or until tender.
- If more browning desired, split open bag to expose breast of bird.
- To make gravy, strain juices in bag.
- Remove fat.
- Add small amount of cornstarch which has been disolved in water.
- Add currant jelly to taste.

Mr. Whitemarsh Seabrook Smith, III

Blind Duck
"Try this!"

Easy
Serve Immediately

Serves: 2
Cook: 5 minutes

1	good friend
1	cold morning
1	duck blind or boat
1	freshly shot duck
1	pocket knife
1	small frying pan

1	can sterno or stove
½	stick butter
4	slices bread
	salt, pepper and garlic powder
1	flask brandy

- Shoot one duck.
- Cut skin down center of breast from neck to tail.
- Peel back skin and filet 2 breasts from bone.
- Heat butter and sauté seasoned breasts until medium rare.
- Serve between bread slices and wash down with brandy.

Mr. J. Conrad Zimmerman, Jr.

Pilot Duck Breast
"You'll love this"

Average
Prepare Ahead

Serves: 6
Marinate: 24 hours
Grill: 12 minutes

6	duck breasts
⅔	cup burgundy wine
⅓	cup soy sauce
1	stick butter

	a little liquid garlic
1	6-ounce jar orange marmalade
1	cup burgundy wine

- Mix ⅔ cup wine and soy sauce for marinade.
- Marinate for 1 day.
- Place duck breast on hot grill, skin side down.
- Combine butter, liquid garlic, marmalade, and 1 cup wine.
- Cook breast 3 minutes, basting with sauce.
- Turn, baste and cook 3 minutes more.
- Repeat for a total of 12 minutes.

Mr. T. Lawrence Lucas (Lukie)

Duck Whoopee
"Hunter's Delight!"

Average
Prepare Same Day
Serve Immediately

Serves: 4
Cook: 1 hour 40 minutes on stove top

4 wild ducks	1 cup flour
water	1 tablespoon Worcestershire sauce
8 strips bacon	4 white potatoes, cubed
2 medium onions, chopped	water
salt and pepper	

- Split ducks in half.
- Place in 5 quart pot and cover with water.
- Par-boil 40 minutes.
- While ducks par-boil, fry bacon, remove from grease and crumble.
- Fry onion until transparent.
- Cut up potatoes and cover with water till ready to use.
- After ducks have par-boiled, remove from pot, wipe dry, then salt, pepper and flour ducks.
- Brown in bacon grease with onions.
- Place potatoes in bottom of empty 5-quart pot.
- Add browned ducks, bacon grease, onions, Worcestershire, crumbled bacon, and salt and pepper to taste.
- Add enough fresh water to half cover the ducks.
- Cook for 1 hour in covered pot over medium low heat on top of stove.
- Take ducks from gravy and serve ducks with gravy over rice.
- Always discard water that ducks are par-boiled in. Par-boiling removes some of the wild flavor.

Mr. Ikey A. Speights, III

Roast Wild Duck

Easy   **Serves:** 4
May Prepare Ahead   **Bake:** 3 hours covered at 325°

2   ducks, cut in half   1   tablespoon Worcestershire sauce
    garlic, salt, pepper to taste   1   tablespoon dry mustard
1   cup chopped celery   ½   tablespoon nutmeg
1   large onion, chopped   juice of 1 small lemon
1   or 2 buttons garlic, chopped   2   cups water
1   cup chili sauce   paprika

♦ Rub duck halves with garlic, salt, and pepper.
♦ Place breast side down in roaster.
♦ Combine other ingredients, except paprika; pour over ducks.
♦ Bake covered at 325° for 3 hours.
♦ When ducks are tender, turn breast side up and sprinkle with paprika.
♦ Bake uncovered until brown.
♦ Serve gravy with ducks.

* If thickened gravy is desired, add a small amount of flour to drippings and
  cook until thickened.

Mrs. Charles E. Miller, Jr. (Sarah R. Gregorie)

Wild Duck
"A real favorite"

Average   **Serves:** 2
May Prepare Ahead   **Bake:** 3 hours at 275°

    salt   2   stalks celery, diced
2   wild ducks   1   apple, diced
    salt and pepper   1   medium onion, diced
2   tablespoons soft butter   4-6 bacon strips
1   orange, cut in small pieces   2   cups cooked wild rice

♦ Rub salt in cavity of ducks and rinse with cold water thoroughly.
♦ Clean ducks well, removing all pin feathers.
♦ Salt and pepper ducks inside and out.
♦ Mix butter with orange, celery, apple, and onion.
♦ Stuff in cavities and close.
♦ Prick skin.
♦ Place breast side up on rack in greased casserole or pan.
♦ Put 2 or 3 strips of bacon on each duck.
♦ Roast covered at 275° for 3 hours or until tender.
♦ Remove meat from bones and serve on bed of cooked wild rice.

Mrs. H. Parker Jones (Josephine Neil)

Duck 'N Orange Sauce
"Goes great with grits or wild rice"

Average
May Prepare Ahead

Serves: 8
Bake: 2 hours at 325°

4	large ducks	3	oranges
2	stalks celery cut into pieces	4	strips bacon
2	onions, quartered	2	cups water
2	apples, quartered	½	cup Worcestershire sauce

♦ Stuff the cavity of each duck with pieces of celery, onion, and apple
♦ Place in roasting pan.
♦ Squeeze the juice from 2 oranges over the ducks.
♦ Lay strips of bacon and slices from 1 orange on top.
♦ Put water and Worcestershire in bottom of pan.
♦ Cover and bake at 325° for 2 hours, basting every 20 minutes.
♦ Remove from pan and slice meat from bones.
♦ Cover with sauce.

Sauce:

⅔	cup brown sugar	2	cups orange juice
⅔	cup white sugar	¾	cup orange marmalade
2	tablespoons flour		

♦ Combine all ingredients in a medium sauce pan.
♦ Simmer until thickened, stirring constantly.

Mrs. Robert H. Hood (Bernie Burnham)

New Street Potted Doves

Easy
May Prepare Ahead

Serves: 4 to 6
Cook: approx. 2 hours

8 - 10	doves		salt, pepper
1	cup water	1	medium onion, sliced
1	cup catsup	3	slices uncooked bacon
3-4	tablespoons Worcestershire sauce		

♦ Place birds in heavy pan with a cover.
♦ Steam on top of stove in small amount of water for 20 minutes.
♦ Add catsup, Worcestershire sauce, salt and pepper.
♦ Lay onion rings, then bacon, on top of birds.
♦ Cook covered on low heat approximately 1½ hours.

Martha J. Lott

Doves With Grapes
"Different, but wonderful"

Average
Partial Prepare Ahead

Serves: 3 doves per person
Cook: approx. 1 hour

doves, whole, with skin on
1 - 1½ cups white seedless grapes,
    cut in half, lengthwise
    juice of one fresh lemon

butter, salt, pepper and flour
½ cup almond slivers
1   piece of toast per bird

- Dry doves.
- Rub thoroughly inside and out with salt and pepper.
- Coat lightly with flour.
- Melt butter in frying pan.
- Slowly brown doves.
- Reduce heat.
- Add a cup of water.
- Cover and cook slowly until doves are tender.
- Add grapes and cook for 25 or 30 minutes.
- Take birds out.
- Pour in almonds and lemon juice.
- Cook 4 or 5 minutes longer.
- Place each bird on a piece of toast.
- Spoon grape sauce over them.

Mr. Ben McC. Moise

J. R.'s Dove Casserole
"Great with rice or grits!"

Easy
Partial Prepare Ahead

Serves: 6
Bake: 1 hour, 20 minutes at 350°

12-18 doves
1   10½-ounce can cream of
    mushroom soup
1   medium onion - diced
¼ to ½ cup sherry

¼ teaspoon oregano
¼ teaspoon crushed rosemary
    salt and pepper to taste
½ pint sour cream

- Place doves, breast side down, in a 15 x 12 baking dish.
- Sauté onions in a little butter.
- Mix onions with soup, sherry, and herbs.
- Pour mixture over doves.
- Cover tightly and cook for one hour, turning occasionally.
- Add sour cream and stir.
- Continue baking for 20 minutes.

Mrs. James H. Rike (Katharyne Hanahan)

Broad Street Dove Breast
"Excellent also as an appetizer!"

Easy
Partial Prepare Ahead

Serves: 4 for dinner or
makes 24 appetizers
Broil: 7 minutes per side

12 slices of bacon, cut in half
12 dove breasts
24 thinly cut pieces of celery about
   ½ inch long

24 thinly cut pieces of onion about
   ½ inch long
   salt and pepper to taste
   onion salt to taste

♦ Fillet dove breast off of each dove-yielding 24 pieces of breast meat.
♦ Place 1 dove breast on the end of a slice of bacon.
♦ Place 1 piece of celery and onion on top of each breast.
♦ Sprinkle each with salt, pepper, and onion salt.
♦ Roll each breast with the slice of bacon it is sitting on and place a toothpick through it.
♦ Place the bundles in a broiler pan and broil for approximately 7 minutes on each side, or until bacon is cooked.
♦ Do not over cook.

Field Doves In Red Wine Sauce

Average
Serve Immediately

Serves: 4 to 6
Cook: 1 to 1½ hours

4 tablespoons butter
1 onion, chopped
16 dove breasts
1 teaspoon salt
1 teaspoon pepper
2 teaspoons parsley

2 teaspoons Worcestershire sauce
¼ teaspoon thyme
½ cup red wine
1 cup beef bouillon
2 tablespoons flour
2 tablespoons softened butter

♦ Melt butter and sauté onions.
♦ Salt and pepper dove breasts and brown both sides.
♦ Add parsley, Worcestershire and thyme to pan.
♦ Reduce heat to simmer.
♦ Arrange breasts so meat side is up.
♦ Add wine and reduce heat to low.
♦ Add bouillon.
♦ Cover and cook 1 to 1½ hrs. or until tender.
♦ Remove doves from skillet.
♦ Mix flour and softened butter to form a roux.
♦ Add to sauce in skillet to thicken.
♦ Arrange doves on platter and pour sauce over them.

Mrs. Grant M. Smith (Hollis Davis)

Sandy's Doves

Easy
Serve Immediately

Serves: 6
Bake: 2 hours at 300°

12 doves
    salt, pepper, and garlic powder
    to taste
 6 slices of bacon - cut in half

1 can of cream of mushroom soup
1 package of Lipton dried onion
   soup mix
1 to 1½ cans of water

♦ Salt, pepper and garlic each dove.
♦ Wrap each dove in bacon and secure with a toothpick.
♦ Place in browning bag.
♦ Add soups and water.
♦ Punch holes in top of bag and place on cookie sheet.
♦ Bake.

Mrs. John A. Stuhr (Bess Cameron)

Stuffed Quail
"Excellent over toast points!"

Average
Serve Immediately

Serves: 4
Bake: 25 minutes at 350°

 1 small package wild and long
    -grain rice, cooked as directed
 8 quail
16 strips uncooked bacon
    butter

½ cup white wine
1 cube beef bouillon
   salt
   pepper
   bunch of green grapes, garnish

♦ Wash quail and pat dry.
♦ Stuff with cooked rice.
♦ Wrap two strips bacon around each quail.
♦ Panfry birds in a little butter (about 1 tablespoon) until slightly brown.
♦ Bake in 350° oven, 25 minutes.
♦ While quails bake, remove most of the oil from the pan (saving ½ cup).
♦ Add wine to pan.
♦ Cook over medium high heat 2-3 minutes.
♦ Add bouillon cube.
♦ Simmer 5 minutes.
♦ Salt and pepper to taste.
♦ When quail are done, place on platter and cover with sauce. Garnish with grapes.

Mrs. Telfair Parker (Hope Haselden)

Mary Blackwell's Quail
"Gravy makes this a real treat!"

Easy
May Prepare Ahead

Serves: 4
Bake: 2½ hours at 350°

8	quail (or doves)	2	sticks real butter
1	cup flour	2	tablespoons flour
1	tablespoon paprika	2	bouillon cubes (chicken for
	salt		quail, beef for dove)
	pepper		

- Heavily salt and pepper quail
- Shake in bag of flour mixed with paprika.
- Melt 2 sticks butter in heavy skillet.
- Brown quail until dark.
- Remove quail and add 2 tablespoons flour and stir.
- Add 2 bouillon cubes and enough water to almost fill pan.
- Simmer 10 minutes.
- Place quail in deep casserole and cover with gravy.
- Cover and bake.
* After baking, birds will be almost "candied". You may want to thin the gravy with a little water.

Mrs. Ivan V. Anderson, Jr. (Josephine Blackwell)

Hunter's Quail

Easy
Prepare Same Day

Serves: 2
Cook: 40 minutes on medium heat

¼	cup butter	1	can condensed consommé
1	small onion, chopped		pinch of thyme
4	quail	½	bay leaf
	salt and pepper	½	cup dry white wine
2	tablespoons flour		

- Melt butter in skillet.
- Add onions and stir.
- Sprinkle birds with salt and pepper.
- Move onions to edge of pan, place the birds in the skillet and brown slowly over medium heat.
- Sprinkle birds with flour.
- Add remaining ingredients and cover skillet tightly.
- Simmer for 40 minutes or until quail are tender.
- Spoon pan juices over quail when serving.

Mrs. William Russell Tyler (Linda Cochran)

Mushroom Sauce
"Great with London broil or any steak."

Average
May Prepare Ahead

Yield: 1½ cups
Cook: 35 minutes

3 tablespoons butter	1 cup canned beef bouillon
1 clove garlic, minced	8 ounces fresh sliced mushrooms
1 slice of onion	¼ teaspoon salt
2 slices carrot	⅛ teaspoon pepper
1 sprig parsley	⅓ cup Burgundy wine
6 whole black peppercorns	2 tablespoons fresh parsley,
1 bay leaf	chopped
2 tablespoons flour	

+ Melt butter in medium skillet.
+ Add garlic, onion, carrot, parsley, peppercorns and bay leaf.
+ Sauté about 3 minutes.
+ Remove from heat and add flour.
+ Stir until smooth.
+ Return to heat and cook, stirring often, until flour is golden. (About 5 minutes.)
+ Remove from heat and gradually add bouillon.
+ Over medium heat, bring to a boil while stirring.
+ Simmer for ten minutes.
+ In separate skillet, sauté mushrooms.
+ Strain bouillon mixture of seasonings and add salt, pepper, Burgundy, parsley and mushrooms.
+ Serve hot.

Mrs. Jules Deas, Jr. (Leigh Tyler)

Mustard Sauce For Baked Ham
"Old family recipe that always receives rave reviews."

Easy
Prepare Ahead

Yield: 4 cups

½ cup sugar	½ cup vinegar
1 tablespoon dry mustard	½ pint whipping cream
2 eggs	

+ In a small saucepan, blend sugar, mustard and eggs.
+ Add vinegar and whipping cream.
+ Place on stove and stir constantly until boiling.
+ Remove from heat, cool and refrigerate.
+ Keeps for 10 days.

Mrs. Thomas M. Walkley (Mary Ellen Dailey)

Sweet Mustard

"Great for sandwiches or ham glaze."

Easy
May Prepare Ahead

Yield: 3 cups
Cook: 10 minutes

½   cup white vinegar
½   cup dry mustard
2   eggs, well beaten

1   cup white sugar
1   cup brown sugar
    pinch of salt

- ◆ Place all ingredients in blender.
- ◆ Blend until well mixed.
- ◆ Pour mixture into medium saucepan.
- ◆ Heat until sugar is dissolved.
- ◆ Use warm or let cool.
- ◆ Store in cabinet in well-sealed jar or refrigerate.

Mrs. William T. Tamsberg (Merle Sparkman)

Sweet And Sour Mustard

Easy
Prepare Ahead

Yield: 1 cup
Cook: 15-20 minutes

1   can Coleman's dry mustard
    (2-ounces)
½ c. cider vinegar

2   eggs
⅛   teaspoon salt
1   cup sugar

- ◆ Pour mustard into measuring cup.
- ◆ Add vinegar to mustard, filling measuring cup to 8 ounces.
- ◆ Let stand one hour.
- ◆ In double boiler, beat eggs well.
- ◆ Add salt and sugar. Stir.
- ◆ Add mustard and vinegar mixture.
- ◆ Cook over boiling water until thick, stirring constantly (about 15 to 20 minutes).

Mrs. Hugh Comer Lane, Jr. (Croft Whitener)

Planter's Duck Sauce
"Delicious over roast duck."

Easy
May Prepare Ahead

Yield: 2 cups
Cook: 10 minutes

1   16-ounce jar currant jelly
½   cup ketchup

2½ tablespoons sherry

♦ Combine all ingredients in saucepan.
♦ Over medium heat, cook until bubbly. DO NOT BURN!
♦ Serve hot.

Mrs. David McCord Smythe (Ruth Ellen Conway)

Bread Sauce
"It enhances the flavor!"

Easy
May Prepare Ahead

Serves: 6-8
Cook: 30 minutes

1   medium onion
5   cloves
2   cups milk

2   cups breadcrumbs
salt and pepper, to taste

♦ Stick the peeled onion with the cloves.
♦ Simmer in the milk for 30 minutes on low heat.
♦ Remove onion and cloves, add the breadcrumbs, salt and pepper.
♦ Mix well.
* Serve with duck and currant jelly.

Mr. J. Conrad Zimmerman, Jr.

Wild Game Sauce
"It's always a hit"

Easy
May Prepare Ahead

Serves: up to 16

1   10-13 ounce currant jelly
½   cup Port wine
2½ tablespoons horseradish

1   can manderin oranges, drained
⅛   teaspoon nutmeg
salt and pepper to taste

♦ In medium saucepan, melt jelly.
♦ Bring to a boil.
♦ Mix remaining ingredients and add to jelly.
♦ Serve hot with game.

Mrs. Telfair H. Parker (Hope Haselden)

SEAFOOD

One of the most popular ways of winter entertaining in the Lowcountry is the oyster roast.

It's a mixture of senses: the glory of figures silhouetted against an orange sky; the smoky smell of oysters being shoveled on the grill; and the divine, salty taste of oysters popped piping hot from the shell.

The host needs add only some beer, crackers and occasionally some cocktail sauce. Then the quest for the perfect oyster takes over amid sounds of lively conversation, laughter and frequent ecstatic exclamations about the fare.

Oyster roasts are held in months with R's in them — months when oysters are best and when it feels good to back up to a fire and warm your hands for a few minutes between batches.

SEAFOOD

Seafood Streudel
"Excellent"

Complicated
Partial Prepare Ahead

Serves: 6-8
Chill: 2 hours
Bake: 50 minutes at 375°

2   tablespoons butter
2   tablespoons flour
½   teaspoon Dijon mustard
    salt
    cayenne pepper
¾   cup milk at room temperature
2   tablespoons whipping cream
¼   cup Parmesan cheese, freshly grated
1   cup bread crumbs
¼   teaspoon dry mustard
1   pound crab, shrimp, scallops, cooked (any one or combination)

½   pound phyllo pastry sheets
½   cup Swiss cheese, grated
2   hard boiled eggs, chopped
¾   cup sour cream
¼   cup parsley, chopped
¼   cup shallots, diced
2   tablespoons chives, chopped
1   large garlic clove, minced
¾   cup butter, melted
2   tablespoons parsley, chopped
2   tablespoons Parmesan cheese, grated

♦ Make thick white sauce with first 6 ingredients.
♦ Add cream.
♦ Cover and chill about 2 hours until firm.
♦ Preheat oven to 375°.
♦ Butter baking sheet.
♦ Combine bread crumbs, ¼ cup Parmesan cheese, dry mustard.
♦ Prepare phyllo according to package.
♦ Brush each sheet generously with melted butter.
♦ Layer on Phyllo - seafood combination, Swiss cheese, and chopped egg.
♦ Dot with sour cream.
♦ Sprinkle with parsley, shallots, chives, and garlic.
♦ Dot with chilled white sauce.
♦ Sprinkle with bread crumb mixture.
♦ Roll and place seam-side down on prepared baking sheet.
♦ Brush with melted butter.
♦ Bake 12 minutes.
♦ Remove from oven and brush with melted butter.
♦ Slice diagonally into 1½ inch pieces.
♦ Reshape loaf.
♦ Add parsley to remaining butter and brush again.
♦ Cook 35-40 minutes, basting 3 times.
♦ Allow to cool 10 minutes.
♦ Transfer to warmed platter.
♦ Dust with 2 tablespoons parsley and 2 tablespoons Parmesan cheese.

Mrs. G. Simms McDowell, III (Elsa Freeman)

173

Seafood Coquille Robert

"My father's version, learned many years ago."

Average
Partial Prepare Ahead

Serves: 4-6
Bake: 20-30 minutes at 350°

12 shrimp, cooked, peeled
   and diced
4 plump scallops
½ cup dry white wine
   bouquet of herbs (parsley,
   chives, dill and tarragon)
   salt and pepper to taste
8 - 10 oysters

½ cup sliced mushrooms
4 tablespoons butter
2 tablespoons flour
2 tablespoons whipping cream
1 egg yolk
4-6 thin slices tomato, peeled
   cheddar cheese, grated
   bread crumbs

♦ Bring to a boil and simmer for 8 minutes, the scallops, wine, herbs, salt and pepper.
♦ Remove scallops; slice them thinly and set aside with shrimp.
♦ Strain stock from scallops.
♦ Return stock to saucepan, adding oysters.
♦ Bring to a boil for 2 minutes.
♦ Remove oysters and reserve stock.
♦ Brown mushrooms in 2 tablespoons butter, reserving stock.
♦ Add cooked mushrooms to shrimp, scallops, and oysters.
♦ Melt 2 tablespoons butter in skillet.
♦ Remove from heat and add 2 tablespoons of flour, stirring well.
♦ Add stock from mushrooms and shellfish, stir, and bring to a boil.
♦ Beat 1 egg yolk with 2 tablespoons cream and stir into mixture.
♦ Simmer several minutes; correct seasoning; add seafood and mushrooms; remove from heat.
♦ Put mixture in large scallop shells or ramekins.
♦ Cover the top of each serving with a tomato slice.
♦ Sprinkle with grated cheese and bread crumbs.
♦ Dot with butter.
♦ Bake for 20-30 minutes at 350° or broil until brown and bubbly.

Mrs. J. Gilbert Baldwin, Jr. (Constance Montague)

Frogmore Stew
"Serves a crowd effortlessly for an outdoor party."

Easy
Serve Immediately

Serves: a crowd
Cook: 30 minutes

½ pound shrimp per person
¼ pound smoked link sausage per
  person, cut in 2-inch pieces
1½ -2 ears corn per person

chopped celery
seafood seasonings
salt

- Bring a large amount of water to boil (there should be roughly twice the volume of water as the volume of ingredients).
- Add ¼ cup salt per gallon of water, chopped celery tied in a cheesecloth, and seafood seasoning.
- Add sausage and boil for 7 minutes.
- Add corn and boil for 7 minutes.
- Add shrimp and cook for 4 minutes. (DO NOT OVERCOOK.)
- Drain and serve in large bowl or tub.

* For variation, raw, cleaned crabs may be added at the time of the corn.

Mr. Ben McC. Moise

Seafood Casserole

Average
May Prepare Ahead
Freezes Well

Serves: 8
Bake: 40 minutes at 350°

2 pounds shrimp, cooked
  and peeled
1 pound claw crab meat
1 pound small scallops
2 cups celery, finely chopped
¾ cup onion, finely chopped

1 cup mayonnaise
1 tablespoon Worcestershire sauce
1 teaspoon black pepper
1½ cups fine bread crumbs
½ stick butter, melted
  lemon wedges

- Toss the shrimp, crab, and scallops in a large bowl.
- In a separate bowl mix together the celery, onion, mayonnaise, Worcestershire and pepper.
- Toss with seafood until well blended.
- Put in an 8 x 12 casserole.
- Mix the bread crumbs and melted butter.
- Sprinkle over casserole.
- Bake about 40 minutes or until bread crumbs are lightly browned.
- Serve with lemon wedges.

* Excellent with red rice from ***Charleston Receipts.***

Mrs. Milon C. Smith (Mary Lou Hodges)

Aunt Jean's Shrimp And Crab

Easy
Serve Immediately

Serves: 8
Bake: 15 minutes at 350°

2 pounds lump crabmeat	1 tablespoon Dijon mustard
1 pound shrimp, cooked and peeled	1 teaspoon salt
	½ teaspoon white pepper
1 green pepper, finely diced	2 eggs, beaten
2 pimentos, chopped	1 cup mayonnaise

♦ Preheat oven to 350°.
♦ Mix all ingredients.
♦ Place in individual scallop shells.
♦ Bake for 15 minutes.
* Good with cold tomato soup.

Mrs. R. Edward L. Holt, III (Kitty Trask)

Shrimp And Crab Casserole

Average
Serve Immediately

Serves: 10-12
Bake: 15 minutes at 400°

1 green pepper, chopped	2 cups cream
2 stalks celery, chopped	1 cup sharp cheddar cheese, shredded
1 medium onion, chopped	dash nutmeg
2 cups water	½ teaspoon salt
1 small jar pimentos, chopped	⅛ teaspoon pepper
2 pounds shrimp, cooked and peeled	½ cup sherry
1 pound crabmeat	1 cup breadcrumbs, buttered
4 hard boiled eggs, sliced	tomato slices
4 tablespoons butter	bacon
4 tablespoons flour	

♦ Preheat oven to 400°.
♦ Combine pepper, celery, onion, and 2 cups of water and cook until tender. Drain.
♦ Add pimento, shrimp, crabmeat, and egg. Set aside.
♦ Melt butter and stir in flour until smooth.
♦ Add cream and cook until thick, stirring constantly.
♦ Add cheese, salt, pepper and nutmeg.
♦ Stir in sherry.
♦ Combine sauce with seafood mixture and place in greased 3 quart dish.
♦ Cover with buttered breadcrumbs.
♦ Top with tomato slices and bacon strips.
♦ Bake.

Mrs. Daniel Ravenel (Linda Compton)

Wappoo Creek Shrimp

Average
Partial Prepare Ahead
Freezes Well

Serves: 8
Bake: 25 minutes at 350°

1½ pounds shrimp, cooked
   and peeled
1 pound crabmeat
4 cups cooked rice
2 cans water chestnuts, sliced
1 cup celery, diced
½ cup onion, diced
1 cup frozen green peas

¾ cup slivered almonds
4 ounces sharp cheese, grated
1 cup Hellmann's mayonnaise
1 cup sour cream
1½ tablespoons Worcestershire
   sauce
½ teaspoon pepper
1 teaspoon salt

♦ Preheat oven to 350°.
♦ Toss first 9 ingredients together (saving a few shrimp and small amount of cheese to garnish).
♦ Mix mayonnaise, sour cream and seasonings in a small bowl.
♦ Toss the two mixtures together very lightly.
♦ Garnish.
♦ Bake in covered, buttered casserole dish for 25 minutes.
♦ Remove cover last 5 minutes to brown.

Mrs. D. William Wallace (Sally Ann Benson)

Shrimp And Crabmeat Delight

Easy
Serve Immediately

Serves: 10
Bake: 30 minutes at 400°

1 cup mayonnaise
4 cups shrimp, cooked and peeled
2 cups crabmeat
2 cups celery, chopped
1½ teaspoons salt
½ teaspoon white pepper
2 teaspoons sugar

1 teaspoon dry mustard
2 tablespoons lemon juice
1 tablespoon Worcestershire sauce
½ cup chopped onion or
   3 teaspoons instant onion
½ cup sharp cheese, grated
   crushed potato chips

♦ Preheat oven to 400°.
♦ Combine all ingredients and place in casserole dish.
♦ Cover with grated cheese.
♦ Top with crushed potato chips.
♦ Bake for 30 minutes or until bubbly.

Mrs. F. L. Hamilton (Keith Chandler)

Crab And Shrimp Shells

Easy
Serve Immediately

Serves: 6
Bake: 30 minutes at 350°

1½ pounds shrimp, cooked
   and peeled
8 ounces crabmeat, picked
4 tablespoons butter
4 tablespoons flour

2 cups half and half
4-6 tablespoons sherry
1 cup cheddar cheese, grated
6-8 pastry shells, cooked according
   to directions

♦ Preheat oven to 350°.
♦ Melt butter in medium sauce pan.
♦ Add the flour.
♦ Slowly add the half and half, stirring constantly.
♦ Cook until thick.
♦ Add sherry to taste.
♦ Add crab and shrimp.
♦ Fill pastry shells and place on cookie sheet.
♦ Top with grated cheese.
♦ Bake for 30 minutes.

Florrie's Seafood Casserole

Easy
Serve Immediately

Serves: 8
Bake: 30-40 minutes at 375°

2 cups tomato juice
2 cups mayonnaise
2 cups rice, cooked
⅔ cup green pepper, chopped
2½ cups fresh crabmeat

2 cups shrimp, cooked and peeled
2 tablespoons horseradish
4 tablespoons butter
1 cup bread crumbs
1 small package slivered almonds

♦ Preheat oven to 375°.
♦ Blend tomato juice and mayonnaise.
♦ Add rice, green pepper, crab, shrimp, and horseradish.
♦ Mix well.
♦ Transfer to greased 2½ quart casserole.
♦ Melt butter.
♦ Toss bread crumbs with butter.
♦ Top casserole with bread crumbs and slivered almonds.
♦ Bake.
* May substitute 2 6½-ounce cans of crab.

Mrs. William T. Tamsberg (Merle Sparkman)

Creamed Lobster And Shrimp

Average
Serve Immediately

Serves: 4-6
Bake: 20 minutes at 350°

5 tablespoons butter	3 lobsters (2 cups), cooked
3 tablespoons flour	1 quart shrimp (2 cups), cooked
1½ cups whipping cream	and peeled
½ teaspoon salt	12 ounce package mushrooms
⅛ teaspoon cayenne pepper	grated Parmesan cheese
½ cup dry sherry	

- Preheat oven to 350°.
- Melt 3 tablespoons of butter. Add flour, and whisk until smooth.
- Warm cream and slowly add to the flour, stirring constantly, until mixture reaches boiling point.
- Add salt, pepper and sherry.
- Mix well; set aside covered.
- Cut lobster into bite-size pieces.
- Add lobster and shrimp to the sauce.
- Sauté mushrooms in two tablespoons of butter. Drain and add to mixture.
- Stir mixture and cook over low heat for several minutes.
- Pour into 2 quart casserole dish.
- Top with Parmesan cheese and dots of butter.
- Bake at 350° for 20 minutes or until bubbly.

* Can be served in pastry shells or over long grain and wild rice.

Mrs. Keating Lewis Simons, Jr. (Julianne Howard Bell)

Franz Witte's Deviled Crab

Average
May Prepare Ahead

Serves: 8 to 10
Bake: 30 minutes at 400°

2 pounds crabmeat	½- ¾ cup cracker meal (more if
¾ cup milk	needed to thicken)
4 hardboiled eggs, finely chopped	5-8 dashes tabasco
10 olives with pimentos, finely chopped	1½ teaspoons seafood seasoning
3 large stalks of celery, finely chopped	4 heaping tablespoons mayonnaise
	⅓ cup lemon juice

- Mix all ingredients together.
- Fill crabshells generously.
- Bake.

Mrs. Bissell J. Witte (Linda Burton)

179

Crab Imperial I

Average
May Prepare Ahead

Serves: 4
Bake: 15 minutes at 350°

⅓ cup green pepper, finely diced	½ teaspoon salt
2 tablespoons pimento, finely chopped	¼ teaspoon white pepper
1½ teaspoons powdered English mustard	1 egg
	¾ cup mayonnaise
	1½ pounds crabmeat

- Mix green pepper, pimento, mustard, salt and pepper.
- In separate bowl, beat egg and add mayonnaise.
- Combine with green pepper mixture.
- Carefully fold in crabmeat.
- Spoon into individual scallop shells and bake for 15 minutes or in casserole dish and bake for 35 minutes.

Mrs. Arthur M. Parker (Catharine Wood)

Crab Imperial II

Average
May Prepare Ahead

Serves: 4 to 6
Bake: 30 minutes at 300°

1 pound lump crabmeat	1 egg, beaten
½ teaspoon Worcestershire sauce	½ cup mayonnaise
1 tablespoon horseradish	1 tablespoon sherry
¼ teaspoon salt	1 cup cheddar cheese, grated
¼ stick butter	

- Mix ingredients and pour into baking dish.
- Sprinkle cheese on top.
- Bake.

Mrs. Joseph A. Coates, III (Susan Dunbar)

Crab Chantilly

Easy
Partial Prepare Ahead
Freezes Well

Serves: 4
Broil: 3-4 minutes

2 tablespoons butter or margarine
2 tablespoons green onion, sliced
1 tablespoon flour
½ teaspoon salt
dash of cayenne pepper
1 cup light cream
¼ cup salad dressing (not mayonnaise)

1 pound crabmeat, picked and drained
1 10-ounce package frozen asparagus, cooked according to package
1 tablespoon grated Parmesan cheese
sherry (optional)

♦ Cook green onion gently in butter until tender.
♦ Stir in flour, salt, and cayenne.
♦ Add cream and stir constantly until thickened.
♦ Remove from heat.
♦ Stir in salad dressing.
♦ Fold in crabmeat.
♦ Season with sherry, if desired.
♦ Arrange cooked asparagus in shallow baking dish.
♦ Spoon creamed crabmeat over asparagus.
♦ Sprinkle with Parmesan cheese.
♦ Broil about 4 inches from heat for 3-4 minutes or until lightly browned and hot. Or, if prepared ahead, heat in 350° oven until lightly browned and hot.

* Creamed crab mixture may be made ahead and frozen.

Mrs. Ritchie H. Belser (Gale Johnson)

Crab In Shells

Average
May Prepare Ahead

Serves: 10 to 12
Bake: 30 minutes at 350°

1 pound lump crabmeat
¾ pound fresh mushrooms, sliced
1 tablespoon butter, melted
1 cup mayonnaise
1 tablespoon dry mustard

1 tablespoon Worcestershire sauce
1 tablespoon lemon juice
3 slices bread, toasted and made into crumbs
paprika

♦ Sauté mushrooms in butter, drain, and set aside.
♦ Combine remaining ingredients, (except paprika).
♦ Stir in mushrooms.
♦ Distribute crab mixture in 10-12 scallop shells.
♦ Sprinkle with paprika.
♦ Bake.

Mrs. James M. Ravenel (Elizabeth Barkley)

Deviled Crab Supreme

Average
May Prepare Ahead
Freezes Well

Serves: 6
Bake: 30 minutes at 350°

4 tablespoons margarine	⅛ teaspoon ground nutmeg
⅛ cup minced green onion, shallots, or mild onion	1 ounce cream sherry
6 tablespoons flour	3 cups loosely packed fresh crabmeat (and roe, if available)
1 pint whipping cream	2 cups fresh buttered bread crumbs (approximately)
½ cup milk	paprika
¼ teaspoon tabasco	
1 teaspoon salt	

♦ Melt margarine and sauté onion until soft.
♦ Remove onion. Add flour and stir until smooth.
♦ Add whipping cream and milk. Stir constantly until thick.
♦ Season with hot sauce, salt, and nutmeg.
♦ Remove from heat. Add sautéed onion and sherry and stir.
♦ Add crab and mix gently.
♦ Place crab mixture into 10-12 cleaned crab shells (or scallop shells), mounding slightly.
♦ Press buttered bread crumbs on top and sprinkle with paprika.
♦ Bake for 30 minutes or until bubbly.

Mrs. Carlton Simons (Etta Ray Longshore)

Crab Casserole Superb

Average
May Prepare Ahead

Serves: 5-6
Bake: 45 minutes at 350°

3 tablespoons butter or margarine	½ cup mayonnaise
¼ cup onion, chopped	juice of ½ lemon
¼ cup celery, chopped	½ cup almonds, sliced
2 tablespoons flour	⅛ cup dry sherry
1 cup light cream	1 pound white crab meat
¼ teaspoon salt	1 cup stuffing mix
¼ teaspoon pepper	1 cup cheddar cheese, grated

♦ Sauté onion and celery in butter until clear.
♦ Add flour and stir until smooth paste.
♦ Pour in cream and heat, stirring constantly until mixture bubbles.
♦ Add remaining ingredients (except cheese) and stir to blend.
♦ Turn into buttered one and a half quart casserole.
♦ Top with cheese.
♦ Bake at 350° for 45 minutes or until bubbly.

Mrs. Thomas E. Thornhill (Mardelle Musk)

Crab Casserole I
"For those in a hurry"

Easy
May Prepare Ahead

Serves: 8
Bake: 30 minutes at 350°

1	pound crabmeat	1	can water chestnuts, sliced
3	eggs, hard-boiled and sliced	3	cups fresh bread, crumbled
2	cups half and half	2	sticks butter
1	cup mayonnaise	2	teaspoons parsley flakes
2	teaspoons grated onion		

+ Mix first six ingredients.
+ Melt butter and stir in bread crumbs and parsley.
+ Blend bread crumbs into mixture, reserving 1 cup.
+ Place mixture in 2-quart greased casserole.
+ Top with remaining crumbs.
+ Bake until bubbly.

Mrs. William Haywood Mapp, Jr. (Mary Louise Owen)

Crab Casserole II

Easy
Prepare Ahead

Serves: 10
Bake: 1 hour at 325°

8	slices bread, crusts removed	1	tablespoon Worcestershire
1½	sticks butter, melted	1	tablespoon salt
1	pound fresh crab meat		dash of tabasco
1	cup celery, chopped	1	pound sharp cheese, grated
⅔	cup mayonnaise	4	eggs
1	tablespoon mustard	2	cups milk

+ Cut bread into strips and coat with butter.
+ Line the bottom of a 9 x 13 casserole dish with the bread strips.
+ Mix crab, celery, mayonnaise, mustard, Worcestershire, salt and tobasco.
+ Spread half of mixture over bread.
+ Top with half of the grated cheese.
+ Repeat layers of crab and cheese.
+ Mix the eggs and milk and pour over the casserole.
+ Chill overnight.
+ Remove from refrigerator 2 hours before baking.
+ Bake in a pan of water.

Mrs. Robert H. Hood (Bernie Burnham)

Crab Cakes

Average
Partial Prepare Ahead

Serves: 4
Fry: 3 to 4 minutes

1   stick butter
2   tablespoons all purpose flour
1   cup milk
1   egg, beaten
1   pound crabmeat

1   tablespoon Worcestershire sauce
½   teaspoon poultry seasoning
¼   teaspoon salt
     dash pepper
     Ritz cracker crumbs

♦ Melt butter; stir in flour; add milk, stirring constantly until slightly thickened.
♦ Add beaten egg to crabmeat and fold into white sauce.
♦ Add Worcestershire, poultry seasoning, salt and pepper.
♦ Refrigerate until set.
♦ Pat into cakes.
♦ Coat with Ritz crackers crumbs.
♦ Fry in hot oil until golden brown.

Mrs. Joseph A. Coates, III (Susan Dunbar)

Crabmeat Casserole
"For elegant appetites."

Average
May Prepare Ahead

Serves: 6 to 8
Bake: 30 minutes

3   tablespoons butter
3   tablespoons flour
2   cups of cream
2   egg yolks, lightly beaten
1   tablespoon lemon juice
1   tablespoon parsley, minced
½   teaspoon paprika

2   tablespoons dry white wine
     (or sherry)
2   cups crabmeat
     salt to taste
1   cup breadcrumbs or Parmesan
     cheese (or both)

♦ Melt butter and add flour and cream, stirring constantly until thickened.
♦ Remove from stove and add egg yolks, lemon juice, parsley, paprika, wine and dash of salt.
♦ Pour sauce into well-greased 5 cup casserole dish.
♦ Blend crabmeat into sauce.
♦ Top with breadcrumbs or Parmesan cheese or both.
♦ Bake.

Mrs. Edward Drummond Izard (Jane Craver)

Crabmeat Tetrazzini

Easy
Partial Prepare Ahead

Serves: 6-8
Bake: 20 minutes at 350°

½ -¾ pound fresh mushrooms,
   sliced
1   stick butter
2   tablespoons flour
2-3 cups half and half
½ -¾ cup sherry (or to taste)

¾ -1 pound crabmeat (claw or
   white)
1   package small egg noodles
½ -¾ cup Parmesan cheese (fresh
   grated is best)
salt and pepper to taste

♦ Sauté mushrooms in butter and remove with slotted spoon.
♦ Add flour to pan, cooking and stirring.
♦ Gradually add half and half, stir until thickened.
♦ Add sherry, salt and pepper, crab and mushrooms.
♦ Cook noodles and mix with crab mixture.
♦ Top with Parmesan cheese.
♦ Bake for 20 minutes or until bubbly.

Mrs. J. Conrad Zimmerman, Jr. (Barbara Hubbard)

Helen's Deviled Crab

Average
May Prepare Ahead
Freezes Well

Serves: 6
Bake: 30 minutes at 400°

1   cup toasted bread crumbs
½   pound butter, melted
1   tablespoon mayonnaise
2   tablespoons sherry
1   teaspoon dry mustard

pinch minced parsley
salt and pepper to taste
1   teaspoon Worcestershire sauce
2   cups crabmeat

♦ Reserving 4 teaspoons of butter, combine remaining butter with
   bread crumbs.
♦ Mix mayonnaise, sherry, mustard, parsley, salt, pepper and Worcestershire.
♦ Add crabmeat gently.
♦ Fill 6 large crab shells (or scallop shells) with crab mixture.
♦ Sprinkle with buttered bread crumbs and pour remaining melted butter
   on top.
♦ Bake.

Mrs. John H. Warren, III (Helen Smith)

Crab Quiche

Average
May Prepare Ahead
Freezes Well

Serves: 4 to 6 as a meal or
16 as an appetizer
Bake: 45 to 60 minutes at 325°

1	deep dish pastry pie shell	½	cup half and half
2	cups fresh lump crabmeat	2	tablespoons flour
2	green onions with tops, sliced thin	½	cup mayonnaise
		¼	teaspoon dry mustard
8	ounces Swiss cheese, grated	½	teaspoon grated lemon peel
2	eggs, beaten	¼	cup sliced almonds (optional)

♦ Prick bottom and sides of pie shell and bake for 10 minutes at 450°.
♦ Spread crabmeat over pie shell. Add onions and then cheese.
♦ Combine eggs, half and half, flour and mayonnaise.
♦ Add mustard and lemon peel to egg mixture and pour over cheese.
♦ Top with almonds.
♦ Bake.

Mrs. Isaac A. Speights, III (Elizabeth Lesesne)

Avocado Crepe With Crabmeat
"Talk About Good"

Average
Partial Prepare Ahead

Serves: 4

2	tablespoons butter	1	cup bechamel sauce *
6	ounces crabmeat	4	ounces cheddar cheese
4	ounces fresh mushrooms, sliced	1	avocado, sliced
1	shallot, chopped		crepes *

♦ Sauté crabmeat, mushrooms, and shallots in butter.
♦ Prepare bechamel sauce and simmer.
♦ Add crab mixture to sauce.
♦ Prepare crepes.
♦ Fold crab mixture into crepe.
♦ Top with slices of avocado and cheddar cheese.

* See index for appropriate listings.

Mrs. Joseph P. Bucknum (Jane Smith)

Crab Cakes Douglas

Average
May Prepare Ahead

Serves: 4 to 6
Fry: 2 minutes

3	tablespoons mayonnaise		dash of mace
1	tablespoon prepared mustard		dash of Worcestershire sauce
1	pound crabmeat, regular or claw	2	tablespoons green pepper,
2	eggs, beaten		chopped (optional)
2	tablespoons onion, minced		butter
¼	cup cracker crumbs		

♦ Mix mayonnaise and mustard together.
♦ Add all other ingredients.
♦ Shape into patties and refrigerate until ready to cook.
♦ Fry in butter over medium heat (350° in electric frying pan) for 2 minutes.
♦ Turn over, cover, and steam cook for 3 minutes.
♦ Serve hot.

Mrs. J. Gilbert Baldwin, Jr. (Constance Montague)

Church Social Deviled Crab
"Divine"

Easy
May Prepare Ahead

Serves: 4 to 6
Bake: 30 minutes at 350°

1	pound crab meat	1	tablespoon ketchup
6	slices bread	1	medium onion, chopped
3	hard boiled eggs, chopped	½	cup mayonnaise
1	teaspoon dry mustard		salt and pepper
2	tablespoons Worcestershire	¼	cup cracker crumbs

♦ Break bread into crumbs.
♦ Add remaining ingredients, cutting eggs into small pieces.
♦ Add crab meat and mix well.
♦ Put in buttered casserole dish.
♦ Put cracker crumbs over top.
♦ Bake at 350° for 30 minutes.

* Serve with tarragon seafood sauce - see index.
* Use less bread if serving fewer people.

Mrs. James Sellers (Winton Chandler)

Fish Stock

Easy
May Prepare Ahead

Yields: 1 quart
May be Refrigerated or Frozen

1 tablespoon butter
1 medium onion, sliced
1 quart water
1½ pounds fish bones, broken into
 medium pieces (don't use skin)
10 peppercorns

2 tablespoons lemon juice or
 1 cup dry white wine
1 bay leaf
 sprig of fresh thyme or
 ¼ teaspoon dried thyme
3-4 stems parsley

♦ Melt butter in a large pot. Sauté onion until soft, but not brown.
♦ Add other ingredients. The bones should be just covered.
♦ Bring to boil slowly, skimming often. Reduce heat and simmer uncovered
 20 minutes.
♦ Strain the stock.
* Essential ingredients for Scallop's Charleston.

Ann W. Dibble

Baked Fish
"Good and Easy"

Easy
Serve Immediately

Serves: 6
Bake: 15-20 minutes at 375°

1 egg, beaten
3 pounds fillet of flounder or sole
1 cup bread crumbs (either corn
 bread or corn flakes prepared)

½ cup butter (no substitute)
 salt and pepper

♦ Dip fish in egg.
♦ Press crumbs all over fish.
♦ Brown butter slightly in oven in large shallow baking dish.
♦ Lower fish into butter and turn over. (Do not crowd fish.)
♦ Salt and pepper to taste.
♦ Baste while baking.
♦ Serve with lemon wedges.

Mrs. Joseph C. Good, Jr. (Virginia Craver)

Stuffed Flounder Fillets

Average
Serve Immediately

Serves: 6-8
Bake: 35 minutes at 400°

2 pounds flounder filets (8 filets)
1 cup Swiss cheese, grated

½ teaspoon paprika

Stuffing

¼ cup onion, chopped
¼ cup butter
1 3-ounce can chopped mushrooms, liquid reserved

½ pound crabmeat, picked
½ cup coarse saltine crackers
2 tablespoons fresh parsley
½ teaspoon salt

Sauce

3 tablespoons butter
3 tablespoons flour
¼ teaspoon salt

½ cup milk
⅓ cup dry white wine

♦ In a skillet, sauté onions in butter until tender.
♦ Stir in mushrooms, crabmeat, crackers, parsley, salt and pepper.
♦ Put 1 tablespoon of stuffing on each flounder filet. Roll filet, secure with toothpick and place seam side down in baking dish.
♦ Prepare white sauce with butter, flour, salt and 1½ cups liquid (add enough milk to reserved mushroom liquid and wine to make 1½ cups).
♦ Cook and stir until mixture thickens and bubbles.
♦ Pour over stuffed fillets.
♦ Bake for 25 minutes.
♦ Remove from oven. Sprinkle with grated cheese and paprika. Return to oven for 10 more minutes or until fish flakes with a fork.

Mrs. Edward W. Riggs (Rebecca Turner)

Parmesan Fish Alaskan

Easy
Serve Immediately

Serves: 4
Marinate: 30 minutes
Broil: 20 minutes

4 fish fillets (sole, flounder, grouper)
1 large lemon
1 cup mayonnaise

1 tablespoon chives, chopped
2 tablespoons parsley, chopped
4 tablespoons Parmesan cheese
2 egg whites, beaten stiff

♦ Marinate fish in juice of lemon for ½ hour.
♦ Combine next 5 ingredients and spread on top of fish.
♦ Cover with foil (do not let foil touch the top).
♦ Broil for 10 minutes.
♦ Remove foil and brown until golden.

Mrs. W. Vaughan Davidson (Salley Barton)

189

Flounder Fillets In Shrimp Sauce
"Great for that special dinner for two."

Average
Partial Prepare Ahead

Serves: 2
Chill: 1 hour
Bake: 25 minutes at 350°

2	6-ounce flounder fillets	1	tablespoon white wine
1	teaspoon lemon juice		

Sauce

2	tablespoons butter	¼	teaspoon dried whole tarragon
2	tablespoons flour	¼	teaspoon Worcestershire sauce
¾	cup milk	1	3 ounce can sliced mushrooms,
2	tablespoons white wine		drained
1½	teaspoons fresh parsley, chopped	½	pound small shrimp, cooked
½	teaspoon salt		and peeled

- Place fillets in a shallow dish.
- Combine lemon juice and wine and pour over fillets.
- Cover and chill for at least an hour.
- Prepare white sauce with butter, flour and milk, stirring constantly until thickened and bubbly.
- Add wine, parsley, salt, tarragon, Worcestershire, mushrooms and shrimp.
- Roll drained fillets.
- Place seam down in lightly greased baking dish.
- Pour sauce on top.
- Bake uncovered for 25 minutes or until fish is flaky, basting occasionally.

Mrs. J. Stanley Claypoole, III (Barbara Pringle)

Broiled Flounder

Easy
Serve Immediately

Serves: 4
Broil: 10-15 minutes

	buttermilk	mayonnaise
	salt, pepper, dill,	Parmesan cheese
	Nature's Seasons to taste	2 pounds flounder fillets

- Place fillets in 9 x 12 baking dish.
- Cover with buttermilk and soak for 15-20 minutes.
- Drain buttermilk.
- Srinkle with seasonings.
- Spread a layer of mayonnaise on top.
- Sprinkle Parmesan cheese on top.
- Broil for 10-15 minutes until done. (If fillets are thick, you may wish to bake at 400°, then broil.)

Sara Turpin

Grilled Grouper

Easy
Serve Immediately

Serves: 6
Grill: 20-30 minutes

1   stick butter or margarine
¼   cup lemon juice
2   tablespoons Worcestershire
2   teaspoons dry mustard
2   small (or 1 large) bay leaf

1   heaping teaspoon seasoned
    pepper
2-3 pounds grouper fillets (any
    game fish will do)

Grill:
- Combine first six ingredients in sauce pan and heat until you smell the aroma of bay leaves.
- Place fish fillets on covered grill at medium heat, skin-side down.
- Baste every 5 minutes until fish is done (about 20-30 minutes).

Oven:
- Place fish in casserole. Pour sauce over and cover.
- Cook at 350° for 20-30 minutes.

Mrs. Michael T. Watson (Mary "Rusty" Thomas)

Bee Dowdy's Salmon Loaf

Easy
May Prepare Ahead
Freezes Well

Serves: 8
Bake: 50 minutes at 350°

1   15½-ounce can salmon, drained
1   tablespoon oil
1   teaspoon lemon juice
2-3 slices white bread, crumbled

2   eggs, beaten
3   tablespoons ketchup
1   small onion, chopped
    salt and pepper to taste

- Combine all ingredients.
- Place in lightly greased loaf pan.
- Bake.

Elizabeth Hayden Blackwell

Salmon Soufflé

Average
Serve Immediately

Serves: 6
Bake: 1 hour at 325°

¼ cup butter	¼ teaspoon pepper
⅓ cup flour	6½ -ounce can salmon
1¼ cups milk	1 teaspoon onion, chopped
4 eggs, separated	(optional)
¼ teaspoon salt	1 cup cheddar cheese, grated

♦ Prepare white sauce with butter, flour and milk.
♦ Beat egg yolks until frothy and stir them into white sauce.
♦ Stir in salt, pepper, salmon (or tuna), and onion (if desired).
♦ Set aside.
♦ Beat egg whites until stiff and fold into mixture.
♦ Grease a 3 quart soufflé dish and pour mixture into it.
♦ Bake for 45 minutes.
♦ Remove from oven, sprinkle with cheese, and return to oven for 15 more minutes.

* Can use fresh or canned tuna.

Mrs. Joseph Gilchrist (Sara Quick)

Fish And Rice
"Use the leftover fish."

Average
Serve Immediately

Serves: 4
Cook: 30-45 minutes

2 cups leftover fish or canned salmon	2 tablespoons flour
2 cups rice, uncooked	2 cups milk
3 raw eggs, beaten	2 hard-boiled eggs, chopped
salt and pepper, to taste	1 cup parsley, chopped
4 tablespoons butter	salt and pepper, to taste

♦ Flake the fish, mix with rice, eggs, salt and pepper.
♦ Oil the top of a double boiler and line with waxed paper. Oil the paper also.
♦ Place fish and rice mixture in lined boiler, fold paper over and steam for 30-45 minutes.
♦ Melt butter, add flour then milk and cook until thick.
♦ Add chopped eggs, parsley, salt and pepper.
♦ Unmold fish and rice, remove paper and pour sauce over it.

Mr. J. Conrad Zimmerman, Jr.

Big Daddy's Trout Almondine
"Wonderful"

Easy
Partial Prepare Ahead
Serve Immediately

Serves: 4
Soak: 1 to 2 hours
Fry

4-6 trout fillets, skinned
1 cup buttermilk
1 egg
1 teaspoon almond extract

2 tubes saltine crackers, crumbled fine
½ cup slivered almonds

- Soak fillets in buttermilk, egg and almond extract, for 1 to 2 hours.
- Drain fillets, do not wipe away any excess.
- Put fillets in crackers and mash down hard so crackers stick well to fish.
- Fry in hot grease.
- Sprinkle slivered almonds on top of each fillet to serve.

Mrs. R. Whitfield Scoggin (Priscilla Robertson)

Grilled Wahoo
"Simple"

Easy
Serve Immediately

Serves: 4
Grill: 20-25 minutes

4 wahoo steaks
1 bottle Italian dressing

1 medium onion

- Soak wahoo steak for 45 minutes in Italian dressing with a slice of onion on top.
- Drain.
- Place on grill with onions on top.
- Grill until done, when fish flakes with a fork.

Mrs. Joseph J. Strickland (Margaret Graybill)

Spanish Mackerel with Olives

Easy
Partial Prepare Ahead

Servings: ½ pound per person
Bake: 25 to 35 minutes at 350°

Fresh Spanish Mackerel,
(whole, cleaned)
1   can plain green olives, pitted
1   can plain black olives, pitted

¼   cup olive oil
¼   cup butter
    salt, pepper, paprika

♦ Stuff cavity of fish with mixture of green and black olives. (Save some to cover fish.)
♦ Pour approximately ¼ cup oil and ¼ cup butter into the bottom of a baking pan.
♦ Sprinkle over the surface of the oil mixture a light amount of salt, pepper, and paprika.
♦ Place fish in pan, and smother with remaining olives.
♦ Cook and baste frequently with oil and butter in pan.

Fried Shark Fingers

Easy
Prepare Ahead

Serves: 6 to 8
Fry: 1 to 2 minutes

buttermilk
1½ pounds shark, skinned and
    cleaned fillets
    juice of 2 lemons
½   cup milk
1   egg, beaten

salt
pepper
4   good dashes paprika
1   cup flour
    oil for frying

♦ Soak shark overnight in buttermilk.
♦ Drain and cut in strips or fingers.
♦ Squeeze juice of 2 lemons over shark in a bowl and let sit for 10 minutes.
♦ Combine milk and egg and dip shark fingers in mixture.
♦ Roll in flour, salt and pepper and paprika.
♦ Fry in hot oil until golden brown.

* House of Autry Seafood Breader mix may be used instead of flour mixture.

Mrs. Isaac A. Speights, III (Elizabeth Lesesne)

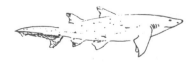

Microwave Fish Henri
"Quick!"

Easy
Serve Immediately

Serves: 4
Cook: 12-16 minutes

2   pounds any fillet of fish
    (½ pound per person)
1   tablespoon butter or margarine,
    cut in small pieces, per fillet

1   fresh lemon
¼   cup white wine
1   can cream of mushroom soup

♦ Place fish in microwave safe dish.
♦ Squeeze lemon juice over and dot with pieces of butter.
♦ Cover dish with plastic wrap and cook on high for 6-8 minutes.
♦ Remove from microwave.
♦ Stir wine into mushroom soup.
♦ Pour over fish.
♦ Return to oven and cook on high 6-8 more minutes.
♦ Serve with rice.

Mrs. Morgan Millis (Joanna Morgan)

Mustard Sauce For Fish

Easy
Serve Immediately

Yield: 1 cup
Bake: 20 minutes at 350°

1   cup sour cream
1   teaspoon mustard

juice of 1 lemon
1   teaspoon Worcestershire sauce

♦ Combine all ingredients.
♦ Spread on flounder or other fish fillets.
♦ Bake at 350° for approximately 20 minutes, until done.

Mrs. Fred J. Attaway, Jr. (Nancy Felder)

Spiced Sauce For Fish

Easy
Serve Immediately

Yield: 1 cup
Bake: 20 minutes at 350°

1   cup mayonnaise
    juice of 1 lemon
2   teaspoons chives, chopped
2   sprigs fresh parsley, cut with
    scissors

1   teaspoon dill or to taste
    pinch of salt

♦ Combine all ingredients.
♦ Spread on flounder or other fish fillets.
♦ Bake at 350° for approximately 20 minutes, or until done.

Mrs. Fred J. Attaway, Jr. (Nancy Felder)

Little Dix Marinade For Grilled Fish

Easy
Freezes Well

Serves: 6-8
Marinate: 2 hours
Grill: until flaky

juice of 1 lime
2 tablespoons soy sauce
4 tablespoons coconut cream
1½ tablespoons dark brown sugar

1 tablespoon sherry
1 garlic clove, pressed
4 tablespoons vegetable oil
3-4 pounds fish

♦ Combine all ingredients.
♦ Marinate fish for 2 hours, covered.
♦ Baste several times while grilling.
* Grilling time depends on the thickness of fish used, 10 to 12 minutes per inch of thickness.
* May freeze fish in marinade.

Mrs. J. Price Cameron, Jr. (Louisa Huger Pringle)

Capers Sauce For Fish

Easy
Serve Immediately

Yield: 1 cup
Bake: 20 minutes at 350°

2 tablespoons butter
1½ tablespoons flour
¾ cup water

1 tablespoon white vinegar
2 tablespoons capers with juice

♦ In a heavy saucepan, melt butter over low heat.
♦ Add flour and blend.
♦ Add water, stirring until sauce begins to thicken.
♦ Add vinegar, capers and salt.
♦ Blend thoroughly and spread on flounder or other fish fillets.
♦ Bake at 350° until done, approximately 20 minutes.

Mrs. Fred J. Attaway, Jr. (Nancy Felder)

Plantation Oyster Pie
"Thanksgiving Family Favorite"

Easy

Serves: 6
Bake: 1 hour at 350°

2	pie crusts (deep dish), pre-cooked	3	tablespoons flour
6	tablespoons bacon drippings	2	pints oysters, drained
1	cup onions, chopped		salt
1	cup celery, chopped		pepper
1	cup green pepper, chopped		tabasco
1	cup parsley, chopped		Worcestershire sauce

♦ Sauté onions in 3 tablespoons bacon drippings.
♦ Add celery, pepper, and parsley. Sauté.
♦ In separate pan, brown flour in 3 tablespoons bacon drippings.
♦ Add to vegetables.
♦ Add oysters and simmer until oysters begin to shrink.
♦ Season with salt and pepper, 2 shots of Worcestershire and 2 dashes of tabasco.
♦ Pour into pie crust.
♦ Top with second crust.
* May use vegetable oil instead of bacon drippings.

Mrs. W.E. Applegate, III (True Gregory)

Giga's Oyster, Sausage And Rice

Easy
May Prepare Ahead

Serves: 4-6
Cook: 20-30 minutes

2½	cups cooked rice	2	small onions, chopped
1	pound bulk sausage (mild or hot)	1	pint oysters, drained
1	cup celery, chopped	1	8-ounce can water chestnuts, sliced

♦ Crumble sausage and cook in a large frying pan until done.
♦ Add the rest of the ingredients and simmer until celery is crisp-tender.
♦ Add rice to frying pan and heat thoroughly.
♦ May keep warm in a double-boiler if not served immediately.

Hayden Blackwell

Lib's Oyster Pie

Average
May Prepare Ahead

Serves: 6 to 8
Bake: 30 minutes at 300°

1   pint oysters
1   small white onion, chopped
24   saltine crackers, crushed
1   egg, beaten
1   cup milk
1   teaspoon lemon pepper
     (or fresh lemon juice to taste)

dash dill weed
1½ sticks butter (one frozen)
salt and pepper to taste
paprika

♦ Drain oysters, reserving liquid.
♦ Sauté onion in 2 tablespoons butter.
♦ Place ½ crushed saltines in bottom of baking dish.
♦ Add ½ oysters and ½ sautéed onions.
♦ Add pats of butter.
♦ Repeat layers.
♦ Combine milk, oyster liquid, beaten egg and seasonings.
♦ Pour over pie (add more milk if pie isn't covered).
♦ Grate frozen butter on top.
♦ Dush with paprika.
♦ Bake at 300° for 30 minutes.

Mrs. Thomas W. Alexander (Patricia Cochrane)

Scalloped Oysters

Easy
Prepare Ahead

Serves: 8
Chill: 3-4 hours
Bake: 45 minutes at 350°

2   cups milk
3-4 eggs
5   slices white bread, crusts
     removed
½   pound sharp cheddar cheese,
     grated

1   quart oysters
4   tablespoons butter
     salt and pepper to taste

♦ Beat eggs and milk together.
♦ Dice bread and mix all ingredients well.
♦ Place in a 3 quart casserole dish.
♦ Generously dot with butter.
♦ Refrigerate for 3-4 hours (uncovered).
♦ Bake.

Mrs. W. David Latimer (Elizabeth Kate Wolfe)

Holiday "Anyday" Oysters

Average
May Prepare Ahead

Serves: 6
Bake: 30 minutes at 350°

1 quart select oysters, thoroughly drained
6 teaspoons fresh lemon juice
salt to taste

white pepper to taste (do not substitute)
3-4 tablespoons butter or margarine
buttered toast crumbs

- Lightly butter 6 individual serving shells.
- Cover the bottom of each shell with a thin layer of buttered crumbs.
- Place 1/6 of drained oysters in each shell.
- Sprinkle 1 teaspoon lemon juice over oysters.
- Add salt and white pepper to taste.
- Cut 1/6 of butter into thin slices and add to each shell.
- Cover with light layer of buttered crumbs.
- Bake in 350° oven for 30 minutes or until bubbled through the center. (Do not overcook or oysters will water.)

Buttered Toast Crumbs:

6 slices of thin white bread, toasted to melba toast stage

- Crumb in blender.
- Melt ½ stick of butter or margarine.
- Add crumbs and stir until all butter is absorbed.
- May prepare ahead and store in refrigerator.

Mrs. Charles Lowndes Mullally (Pauline "Punch" Slay)

Oyster Casserole

Easy
May Prepare Ahead

Serves: 6 to 8
Bake: 10 minutes at 350°

1 quart oysters
¼ teaspoon pepper
½ teaspoon salt

¼ teaspoon mace
12 saltine crackers, crushed
1 stick butter or margarine

- Drain oysters and place in shallow baking dish.
- Sprinkle salt, pepper and mace on top.
- Cover with crushed saltines.
- Dot with butter.
- Heat at 350° until hot - about 10 minutes.

Mrs. Randell C. Stoney (Adela Holmes)

Cheesy Scallops

Easy
Serve Immediately

Serves: 3-4
Bake: 30 minutes at 350°

2 tablespoons butter
2 tablespoons onion, chopped
¼ pound small mushrooms, sliced
1 pound fresh sea scallops
1 10¾-ounce can condensed cheddar cheese soup
2 tablespoons lemon juice

dash pepper
dash thyme leaves
dash ground marjoram
2 tablespoons buttered bread crumbs
¼ cup white wine

♦ Preheat oven to 350°.
♦ In skillet, sauté onion and mushrooms until tender.
♦ Add scallops and cook 3-4 minutes.
♦ Place mixture in shallow baking dish.
♦ Combine undiluted soup, lemon juice and seasonings.
♦ Pour over scallops and bake for 15 minutes.
♦ Stir well.
♦ Top with breadcrumbs and wine.
♦ Bake for 15 more minutes.

Mrs. Thomas J. Parsell (Susan Poston)

Scallops Supreme

Easy
Serve Immediately

Serves: 4-6
Cook: 10-15 minutes

1 clove garlic, minced
4 tablespoons butter
1 cup dry white wine

1 fresh lemon (juice only)
1 pound medium to large scallops

♦ Sauté garlic in butter until soft.
♦ Add wine, lemon juice and stir.
♦ Add scallops and cook on medium heat until they turn white and are done, stirring constantly.
♦ Serve with curried rice.

Mrs. William F. Fuller (Ann Colwell)

Scallops Charleston

"Don't let the fish stock scare you—it's simple and enhances the flavor."

Average
Partial Prepare Ahead

Serves: 4
Bake: 15 to 20 minutes at 400°

1 pound scallops	1 onion, finely chopped
pinch salt	3 tablespoons flour
2 cups fish stock (see index)	½ cup heavy cream
⅓ cup water	4 tablespoons bread crumbs
2 tablespoons lemon juice	3 tablespoons melted butter
6 ounces mushrooms	salt and pepper to taste
3 tablespoons butter	

- Preheat oven to 400°.
- Rinse scallops in water and drain well.
- Cover scallops with stock and pinch of salt and cover pot.
- Cook 1-3 minutes or until scallops are no longer clear in middle. Do not overcook!
- Drain, reserving liquid.
- Cut scallops into 2 or 3 pieces.
- Cut mushrooms in quarters, put in sauce pan and add ⅓ cup water and lemon juice, and salt and pepper. Cover and cook over high heat until tender (3-5 minutes). Drain, reserving liquid.
- Melt butter in sauce pan and add onion, cooking until soft, but not brown. Add flour, stirring constantly and cooking well. Whisk in reserved liquids from scallops and mushrooms. Bring to a boil, whisking constantly and then simmer 2 minutes.
- Add cream and boil gently until sauce is thick enough to coat the spoon.
- Stir in mushrooms and scallops. Correct seasoning.
- Butter 4 ramekins or ceramic shells and fill with scallop mixture.
- Sprinkle with bread crumbs and butter. Bake on cookie sheet for 15-20 minutes or until bubbling and browned.

Ann W. Dibble

Marinated Conch

Average
Prepare Ahead

Serves: 4
Marinate: 3 days

1   pound fresh conch
     chopped onion, to taste
     chopped green pepper, to taste
1   garlic clove, mashed

mixture of ½ fresh squeezed
lime juice and ½ white wine (to
cover conch and vegetables)

♦ Extract the conch animal from the shell.
♦ Rub the dark skin off (scald and rub off with a wire brush or pot cleaner).
♦ Discard all parts except the white meat "foot" of the conch.
♦ Cut the "foot" into paper-thin slices and place in glass or ceramic bowl with chopped vegetables.
♦ Cover with lime juice and wine mixture.
♦ Refrigerate, covered, for 3 days. (Lime juice "cooks" conch.)

Mr. Ben McC. Moise

Brandied Rock Shrimp

Easy
Prepare Ahead

Serves: 6
Chill: overnight

2   quarts water (salted or unsalted)
3   pounds rock shrimp
5   tablespoons sour cream
5   tablespoons mayonnaise

3   tablespoons chili sauce
3   tablespoons fresh dill
2   tablespoons brandy
     freshly grated pepper

♦ Boil rock shrimp in water until they turn pink.
♦ Pour off water and let them cool.
♦ Remove shells and veins.
♦ Slice in half, if desired.
♦ Chop dill and combine all ingredients except shrimp.
♦ Add shrimp.
♦ Refrigerate overnight, covered.
♦ Stir once or twice.
♦ Serve cold.

Mrs. Jordan T. Jack (Josephine Bennett Pierrepont)

Hampton Plantation Shrimp Pilau

*"A favorite from **Charleston Receipts**."*

Average
Serve Immediately

Serves: 6
Cook: about 30 minutes

4 strips bacon	2 cups raw shrimp, peeled
1 cup raw rice	1 teaspoon Worcestershire sauce
1 teaspoon salt	1 tablespoon flour
3 tablespoons butter	salt and pepper to taste
½ cup celery, chopped fine	
2 tablespoons chopped bell pepper	

- Fry bacon until crisp. Drain.
- Add bacon grease and salt to water to cook rice.
- In large frying pan, melt butter and sauté onions and peppers.
- Sprinkle shrimp with Worcestershire and dredge in flour.
- Add shrimp to pan and simmer until flour is cooked.
- Season with salt and pepper.
- Add cooked rice and mix well.
- Stir in crumbled bacon.

* You may add more butter.

Mrs. Paul Seabrook (Harriott Horry Rutledge)

Bobbie's Shrimp And Rice

Easy
Serve Immediately

Serves: 6
Cook: 15 minutes

¼ pound butter	1 cup rice, cooked
2-3 bunches green onions, chopped	1 10-ounce package frozen green peas, prepared according to directions
8 ounces fresh mushrooms, sliced	
1½ pounds shrimp, peeled and deveined	soy sauce

- Melt butter in frying pan.
- Sauté onions until clear.
- Add mushrooms and sauté until soft.
- Add shrimp and sauté until pink.
- Add cooked rice to shrimp mixture.
- Add cooked green peas.
- Season with soy sauce to taste.

Mrs. James A. Lester Glenn (Lucy Robson)

Shrimp Curry á la Richards

Easy
Serve Immediately

Serves: 4
Cook: 20 minutes

1 medium onion, minced
2 tablespoons butter or margarine
2 teaspoons curry powder
1 cup celery, chopped
½ bell pepper, chopped
1 14-ounce can mixed Chinese vegetables, drained
3 tablespoons flour

1 cup milk
tabasco and Worcestershire to taste
1 tablespoon ketchup
salt and pepper to taste
1½ - 2 pounds shrimp, cooked and peeled

- Brown onion in butter.
- Add curry powder.
- Add celery, bell pepper, and Chinese vegetables.
- Make a paste of flour and milk, seasoned with tabasco, Worcestershire, ketchup, salt, and pepper.
- Add to vegetable mixture and add shrimp.
- Serve as soon as heated over rice.
- Suggested condiments: chutney, chopped egg, toasted coconut, bacon, peanuts, chopped onion, etc.

Mrs. John C. Wilson (Nancy Rhett)

Shrimp au Vin

Average
Serve Immediately

Serves: 4
Cook: 20 minutes

¼ cup onion, chopped
2 tablespoons margarine
1½ cups milk
1 8-ounce package cream cheese, cubed
2 cups shrimp, cooked and peeled (may use more or less)
2 tablespoons white wine or sherry

1 3-ounce can sliced mushrooms, drained
2 tablespoon parsley, chopped
¼ teaspoon salt
⅛ teaspoon pepper
¼ teaspoon seasoned salt
flour, if desired

- Sauté onion in margarine until tender.
- Add milk and cream cheese and stir until cheese is melted.
- Add shrimp, mushrooms, parsley, and seasonings and heat.
- If desired, add flour to thicken.
- Serve over rice or toast points.

Mrs. Charles Talmadge Cole, Jr. (Joanne Gilmer)

Shrimp Curry
"Great for a dinner party."

Average
Prepare Ahead

Serves: 8-10
Cook: 20 minutes
Chill: overnight

¾ cup all-purpose flour
1½ teaspoons curry powder
2 teaspoons salt
½ teaspoon ginger
2 teaspoons granulated sugar
1 cup onions, minced
1 cup green apples, diced and pared

¾ cup butter
1 quart chicken broth
2 cups milk
2½ pounds shrimp, cooked and peeled
10 ounces button mushrooms
2 tablespoons lemon juice

Day Before:
♦ Mix together first 5 ingredients. Set aside.
♦ In large skillet, sauté onion and apple in butter until tender.
♦ Blend in flour mixture.
♦ Slowly stir in chicken broth and milk.
♦ Cook, stirring often until thick.
♦ Remove from heat.
♦ Add cooked shrimp.
♦ Add lemon juice and mushrooms.
♦ Refrigerate overnight.

Before Serving:
♦ Cook desired amount of rice.
♦ Reheat curry.
♦ Serve with condiments – chutney, chopped peanuts, raisins, coconut, etc.

Mrs. Gerard Stelling, Jr. (Jane Riley)

Garlic Broiled Shrimp
"Simply Delicious"

Easy
Serve Immediately

Serves: 4-6
Broil: 10-15 minutes

2 pounds raw shrimp, peeled
1 stick butter
2 lemons

garlic salt
paprika

♦ Melt butter in large sheet pan with ½-inch sides.
♦ Add juice of 2 lemons.
♦ Place shrimp in pan and liberally sprinkle with garlic salt and paprika.
♦ Broil until shrimp are pink and firm (approximately 10-15 minutes).
♦ Serve with grits and sliced tomatoes.

Mrs. Isaac A. Speights, III (Elizabeth Lesesne)

Feta-Tomato Sauce With Shrimp
"Variation of Greek recipe"

Easy
Serve Immediately

Serves: 4
Cook: 30 minutes

½ cup onion, finely chopped
2 tablespoons butter
1 tablespoon Dijon-style mustard
½ teaspoon dried tarragon leaves
1 small garlic clove, finely minced
½ teaspoon salt

½ teaspoon pepper
4 medium tomatoes, peeled, seeded, and chopped
4 ounces feta cheese
1 pound raw shrimp, peeled
fresh parsley

♦ In a deep skillet, melt butter.
♦ Add mustard, tarragon, garlic and onion and sauté for 5 minutes.
♦ Add tomatoes, salt and pepper and simmer for 10-15 minutes until sauce has thickened.
♦ Add feta cheese and simmer 10 minutes.
♦ Just before serving, add shrimp and cook over low heat until shrimp are pink.
♦ Garnish with parsley.
♦ Serve over noodles.

Dr. René Ravenel

Lizzie Green's Shrimp Creole

Average
May Prepare Ahead

Serves: 20
Cook: 2 hour

2 sticks margarine (or 1 stick margarine and 1 cup bacon drippings)
8 green peppers, finely chopped
3 pounds onions, chopped
1 large stalk celery, chopped
1 garlic clove, chopped
2 quart cans tomatoes

2 small cans tomato paste
salt, pepper, thyme, to taste
1 tablespoon Worcestershire sauce (optional)
4 pounds raw shrimp, peeled
1 large can mushrooms
1 #2 can green peas, optional

♦ Cook green peppers in butter (or grease) for 20 minutes.
♦ Add onions, celery and garlic separately every 20 minutes.
♦ Add tomatoes and cook 15 minutes.
♦ Add tomato paste and simmer 1 hour.
♦ Add salt, pepper, and thyme to taste.
♦ Add 1 tablespoon Worcestershire sauce (optional).
♦ 20 minutes before serving, add shrimp, mushrooms, and green peas.
♦ Serve over rice or spaghetti.
* Serves a crowd with salad and French bread.

Mrs. Benjamin O. Turnage (Frances "Fronnie" Baker)

Shrimp Chef Monteur

Average
Serve Immediately
Freezes Well

Serves: 6
Cook: 30 minutes

1 pound raw, jumbo shrimp, peeled and deveined	¼ teaspoon white pepper
½ teaspoon salt	½ teaspoon oregano
½ cup olive oil	1 small onion, minced
3 garlic cloves, mashed	2 tablespoons butter
½ cup brandy	½ cup dry white wine
1 cup heavy cream	2 16-ounce cans peeled tomatoes, drained and chopped

- Split the shrimp down the back and sprinkle with salt.
- Heat oil in a large skillet.
- Add garlic and cook 2-3 minutes.
- Add shrimp and cook for 5 minutes.
- Add brandy and cook 3-4 minutes.
- Add cream, cook, and stir constantly until brandy and cream are cooked down.
- Sauté onion in 2 tablespoons butter. Add to shrimp mixture along with pepper, oregano, wine, and tomatoes.
- Cook 10 minutes longer.
- Serve over rice, noodles, or toast points.

Mrs. Edward Wilson Riggs (Rebecca Turner)

Tom Chason's Shrimp Capers

Easy
Serve Immediately

Serves: 6 to 8
Bake: 7-9 minutes at 350°
Heat: 10 minutes

3 pounds small-medium shrimp, peeled	4 fresh lemons
½ pound butter	¼ cup Worcestershire sauce
1 3 ounce jar capers	2 tablespoons garlic salt

- Melt butter and add juice of lemons, garlic salt and Worcestershire sauce.
- Drain capers and add to sauce. Set aside.
- Bake peeled shrimp at 350° until pink (7-9 minutes).
- Remove shrimp and drain all liquids.
- Put shrimp in capers butter sauce and let stand for 10 minutes.
- Serve shrimp and sauce over a bed of hot rice.

Mrs. William Tamsberg (Merle Sparkman)

Shrimp And Lemon Rice

Easy
Partial Prepare Ahead

Serves: 6
Bake: 40 minutes at 350°

1 cup cooked rice	½ teaspoon salt
2 teaspoons ground tumeric	1 cup dry white wine
1 teaspoon mustard seed	2 tablespoons lemon juice
½ cup butter or margarine	
2 pounds raw shrimp, peeled and deveined	

- In a large skillet, sauté tumeric and mustard seed in butter for 3 minutes.
- Stir in shrimp and sauté for 5 minutes.
- Remove shrimp with a slotted spoon, reserving drippings.
- Place shrimp in a 2½ quart casserole dish.
- Stir rice into drippings. Heat slowly, stirring constantly, until rice is coated.
- Spoon into casserole.
- Add salt, wine, lemon juice and toss all ingredients together.
- Cover and chill until an hour before serving.
- Bake.

Mrs. Nathaniel A. Davis (Susan Reid Perry)

Shrimp Pilau

Easy
May Prepare Ahead

Serves: 8
Bake: 45 minutes at 350°

2 cups raw rice	1 onion, chopped
1 cup mayonnaise	1 bell pepper, chopped
1 cup ketchup	2 pounds shrimp, cooked and peeled
1 teaspoon salt	
½ teaspoon pepper	4 slices bacon, cut in small pieces

- Cook rice in steamer.
- Combine mayonnaise, ketchup, salt, and pepper, and stir into warm rice to thoroughly moisten.
- Add onion, bell pepper, and shrimp.
- Place in casserole and cover with pieces of bacon.
- Sprinkle top with pepper.
- Cook 30 minutes covered.
- Uncover for last 15 minutes to crisp bacon.

Mrs. Charles C. Geer (France Voigt)

Shrimp Etouffee

Easy
May Prepare Ahead
Freezes Well

Serves: 4-6
Cook: 45 minutes

2 pounds medium raw shrimp, peeled	1/4 cup green pepper, chopped
1/4 cup margarine	3/4 cup celery, chopped
3 tablespoons flour	1 cup onion, chopped
1 clove garlic, minced	1/2 cup water
2 tablespoons dill weed	1/2 teaspoon salt
2 tablespoons green onion, chopped	1/2 teaspoon cayenne pepper
	1 tablespoon lemon juice

♦ Melt margarine in a large frying pan.
♦ Blend in flour.
♦ Add garlic, dill weed, green onion, green pepper, celery, and onion.
♦ Cover and cook 8 minutes or until tender.
♦ Add water and stir.
♦ Add salt, pepper, and lemon juice.
♦ Push vegetables to side of pan.
♦ Add raw shrimp and spoon vegetables over.
♦ Cover and cook over low heat until shrimp are pink and tender.
♦ Serve over rice.

* May substitute scallops or use a combination.

Mrs. Michael Piepenbring (Lee Caughman)

Davy's Shrimp
"Excellent"

Easy
Serve Immediately

Serves: 6
Bake: 20 minutes at 400°

2 pounds raw shrimp, peeled and cleaned	1 stick butter
juice of 2 limes	6 ounces cream cheese
	2 ounces blue cheese

♦ Arrange shrimp in bottom of casserole dish and sprinkle lime juice on top.
♦ In heavy pan, melt butter, cream cheese, and blue cheese.
♦ Pour over shrimp.
♦ Bake in preheated 400° oven for 20 minutes.
♦ Serve over pasta or rice.

Mrs. Whitemarsh Seabrook Smith, III (Anne Frampton)

Shrimp In Mustard Sauce

Average
Serve Immediately

Serves: 6 to 8
Cook: 10 minutes

4   tablespoons butter
2   pounds medium shrimp, peeled
½   cup shallots, chopped
2   teaspoons tarragon, chopped
¼   cup dry sherry
1½ cups heavy cream

2   tablespoons soft butter
1   tablespoon prepared Dijon
    mustard
    salt and pepper, to taste
    chopped fresh parsley

♦ Melt 4 tablespoons butter in heavy skillet.
♦ When hot, add shrimp. Turn and sauté very lightly, being careful not to overcook.
♦ Remove shrimp with slotted spoon and set aside.
♦ Sauté shallots in residue in same pan for 2-3 minutes.
♦ Deglaze pan with sherry, reducing to ½.
♦ Add cream, bring to a boil and reduce heat to thicken.
♦ Swirl in soft butter, mustard, salt and pepper to taste.
♦ Pour on serving dish and arrange shrimp on or around sauce.
♦ Sprinkle with chopped parsley.
♦ Serve with hot white rice or pasta.

Mr. G. Marshall Mundy

Broiled Marinated Shrimp

Easy
Prepare Ahead
Serve Immediately

Serves: 3-4
Marinate: 1 hour
Broil: 5-10 minutes

2   tablespoons Dijon mustard
2   tablespoons sugar
1   tablespoon lemon juice
1   tablespoon vinegar

    scant ½ cup salad oil
    salt and pepper, to taste
1½ tablespoons dill weed
1   pound raw shrimp, peeled

♦ Combine in jar: mustard, sugar, lemon juice, vinegar, oil and seasonings.
♦ Shake well and let stand a while.
♦ Place shrimp in small baking pan.
♦ Pour sauce over and chill one hour.
♦ Place under broiler and cook until pink and sizzling (5-10 minutes).

Mrs. Edward Walker (Hildreth Wilson)

My Mother's Parsley Shrimp
"Simple and Good."

Easy
Serve Immediately

Serves: 3-4
Cook: 10 minutes

1 pound raw shrimp, peeled	1 clove garlic, pressed
4 tablespoons olive oil	4-5 tablespoons lemon juice
½ teaspoon salt	½ cup parsley, chopped
pepper to taste	

- Heat oil in large skillet.
- Add garlic, salt and pepper.
- Add shrimp.
- Add parsley.
- Stir and cook until shrimp is pink and tender.

Mrs. Andrew Drury, Jr. (Margaret Reeves)

Celestial Shrimp
"Heavenly."

Average
Serve Immediately

Serves: 6-8
Heat: 30 minutes

2 pounds shrimp, cooked and peeled	2 tablespoons butter
½ pound walnut halves	2½ cups hot chicken stock
6 green onions, sliced thinly and diagonally	3 tablespoons cornstarch
	3 tablespoons soy sauce

- Cook walnuts in 450° oven for 6 minutes.
- Rub off brown skins.
- Cook onions in butter in heavy skillet for a minute.
- Pour in hot stock. Bring to a boil.
- Combine cornstarch and soy sauce and add to stock.
- Cook until thickened and clear.
- Add shrimp and walnuts.
- Heat and serve over rice.

* Good served with grapefruit and orange salad and snow peas.

Mrs. Greenfield Polk

Shrimp Supreme

Average
Serve Immediately

Serves: 4-6
Cook: 45 minutes

2 tablespoons olive oil
1-2 medium onions, sliced (or 3-6 spring onions, chopped)
1 - 1½ pounds raw shrimp, peeled
1 green pepper, diced
1 cup celery, chopped
1 lemon

salt, pepper, tabasco, to taste
3 cups cooked rice
½ cup Parmesan cheese
1 small jar pimentos, sliced
lemon slices
parsley

♦ Sauté onion in olive oil until clear.
♦ Add shrimp and sauté until pink.
♦ Reduce heat and add green pepper and celery.
♦ Stir and cover to heat.
♦ Add the juice of one lemon and season with salt, pepper, tabasco.
♦ Stir in cooked rice.
♦ Turn onto serving platter or bowl.
♦ Sprinkle with Parmesan cheese.
♦ Garnish with pimentos, lemon slices, and parsley.

Dr. Jack W. Simmons, Jr.

Shrimp Gumbo

Average
May Prepare Ahead

Serves: 6
Cook: 1½ hours

3 strips of bacon
1 small onion, chopped
3 cups fresh okra, chopped
2 ears fresh corn, cut off cob
1 20-ounce can tomatoes (or 14-ounce can and 4-5 very ripe fresh tomatoes)

1 teaspoon sugar
1 teaspoon salt
½ teaspoon thyme
½ pound raw shrimp, peeled

♦ In a large pot or dutch oven, fry bacon and reserve 2 tablespoons drippings.
♦ Sauté onion in bacon drippings until clear.
♦ Add okra and cook 10 minutes.
♦ Add corn and continue cooking and stirring 10 minutes.
♦ Add tomatoes and spices.
♦ Reduce heat to low and simmer 45-60 minutes.
♦ Before serving, return gumbo to a boil and add raw shrimp. (Shrimp should be done in 5 minutes or less.)
♦ Serve over rice in bowls.

Mrs. Barry Gumb (Beverly Brooks)

Helen's Shrimp Casserole

Easy
Prepare Ahead
Freezes Well

Serves: 6-8
Chill: overnight
Bake: 1 hour at 350°

6 slices white bread, cubed
1½ - 2 pounds shrimp, cooked and peeled
½ pound sharp cheese, cubed
½ cup butter, melted
½ teaspoon dry mustard (or 1½ teaspoons hot prepared mustard)

½ teaspoon salt
3 eggs, beaten
2 cups milk
a little madeira (optional)

♦ Mix shrimp, bread, cheese and butter.
♦ Add mustard and salt to beaten eggs and combine with shrimp.
♦ Add milk (and madeira, if used).
♦ Place mixture in greased dish. (Allow 2 inches for casserole to rise.)
♦ Refrigerate overnight.
♦ Bake.

Mrs. Richard S. Lovering (Errol Cropper)

Rockville Shrimp Pie
"Easy to increase."

Easy
Serve Immediately

Serves: 6-8
Bake: 30 minutes at 350°

1 large onion, chopped
1 large green pepper, chopped
3 ribs celery, chopped
1 stick margarine
8 ounces sharp cheese, grated
1 teaspoon sugar
1 tablespoon Worcestershire sauce

8 drops tabasco sauce
2 cups canned tomatoes, crushed
1 teaspoon salt
good dash of black pepper
1½ pounds shrimp, cooked and peeled
4 slices white bread, crumbled

♦ Sauté onion, green pepper, and celery in margarine.
♦ Add remaining ingredients and mix well, reserving enough cheese for top of casserole.
♦ Pour into greased 1½-quart casserole.
♦ Top with remaining cheese and bake until bubbly hot.
* Serve over rice.

Mrs. John C. Townsend (Margaret Virginia Smith)

Tradd Street Shrimp

Easy
May Prepare Ahead

Serves: 6-8
Bake: 20 minutes at 375°

2-3 pounds shrimp, cooked and peeled
1 box wild and white rice mix, cooked
1 cup cheddar cheese, grated
1 cup Swiss cheese, grated
1 can cream of mushroom soup
1 cup onion, chopped

1 cup green pepper, chopped
1 cup celery, chopped
6 tablespoons butter
4 lemons, thinly sliced
salt to taste
black pepper, freshly ground, to taste

- Mix together first five ingredients. Set aside.
- Sauté onions, pepper and celery in butter until soft.
- Add to shrimp mixture.
- Place in a long flat 3 quart casserole dish.
- Season to taste with salt and pepper.
- Cover the top completely with lemon slices.
- Sprinkle with more pepper.
- Cover with foil.
- Bake until thoroughly heated (about 20 minutes).

* 3-4 cups of cooked chicken can be substituted or a mixture of both.

Mrs. Horry Heriot Kerrison (Dorothy Barnwell)

Herbed Shrimp in Garlic Butter

Easy
Partial Prepare Ahead

Serves: 6-8
Chill: 20 minutes
Bake: 12-15 minutes at 375°

36 large shrimp, peeled, deveined, and uncooked
1 tablespoon salt
1 teaspoon oregano
1 teaspoon thyme

1 stick butter, softened
4 garlic cloves, crushed
1 tablespoon minced parsley
¼ pound fresh mushrooms, sliced
2 tablespoons butter

- Toss shrimp with salt, oregano, and thyme.
- Chill shrimp (covered) for at least 20 minutes.
- Cream together butter, garlic cloves, and parsley.
- In a skillet, sauté mushrooms in butter.
- Place shrimp in baking dish. Top with mushrooms.
- Dot mushrooms with garlic butter.
- Bake at 375° until shrimp are pink (about 12-15 minutes).
- Serve with rice (white or wild) if desired.

Mrs. W. Vaughan Davidson (Salley Barton)

Shrimp Casserole
"Easy"

Easy
Partial Prepare Ahead

Serves: 6
Bake: 40 minutes at 350°

½ cup butter	1 10¾-ounce can cream of shrimp soup
½ cup celery, finely chopped	1 cup herb stuffing
½ cup onion, chopped	1 cup cooked rice
½ cup bell pepper, chopped	salt and pepper, to taste
1 pound raw shrimp, peeled	

- Sauté celery, onion, bell pepper, and shrimp in butter.
- Add cream of shrimp soup and rice.
- Mix and pour in buttered 2-quart casserole dish.
- Sprinkle with herb stuffing.
- Bake.

Mrs. J. Walker Coleman, Jr. (Anne Frizelle)

Shrimp Pie

Average
Serve Immediately

Serves: 3-4
Bake: 30 minutes at 350°

3 slices of bread, toasted	1 pinch dry mustard
½ cup tomato juice	1 slice bell pepper, chopped
1 tablespoon sherry	1 pound small shrimp, cooked and peeled
1 teaspoon Worcestershire sauce	4 tablespoons butter, melted
¼ teaspoon salt	½ cup cracker crumbs
⅛ teaspoon pepper	

- Knead toast in tomato juice in large mixing bowl.
- Add sherry, Worcestershire, salt, pepper, mustard, and bell pepper. Mix well.
- Melt butter and pour into mixture, reserving one tablespoon for top.
- Add shrimp and mix well.
- Place mixture in greased 9-inch glass pie dish.
- Drip remaining tablespoon of butter over mixture and cover with cracker crumbs.
- Bake.

Mrs. W. Foster Gaillard (Susan Street)

Oven Shrimp Perdito

"Have lots of napkins on hand."

Easy
Serve Immediately

Serves: 20
Bake: 20 minutes at 400°

1	pound butter	4	teaspoons salt
1	pound margarine		juice of 4 lemons
1	teaspoon rosemary	1	teaspoon tabasco
6	ounces Worcestershire sauce	10	pounds shrimp (in shells)
5	tablespoons black pepper		French bread

♦ Bring first 8 ingredients to a boil.
♦ Place shrimp in bottom of large roasting pan.
♦ Pour boiled ingredients over shrimp and bake at 400° for 20 minutes.
♦ Serve with French bread which you can dip into sauce.

* Halves easily.

Mrs. F. Avery Burns (Susan Crabtree)

Smith Street Shrimp

Average
Serve Immediately

Serves: 4
Bake: 40 minutes at 350°

1	pound shrimp, cooked and peeled	¾	cup medium cheddar cheese, cubed
2	medium onions, sliced	1	cup milk
2	large tomatoes, sliced	¼	cup white wine
2	tablespoons butter or margarine	1	6-ounce package provolone cheese, sliced
2	tablespoons flour	2	slices white bread, crumbled
¼	teaspoon salt		
	pinch pepper		

♦ Boil onions gently for 5 minutes. Place in bottom of 8 x 8 casserole.
♦ Layer tomato slices over onions and add shrimp.
♦ Prepare cheese sauce by melting butter in medium sauce pan. Stir in flour, salt, and pepper. Add milk until sauce thickens. Add cheese and stir until melted. Add wine.
♦ Pour cheese sauce over shrimp.
♦ Cover casserole with provolone cheese slices and top with bread crumbs.
♦ Cook at 350° for 40 minutes or until the bread crumbs are brown and sides are bubbly.

Mrs. Clarence M. Condon, III (Dorsey Glenn)

Basil Shrimp With Creme Fraiche
"Divine"

Complicated
Prepare Ahead

Serves: 4
Chill: 36 hours
Sauté: 6 to 8 minutes

1¾ pounds shrimp, peeled
2 garlic cloves, minced
   handful fresh basil leaves, cut
   into narrow ribbons
3-4 tablespoons virgin olive oil
   salt and pepper

2 cups shelled fresh peas (or
   asparagus, green onions,
   spinach, or leeks may be
   substituted)
¾ cup creme fraiche
   spaghetti for 4

- Sauté shrimp in hot olive oil.
- Season with salt and pepper.
- Lower heat and add garlic and peas.
- Cook for 1 minute.
- Add the creme fraiche and basil and cook another minute or so.
- Cook the pasta and add.
- Mix well and adjust seasoning.
- Garnish with fresh basil.

Creme Fraiche

1 cup heavy or whipping cream

1 cup dairy sour cream

- Whisk the two creams together until thoroughly blended.
- Pour into a jar, cover and let stand in a warm place until thickened - about 12 hours.
- Stir well and refrigerate covered for 36 hours before using.
- May store in refrigerator for 7-10 days.

Mr. G. Marshall Mundy

Hot Cocktail Sauce
"Great with boiled shrimp or oysters."

Average
May Prepare Ahead

Yield: about 4 cups

- 2 cups chili sauce
- 2 cups catsup
- ½ cup prepared horseradish
- 1 teaspoon hot mustard
- 2 tablespoons Worcestershire sauce
- 4 tablespoons lemon juice

- ½ teaspoon tabasco sauce
- ½ teaspoon salt
- 2 tablespoons parsley, finely chopped
- ½ cup minced onion
- 3 stalks celery, finely chopped

♦ Combine all ingredients in blender and mix well.

Mrs. Isaac A. Speights, III (Elizabeth Lesesne)

Mustard Watercress Sauce
"Good on fish, vegetables, chicken salads."

Easy
May Prepare Ahead

Yield: 1½ cups

- 1 ounce watercress, including stems
- ¼ cup Dijon mustard
- ½ cup mayonnaise

- ½ cup sour cream
- 2 tablespoons lemon juice
  salt, pepper

♦ Combine watercress and mustard in blender or food processor.
♦ Blend/process until puréed, scraping bowl as necessary.
♦ Add remaining ingredients and blend by turning machine on and off several times.
♦ Refrigerate.

Tarragon Seafood Sauce
"Great with deviled crab"

Easy
May Prepare Ahead

Yields: 1 cup
Chill

- 1 cup mayonnaise
- 3 tablespoons tarragon vinegar
- 1 tablespoon lemon juice

- 2 tablespoons chili sauce
- 1 tablespoon onion, grated, optional

♦ Mix.
♦ Shake well.
♦ Store in jar in refrigerator.

* Can also be used with fried shrimp or as a salad dressing.

Mrs. James Sellers (Winton Chandler)

Charleston is a study in contrasts. From a perch atop the historic Calhoun Mansion, you can see stately church spires juxtaposed with the soaring, modern bridges that span the Cooper River.

It's a city associated with traditions and history. It attracts thousands of people each year to see its graceful beauty and pre-Revolutionary charm.

But it's also a city keeping pace with the 20th century. It attracts thousands of people each year to run in the Cooper River Bridge Run — a race that attracts everyone from top-flight runners who take the spans without as much as a labored breath to sedentary strollers who enter for the fun of it.

VEGETABLES

Missy's Green Beans

Average
May Prepare Ahead

Serves: 6
Cook: 25 minutes

6 ounces bacon, cooked and diced	1 cup water, boiling
1 onion, minced	3 tablespoons white vinegar
2 pounds green beans	3 tablespoons butter
1 teaspoon red pepper	salt and pepper to taste

♦ Sauté onion in bacon grease until tender.
♦ Add green beans and sauté over medium heat for 2 minutes, stirring frequently.
♦ Add boiling water to pan and cover.
♦ Steam, shaking pan occasionally for 15 minutes or until beans are tender.
♦ Transfer to serving dish.
♦ Add vinegar, butter and salt and pepper.
♦ Toss and sprinkle with bacon.

Mrs. James H. Rike (Katharyne Hanahan)

Sweet And Sour Beans

Easy
May Prepare Ahead

Serves: 4
Cook: 15 minutes

4 slices bacon, fried crisp	2 tablespoons sugar
½ cup onion, chopped	¾ cup bean liquid
1 tablespoon flour	1 teaspoon salt
¼ cup vinegar	2 cups green beans, cooked

♦ Brown onion in bacon drippings.
♦ Stir in flour.
♦ Add remaining ingredients except beans.
♦ Bring mixture to a boil.
♦ Stir in beans - heat thoroughly.
♦ Top with crumbled bacon.

Mrs. Bissell Jenkins Witte (Linda Burton)

Christina's Greek Beans

Easy
Serve Immediately

Serves: 6
Cook: 35-45 minutes

1 pound fresh green beans (half runners are best)
3 tablespoons olive oil
½ teaspoon dill weed
1 garlic clove, peeled and left whole

2 green onions, chopped
2 bouillon cubes
½ teaspoon Worcestershire sauce
1 bay leaf

◆ Snap ends off beans.
◆ Cover with water plus 2 inches.
◆ Add rest of ingredients.
◆ Bring to a boil and turn down to medium.
◆ Cover - cook 35-45 minutes.
◆ The water cooks down and makes a sauce.

Mrs. William Wallace (Sally Benson)

Grandmother's Spiced Beets
"Good as a side dish for a cold buffet."

Easy
Prepare Ahead

Serves: 6-8
Cook: 10 minutes
Chill: 24 hours

2 no. 2 cans sliced beets
1 cup vinegar
1 cup sugar
2 sticks cinnamon

peppercorns
1 teaspoon mustard seed
8 cloves
1 clove garlic or 1 sliced onion

◆ Drain beets, reserving 1 cup beet juice, and set aside.
◆ Combine beet juice with remaining ingredients.
◆ Bring to a boil.
◆ Simmer 10 minutes.
◆ Pour over beets in glass or enamel dish.
◆ Refrigerate at least 24 hours before serving.
◆ Serve cold.

Mrs. J.G. Blaine Ewing, III (Phyllis Walker)

Golden Cheddar Broccoli Casserole
"Fresh corn makes it even better."

Average
May Prepare Ahead

Serves: 8
Bake: 30 minutes at 350°

1½ bunches of fresh broccoli or 2 10-ounce packages of frozen broccoli spears
4 tablespoons butter or margarine
2 tablespoons flour
¼ teaspoon salt
¼ teaspoon white pepper
1½ cups milk

8 ounces sharp cheddar cheese, grated
1 cup corn flakes, crushed, divided
1 12-ounce can whole kernel corn, drained
2 tablespoons butter or margarine paprika

♦ Cut broccoli into spears.
♦ Put broccoli in large saucepan with ½ cup water. Bring to boil, turn to low, cover and cook 10 minutes.
♦ Drain broccoli. (If using frozen broccoli, cook according to package directions.)
♦ While broccoli is cooking, make sauce.
♦ Melt 2 tablespoons butter or margarine.
♦ Stir in flour, salt and pepper.
♦ Gradually add milk, stirring until smooth.
♦ Cook over medium heat until sauce boils, stirring constantly.
♦ Gradually add cheese and stir until cheese melts.
♦ Mix in ½ cup corn flakes and corn.
♦ Arrange broccoli spears crosswise in 9 x 13 pan or baking dish.
♦ Pour sauce over broccoli.
♦ Melt 2 tablespoons butter or margarine and mix in ½ cup corn flakes.
♦ Sprinkle mixture over casserole.
♦ Sprinkle with paprika.
♦ Bake uncovered at 350° for 30 minutes.

Mrs. Gary Graupmann (Lynn DuBois)

Broccoli Casserole

Easy
May Prepare Ahead

Serves: 8
Bake: 30 minutes at 350°

2	6-ounce packages frozen, chopped broccoli
1	cup Swiss cheese, grated
1	10½-ounce can cream of celery soup
2	eggs, beaten

1	tablespoon onion, grated
1	tablespoon lemon juice
2	teaspoons salt
1	cup mayonnaise
1	cup seasoned breadcrumbs

- Cook broccoli until tender. Drain.
- Combine with cheese, soup, eggs, onion, lemon juice, salt and mayonnaise.
- Pour into casserole dish and top with breadcrumbs.
- Bake at 350° for 30 minutes.

Mrs. James H. Rike (Katharyne Hanahan)

Cabbage Casserole

Average
May Prepare Ahead

Serves: 12
Bake: 15 to 20 minutes at 350°

1	medium cabbage
1	medium onion, diced or sliced
	salt
1	can water chestnuts, sliced

1	small jar diced pimento
1	can cream of celery soup
	cheddar cheese, grated
1	can French fried onions

- Boil sliced medium cabbage and diced or sliced onion in salted water.
- Drain cabbage and onion and put in greased 3 quart baking dish.
- In layers, add sliced water chestnuts, evenly spreading them.
- Add diced pimento, evenly spreading them.
- Add cream of celery soup.
- Sprinkle grated cheese on top of soup and then sprinkle the French fried onions on top.
- Bake uncovered in 350° oven until it bubbles.

Mrs. Thomas P. Lesesne, III (Doris Clary)

Scalloped Carrots

Easy
May Prepare Ahead

Serves: 6
Bake: 20 minutes at 350°

2 pounds carrots, sliced thin	1 medium onion, chopped
1 can cream of celery soup	1 8-ounce package sliced cheddar cheese
½ can milk	
⅛ teaspoon dry mustard	buttered breadcrumbs
1 tablespoon butter	salt to taste

- Cook carrots until tender, drain.
- Dilute soup with ½ can milk.
- Add salt and mustard.
- Sauté onion in butter, add to soup mixture.
- Arrange layers of carrots and cheese in 2 quart casserole dish.
- Pour soup mixture over carrots and cheese, top with buttered crumbs.
- Bake at 350° until cheese melts or bubbles.

Mrs. J. Marcus Harris (Ann Allen)

Company Carrots
"Adds color to a company menu."

Easy
May Prepare Ahead

Serves: 6
Bake: 20 minutes at 350°

2 pounds peeled carrots	¼ cup fine breadcrumbs
boiling salted water	2 tablespoons margarine, softened
¼ cup cooking liquid from carrots	paprika
½ cup mayonnaise	chopped fresh parsley
1 tablespoon minced onion	salt and pepper to taste
1 tablespoon prepared horseradish	

- Cook carrots in salted water until tender.
- Save ¼ cup cooking liquid.
- Cut carrots lengthwise, arrange in shallow baking dish.
- Combine ¼ cup cooking liquid with mayonnaise, onion, horseradish, salt and pepper.
- Pour sauce over carrots.
- Sprinkle crumbs on top before cooking.
- Dot with margarine and paprika and chopped parsley.
- Bake uncovered at 350° for 20 minutes.

Mrs. Hugh M. Doherty (Mary Pierce)

223

Curried Baked Cauliflower
"Very rich and very spicy."

Easy
May Prepare Ahead

Serves: 8-10
Bake: 30 minutes at 350°

1	large head cauliflower, separated into flowerets	½	teaspoon salt
1	10½-ounce can cream of chicken soup	½	teaspoon cayenne pepper
⅓	cup mayonnaise	14	ounces cheddar cheese, grated
1	tablespoon curry powder	2	tablespoons butter, melted
		¼	cup breadcrumbs, dried

♦ Cook cauliflower in 1 inch boiling water for 10 minutes, covered.
♦ In 2 quart casserole, stir together soup, mayonnaise, curry powder, salt, pepper and cheese.
♦ Add cauliflower and mix well.
♦ Combine the breadcrumbs and butter and sprinkle on top of casserole.
♦ Bake uncovered for 30 minutes or until bubbly.

Mrs. Carlisle C. Howard

Cauliflower Parmesan

Average
Serve Immediately

Serves: 6
Fry: 5 minutes

2	cups cauliflower flowerets	1	tablespoon parsley
½	cup water	1	teaspoon oregano
1	teaspoon lemon juice	1	teaspoon finely grated lemon peel
	dash hot pepper sauce		vegetable oil
⅓	cup all purpose flour		salt
⅓	cup grated Parmesan cheese		paprika
1	egg, slightly beaten		

♦ Blanch cauliflower in boiling water until tender. Refresh in cold water - drain.
♦ Combine water, lemon juice and hot pepper sauce. Beat in flour, cheese, egg, parsley, oregano and lemon peel.
♦ Dip florets in batter and fry (5 minutes). Drain and keep warm.
♦ Salt and dust with paprika.

Mrs. John Graham Smith

Baked Cauliflower Pureé

Easy
May Prepare Ahead

Serves: 8
Bake: 15 minutes at 350°

1 large cauliflower, separated into flowerets
1 medium onion, chopped
½ cup buttermilk

salt and pepper to taste
3 tablespoons butter
parsley, chopped

♦ Preheat oven to 350°.
♦ Boil cauliflower and onions until tender. Drain.
♦ Put in blender and mix until smooth.
♦ Slowly add buttermilk, then seasonings.
♦ Add butter and pureé until butter melts.
♦ Place in buttered soufflé dish.
♦ Bake for 15 minutes.
♦ Garnish with parsley.

Mrs. G. Simms McDowell, III (Elsa Freeman)

Far East Celery

Easy
May Prepare Ahead

Serves: 4-6
Bake: 20 minutes at 350°

3 cups celery, cut into 1 inch pieces
1 4-ounce can water chestnuts, sliced
1 6-ounce can mushrooms, sliced

1 cup canned chicken stock
½ cup light cream
3 tablespoons butter
1 cup breadcrumbs, fine

♦ Cook celery in salted water for 8 minutes.
♦ Combine celery, water chestnuts, mushrooms, stock and cream.
♦ Melt butter, toss crumbs in butter.
♦ Pour celery mixture into 2 quart casserole.
♦ Spread bread crumbs over celery.
♦ Bake at 350° until crumbs are golden brown and bubbly.
* Can substitute cream of chicken soup.

Mrs. Henry B. Fishburne (Amy Allston)

Scalloped Corn

Easy
May Prepare Ahead

Serves: 4-5
Bake: 40-50 minutes at 350°

1	16-ounce can whole kernel corn (or 2 cups fresh cut corn)	1	teaspoon salt
1	cup evaporated milk		pepper to taste
2	tablespoons butter	2	eggs, beaten
2	tablespoons flour	½	cup buttered crumbs
			paprika

- Drain corn and save liquid.
- Add milk to liquid to measure 1 cup.
- Melt butter, add flour, salt and pepper. Blend.
- Add liquid and cook until thickened.
- Remove from heat. Add corn.
- Slowly add eggs.
- Put in greased baking dish.
- Put crumbs and paprika on top.
- Put baking dish in shallow pan of water.
- Bake at 350° 40 to 50 minutes.

Mrs. William Wallace (Sally Benson)

Savory Stuffed Eggplant

Average
May Prepare Ahead
Freezes Well

Serves: 6
Bake: 30 minutes at 350°

1	medium to large eggplant	½	cup cheddar cheese, grated
¼	cup onion, chopped	1	cup fresh bread, cubed
1	clove garlic, chopped or pressed	1	egg
¼	cup butter		salt and pepper to taste

- Cut eggplant in half lengthwise.
- Put cut side down in frying pan in one inch of water.
- Simmer for 10 minutes, covered. Cool slightly.
- Remove meat to ½ inch of shell and save shell. Chop meat.
- Melt butter in skillet and add onion, garlic and eggplant.
- Sauté 5 minutes.
- Add cheese, bread, egg, salt and pepper.
- Put mixture into shells.
- Put filled shells in baking pan and add ½ inch water.
- Bake 30 minutes at 350°.
- Shell is tender and edible.

Mrs. Berkeley Grimball (Emily Kirkland)

Wadmalaw Island Eggplant Pie
"Great to take out of the freezer."

Easy
May Prepare Ahead
Freezes Well

Serves: 5-6
Bake: 45 minutes at 350°

2 medium eggplants, pared and cubed	1 cup cheddar cheese, shredded
1 egg, slightly beaten	1 teaspoon Worcestershire sauce
½ small onion, chopped	¼ teaspoon onion powder
½ small bell pepper, chopped	salt and pepper, to taste
	cheese, shredded to cover top

♦ Cook eggplant in large sauce pan on top of stove for approximately 15 minutes.
♦ Drain well and mash.
♦ Add remaining ingredients except cheese to cover top, and mix together well.
♦ Pour into one quart casserole and top with cheddar cheese.
♦ Bake uncovered at 350° for 45 minutes.

Mrs. James M. Ravenel (Elizabeth Barkley)

Eggplant And Zucchini Oriental
"An interesting combination of two vegetables."

Average
Serve Immediately

Serves: 6
Cook: 25 minutes
Bake: 5-10 minutes at 350°

2 tablespoons oil	1 bell pepper, chopped
3 small shallots or onions, cut up	½ pound zucchini (4 large or 6 small), cut into bite size pieces
3 medium tomatoes, skinned, cut up	1 large eggplant, cut into bite size pieces
6 large mushrooms, cut up	12 ounces Monterey Jack cheese, shredded
1 clove garlic, chopped	
1 bay leaf	

♦ In heavy fry pan, put 2 tablespoons oil, onions, tomatoes, mushrooms, garlic, bay leaf and bell pepper.
♦ Cook covered for 10 minutes.
♦ Add zucchini and eggplant.
♦ Cook for 15 minutes covered tightly.
♦ Pour into large baking dish.
♦ Cover with cheese and bake at 350° for 5-10 minutes.

Mrs. Batson L. Hewitt (Ann Turner)

Meatless Moussaka (Baked Eggplant)
"Worth all the time and effort"

Complicated
May Prepare Ahead

Serves: 10 to 12
Bake: 30 minutes at 375°

2 medium eggplants, sliced ½-inch thick, but not peeled	4 tablespoons parsley, chopped
4 tablespoons olive oil	1 tablespoon mint, chopped
2 medium onions, chopped	1 teaspoon sugar
1 clove garlic, minced	½ teaspoon oregano
1 cup tomato sauce	½ teaspoon basil
1 cup water	¼ teaspoon cinnamon
1 teaspoon salt	vegetable oil
⅛ teaspoon pepper	1 cup Romano cheese, grated

Filling

1½ cups cottage cheese
1 egg, slightly beaten

½ teaspoon salt

- Slice eggplants; soak in deep bowl of salt water for 30 minutes.
- Heat olive oil and sauté onion until transparent.
- Add garlic and sauté 2 to 3 more minutes.
- Add tomato sauce, water, salt, pepper, parsley, mint, sugar, oregano, basil and cinnamon.
- Simmer, covered, 30 minutes.
- Drain eggplant and squeeze slices with paper towels to absorb excess moisture.
- Brush with vegetable oil.
- Broil 4 minutes on each side, 4 inches from heat.
- Mix cottage cheese, egg and salt and set aside.
- Grease 13 x 9 x 2 pan.
- Spread ½ the tomato sauce over the bottom of pan.
- Sprinkle with ½ cup Romano cheese.
- Arrange ½ the eggplant slices on top, overlapping slices.
- Spread cheese filling over this.
- Place remaining eggplant slices over cheese filling.
- Cover with remaining tomato sauce.
- Sprinkle with ½ cup Romano cheese.
- Bake 375°, for 30 minutes.
- Let stand 15 minutes before cutting into squares.

Mrs. J. Michael Grayson (Hope Gazes)

Easy Eggplant

Easy　　　　　　　　　　　　　　　**Serves:** 2 slices per person
Serve Immediately　　　　　　　　　**Bake:** 8-10 minutes at 450°

eggplant, peeled and cut　　　　　　lemon pepper
into ⅜-inch slices　　　　　　　　　Parmesan cheese
mayonnaise

♦ Coat each side of eggplant with mayonnaise and dust with lemon pepper and
   Parmesan cheese.
♦ Place on a teflon coated pan and bake at 450° for 8-10 minutes.

Mrs. R.W. Sills (Lucretia Hill)

Mushroom Casserole
"Good with roast beef or steak."

Average　　　　　　　　　　　　　**Serves:** 4-5
Serve Immediately　　　　　　　　　**Bake:** 20 minutes at 375°

1½ pounds fresh mushrooms, sliced　　⅛ teaspoon pepper
¼ cup butter　　　　　　　　　　　2 cups milk
¼ cup flour　　　　　　　　　　　　1 tablespoon dry sherry
1 tablespoon parsley, chopped　　　　2 cups seasoned croutons
½ teaspoon salt　　　　　　　　　　　paprika

♦ Sauté mushrooms in butter and drain.
♦ Melt butter in small sauce pan.
♦ Stir in flour, parsley, salt and pepper.
♦ Add milk to sauté pan and heat until milk is warm.
♦ Blend milk into flour mixture.
♦ Cook over moderate heat, stirring until mixture thickens.
♦ Blend in sherry.
♦ Place half of the croutons in buttered casserole dish.
♦ Top with half of the mushrooms.
♦ Pour half of the white sauce over mixture.
♦ Repeat the two layers.
♦ Sprinkle with paprika.
♦ Bake at 375° for 20 minutes in one quart casserole.

Mrs. James Austin Hufham, III (Cathy Brooks)

Mushroom Strudel
"Absolutely fabulous."

Complicated
Prepare Ahead
Freezes Well

Serves: 16
Bake: 25 minutes at 375°

3	tablespoons butter	½	cup yogurt
1	pound mushrooms, sliced	½	cup sour cream
¼	onion, chopped	⅓	cup parsley, chopped
1	tablespoon sherry	2	large cloves garlic, minced
1	teaspoon salt		juice of one lemon
8	ounces cream cheese, room temperature	½	teaspoon pepper
		1	cup butter, melted
1	cup breadcrumbs	20	phyllo sheets

♦ Over medium heat, sauté onions and mushrooms in 3 tablespoons butter.
♦ Stir in sherry and salt and cook until absorbed.
♦ Remove from heat and drain well.
♦ Return to skillet. Cut cream cheese into small pieces.
♦ Add cream cheese to pan and stir until melted.
♦ Blend in crumbs, yogurt, sour cream, parsley, garlic, lemon and pepper.
♦ Preheat oven to 375°.
♦ Grease baking sheet.
♦ Place one phyllo sheet on work surface and brush with melted butter.
♦ Repeat to form stack of 10 sheets.
♦ Spoon half of mushroom filling in strip along long edge of phyllo, leaving 3-inch margin at each end.
♦ Roll up to enclose, tucking in ends.
♦ Put seam side down on baking sheet.
♦ Brush with butter.
♦ Repeat for second roll.
♦ Bake until crisp and browned (about 25 minutes).
♦ Cool 5 minutes and cut into 8 pieces to serve.

* Keep phyllo moist with a damp towel.

Mrs. G. Simms McDowell, III (Elsa Freeman)

Baked Vidalia Onions

Easy
Serve Immediately

Serves: 4
Bake: 1 hour at 375°

4 large vidalia onions
4 tablespoons butter or margarine
1 teaspoon salt

⅛ teaspoon pepper
   Parmesan cheese

- Trim and peel each onion.
- Cut each onion as if quartering, but don't cut all the way through.
- Press 1 tablespoon of butter or margarine into each onion.
- Sprinkle with salt and pepper followed by a generous amount of cheese.
- Wrap each onion in aluminum foil.
- Bake at 400° for one hour.

Mrs. Clarence M. Glenn (Ferne Fulton)

Vidalia Onion Pie

Easy
Serve Immediately

Serves: 4
Bake: 10 minutes at 450°—
          30 minutes at 300°

3 vidalias, thinly sliced
2 tablespoons melted butter
3 eggs
1 cup sour cream
1 teaspoon salt

¼ teaspoon pepper
1 teaspoon dill, celery seed
   or basil
1 9-inch pie shell, baked
   crisp bacon, crumbled

- Sauté onions in butter until clear.
- Combine eggs, sour cream, salt and pepper and spice over low heat to blend well.
- Then add to cooled onions.
- Pour into baked pie shell.
- Top with crumbled bacon.
- Bake at 450° for 10 minutes, then 300° until crust is light brown.

Mrs. Stuart Whiteside (Frances Brunson)

Game Chips
"Perfect with game or fish."

Easy
Serve Immediately

Serves: any number
Fry: 3 minutes

cooking oil
baking potatoes

salt

♦ Heat oil in fryer to 375°.
♦ Process washed potatoes (not peeled) through thin blade of a processor.
♦ Place in a bowl of water to keep from turning brown.
♦ Dry with a cloth towel and fry in small batches until golden.
♦ Salt and keep warm in oven.
♦ Serve with fish or game.

Mr. J. Conrad Zimmerman, Jr.

Fancy Stuffed Potatoes
"A splendid addition to any freezer!"

Easy
May Prepare Ahead
Freezes Well

Serves: 6 to 8
Bake: 1 hour at 400° / 15 to 20 minutes at 350°

4	large baking potatoes		1	cup sour cream
8	slices of bacon		1	teaspoon salt
3	tablespoons bacon drippings		½	teaspoon pepper
½	cup chopped green onions			paprika
4	tablespoons Parmesan cheese			

♦ Bake potatoes in 400° oven for 1 hour or until cooked thoroughly.
♦ Fry bacon until crisp, drain on paper towels, and crumble.
♦ In bacon drippings, sauté green onions until tender.
♦ Cut potatoes in half lengthwise. Spoon out the inside of potato, being careful not to puncture the skin.
♦ Add potato pulp to onion in skillet, then add cheese, sour cream, salt, pepper.
♦ Mash and blend well. Add bacon.
♦ Heat over low heat.
♦ Stuff potato skins with this mixture and sprinkle tops with paprika.
♦ Place on baking sheet and bake at 350° for 15-20 minutes.

Ann W. Dibble

Gratin Potatoes

Easy
Serve Immediately

Serves: 6
Bake: 50 minutes at 375°

4 cups thinly sliced potatoes	1½ cups Gruyére cheese, grated
1 teaspoon salt	4 tablespoons butter
¼ teaspoon pepper	2 eggs, beaten
⅛ teaspoon nutmeg	1 cup heavy cream
1 clove garlic, minced fine	3 tablespoons Parmesan cheese

- Preheat oven to 375°.
- Toss potatoes with seasonings to coat.
- Place ⅓ of the potatoes in a buttered shallow baking dish.
- Sprinkle ⅓ of the Gruyére and ⅓ of the butter on potatoes.
- Repeat twice.
- Beat eggs and cream together slightly.
- Pour over potatoes and add Parmesan cheese.
- Bake covered for 40 minutes then uncovered for 10 minutes until top is golden.

Mrs. Jules Deas (Leigh Tyler)

Stuffed Potatoes With Broccoli And Cheese
"A great do-ahead!"

Average
May Prepare Ahead

Serves: 6 to 8
Bake: 1 hour and 10 minutes at 425°

6 large baking potatoes	1½ cups grated cheddar cheese
2 tablespoons butter (at room temperature)	1 10-ounce package frozen chopped broccoli
⅓ cup milk	salt and pepper to taste

- Bake potatoes in preheated oven (425°) for 1 hour.
- Cook broccoli according to directions on package, drain broccoli well.
- Cut potatoes in half, and scoop out pulp, being careful not to pierce the skin.
- Force the pulp through a sieve or ricer into a large bowl.
- Heat the milk.
- Add milk, butter, and salt and pepper to the potatoes.
- Beat the mixture until fluffy.
- Stir in broccoli and cheese and fill the shells.
- Bake the potatoes again at 425° for 10 minutes, or for 20 minutes if they've been refrigerated.

Ann W. Dibble

Potato "Pears"

"An attractive, delicious side dish or cocktail fare."

Complicated
May Prepare Ahead

Yield: 35 croquettes
Bake: 1 hour
Fry: 2 minutes

2   pounds russet potatoes,
     scrubbed
1½ sticks unsalted butter, cut in
     small pieces and softened
3   large eggs
1¼ cups freshly grated very best
     Parmesan

salt and pepper, to taste
dried rosemary for garnish
oil for frying
2   cups fresh bread crumbs

♦ Bake potatoes in preheated 425° oven for 1 hour. (Prick several times after 30 minutes.)
♦ Cool. Scoop out pulp. Save skins for another use.
♦ Force potatos through a ricer into a large bowl.
♦ Add butter and 1 lightly beaten egg. Heat well.
♦ Add Parmesan, salt and pepper.
♦ Form rounded tablespoons into "pears".
♦ Dip "pears" in remaining 2 eggs (beaten well) letting excess drip off.
♦ Coat well with bread crumbs.
♦ Stick a rosemary sprig in top of each "pear".
♦ Fry in batches in 3 inches of hot oil for 2 minutes or until golden.
♦ Drain. Keep warm in a preheated 250° oven.

Mrs. Greenfield Polk

Oven Fries

"Easy and children love them."

Easy
Serve Immediately

Serves: 4
Bake: 45 minutes at 400°

4   medium potatoes
½ cup cooking oil
½ teaspoon salt

½ teaspoon paprika
¼ teaspoon garlic powder
¼ teaspoon pepper

♦ Cut potatoes lengthwise in long strips, leaving on skin. (Like triangles.)
♦ Arrange on a cookie sheet skin side down.
♦ Mix oil and spices together and brush on potatoes to coat.
♦ Bake at 400° for 45 minutes basting every 15 minutes.

Mrs. Wade H. Logan, III (Eunice Smith)

Sweet Potato Soufflé With Sherry

"Serve with sausage and a salad."

Easy
May Prepare Ahead

Serves: 6
Bake: 30 minutes at 350°

2	large sweet potatoes, boiled	1	teaspoon almond extract
½	cup sugar	4	tablespoons cream
3	tablespoons butter, divided	½	cup sherry
½	teaspoon salt	¾	cup pecans, chopped
	pinch nutmeg		

- Mash the potatoes or process to make smooth.
- Add sugar, 2 tablespoons butter, salt, nutmeg, almond extract, cream and sherry.
- Mix well.
- Brown pecans in 1 tablespoon of butter, stirring well.
- Add nuts to potato mixture and stir well by hand.
- Pour into a 3 quart rectangular baking dish.
- Bake at 350° for 30 minutes or until light brown on top.

Mrs. T. Ladson Webb (Ann Moore)

Sweet Potato Soufflé

"Delicious with Thanksgiving turkey."

Easy
May Prepare Ahead

Serves: 6-8
Bake: 30-35 minutes at 350°

3	cups hot sweet potato	1	tablespoon vanilla
1	stick margarine	¼	cup milk

Topping:

1	cup brown sugar, packed	⅓	cup plain flour
⅓	cup melted butter	1	cup chopped nuts

- In a mixer, mix sweet potatoes, margarine, vanilla and milk.
- Bake in 2 quart buttered dish at 350° for 15-20 minutes.
- Mix and spread topping over potato mixture.
- Bake 15 minutes longer.

Mrs. F. J. Martschink (Linda Lockwood)

235

Spinach And Spaghetti
"Even the Italians raved!"

Average
Partial Prepare Ahead

Serves: 4
Bake: 30 minutes at 350°

1   10-ounce package frozen
chopped spinach
1   egg, beaten
½   cup sour cream
¼   cup milk
4   tablespoons Parmesan cheese,
grated and divided

2   teaspoons dried minced onion
½   teaspoon salt
dash pepper
2   cups Montery Jack cheese,
grated (8 ounces)
4   ounces spaghetti, cooked and
drained (2 cups)

- Cook spinach and drain well.
- Combine egg, sour cream, milk, 2 tablespoons Parmesan cheese, onion, salt and pepper.
- Add Monterey Jack cheese and mix well.
- Add drained spinach and mix well.
- Pour mixture into an ungreased 10 x 6 x 2 baking dish.
- Sprinkle with remaining Parmesan cheese.
- Bake covered for 15 minutes.
- Continue to bake uncovered for 15 minutes longer or until firm.
- Serve over spaghetti.

Mrs. Frank Murphy (Amy Bain)

Herb Spinach

Easy
May Prepare Ahead

Serves: 6-8
Bake: 25 minutes at 350°

1   10-ounce package frozen
chopped spinach
1   cup herb rice, cooked
1   cup sharp cheddar cheese,
grated
2   eggs, slightly beaten

2   tablespoons butter, softened
⅓   cup milk
2   tablespoons onion, chopped
½   teaspoon Worcestershire sauce
1   teaspoon salt
¼   teaspoon rosemary or thyme

- Cook and drain spinach according to directions on package.
- Mix with remaining ingredients.
- Pour into 10 x 6 shallow baking dish.
- Bake at 350° for 25 minutes.

Sarah W. Wilson

Spinach Casserole I

Easy
May Prepare Ahead

Serves: 6-8
Bake: 30 minutes at 350°

2   packages frozen spinach, chopped
2   8-ounce packages cream cheese, softened

¼   pound butter or margarine, softened
¼   teaspoon salt
1½ cups Parmesan cheese

- Preheat oven to 350°.
- Cook spinach until just done.
- Drain well.
- Mix spinach with cream cheese, butter and salt.
- Put into casserole and cover with Parmesan cheese.
- Bake at 350° for 30 minutes or until cheese melts.

Mrs. C. Deas Gadsden (Lou Kidder)

Spinach Casserole II
"Very tasty!"

Average
May Prepare Ahead

Serves: 4
Bake: 20 minutes at 350°

1   bag fresh spinach
2   tablespoons butter
¼   cup flour
½   cup milk

¼   teaspoon nutmeg
2   tablespoons Parmesan cheese
    salt and pepper to taste
1   hard boiled egg

- Preheat oven to 350°.
- Wash spinach and break into bite size pieces.
- Place in covered pot and steam for 5 minutes.
- Drain spinach and chop finely
- Melt butter in saucepan.
- Make roux with flour.
- Add milk slowly, stirring constantly.
- Add spinach to sauce and stir well.
- Add nutmeg, cheese, salt and pepper.
- Stir until cheese melts.
- Pour into 2 quart casserole.
- Top with hard boiled egg.
- Bake at 350° for 20 minutes.

Mrs. A.A. Burris, III (Anne Cogswell)

Spinach-Artichoke Casserole

Average
May Prepare Ahead

Serves: 6
Bake: 40 minutes at 350°

1½ cups artichoke hearts
2 packages frozen spinach -
   thawed and drained
1 8-ounce cream cheese
1 8-ounce can sliced mushrooms -
   drained

½ cup milk
2 tablespoons margarine
   salt
   pepper
   dill weed
   Parmesan cheese

♦ Butter bottom and sides of 1 quart casserole dish.
♦ Place artichokes in bottom, mushrooms on top, then drained spinach.
♦ In a separate bowl, whip cream cheese, margarine, salt, pepper, dill weed and milk until smooth. Spread this mixture over spinach.
♦ Sprinkle with Parmesan cheese, cover and bake in 350° oven for 30 minutes.
♦ Remove cover and continue to bake 10 minutes to brown cheese.

Pamela J. Edwards

Squash Supreme
"The carrots make the texture."

Easy
May Prepare Ahead

Serves: 8
Bake: 45 minutes at 350°

1½ pounds yellow squash
1 small onion, chopped
1½ -2 carrots, grated
1 (8-ounce) sour cream

1 (10¾-ounce) can cream of
   chicken soup
½ cup stuffing mix crumbs

♦ Cook squash uncovered until tender. Drain, then mash.
♦ Combine squash, onion, carrots, sour cream and cream of chicken soup in a buttered 1½ quart casserole.
♦ Top with crumbs.
♦ Bake at 350° for 45 minutes, uncovered.

Mrs. Thomas E. Thornhill (Mardelle Musk)

Church Street Squash

Easy
May Prepare Ahead
Freezes Well

Serves: 6
Bake: 30 minutes at 350°

2 pounds yellow or zucchini squash
1 medium onion, chopped
4 tablespoons butter, divided
¾ cup sharp cheddar cheese, grated
1 cup sour cream

1 teaspoon salt
½ teaspoon pepper
1 egg, whisked
½ cup Pepperidge Farm stuffing mix, plain
1 tablespoon paprika

◆ Cook squash until tender.
◆ Mash with fork after draining.
◆ Let stand until cool.
◆ Sauté onion in 2 tablespoons butter until yellow, not brown.
◆ Mix squash, onions, cheese, sour cream, salt, pepper and egg.
◆ Gently pour into greased casserole.
◆ Sprinkle stuffing mix on top and dot with 2 tablespoons butter.
◆ Sprinkle paprika on top.
◆ Cook uncovered 30 minutes at 350° or until bubbly.

* It does freeze well after cooking and covered.

Mrs. Thomas L. Webb (Ann Moore)

Squash And Zucchini Casserole
"Great dish for a Mexican dinner."

Easy
Serve Immediately

Serves: 8
Cook: 15-20 minutes

6 strips of bacon, fried and cut into small pieces
15 medium yellow squash, sliced thin

6 zucchini, sliced thin
salt and pepper to taste
water

◆ Sauté vegetables in bacon grease over medium-low heat.
◆ Add enough water to cover vegetables and stew until vegetables are tender.
◆ Keep adding water as needed.
◆ Salt and pepper to taste.
◆ Place the squash and zucchini in a casserole and cover with bacon bits.
◆ Warm in 300° oven until time to serve.

Mrs. Michael Smoak (Beth Easterling)

Squash Casserole

Easy
May Prepare Ahead

Serves: 6
Bake: 30 minutes at 350°

1 pound yellow squash, cut fine
2-3 white onions, cut fine
1 stick butter
1 egg, beaten
6 tablespoons cream

½ cup almonds, chopped
salt and pepper to taste
1 cup breadcrumbs, toasted
(optional)

♦ Cook squash and onions in saucepan with butter over medium heat until mixture is mush.
♦ Remove pan from heat and add egg, cream and almonds.
♦ Mix well and add salt and pepper.
♦ Place in a 1½ quart casserole and top with breadcrumbs.
♦ Bake at 350° for 30 minutes or until bubbly.

Mrs. Joseph C. Moore, Jr. (Llewellyn Kooken)

3 Squash Casserole

Easy
May Prepare Ahead

Serves: 6
Bake: 30 minutes at 350°

4 small zucchini squash
4 small yellow squash
4 small white squash
1 large onion, chopped
4 tablespoons butter, melted
⅛ teaspoon chervil

¼ teaspoon Beau Monde
⅛ teaspoon Fines herbs
1 cup cheddar cheese croutons, crushed
2 cups sour cream
salt and pepper to taste

♦ Boil or steam squash and onion until tender.
♦ Drain.
♦ Mix with other ingredients except save ½ cup croutons for topping.
♦ Bake at 350° 30 minutes or until bubbly.

Mrs. Henry Fishburne, Jr. (Lurline Stedman)

Vinegarette Tomatoes
"A good cold vegetable dish for summer supper"

Easy
Prepare Ahead

Serves: 10-12
Marinate: overnight

1 clove garlic, diced	1 bottle Italian dressing
1 medium onion, diced	12 tomatoes, peeled and sliced
1 small green pepper, diced	1 small box fresh mushrooms,
½ cup celery, diced	peeled and sliced
½ teaspoon salt	1 tablespoon sugar
½ teaspoon pepper	3-4 tablespoons fresh parsley, cut
1 teaspoon mustard	up fine

♦ Mix together first 8 ingredients.
♦ Set aside.
♦ Place in a 9 x 13 pan, tomatoes topped with mushrooms.
♦ Sprinkle on sugar and parsley.
♦ Top with Italian dressing mixture.
♦ Chill overnight in refrigerator.
♦ Drain some of liquid when serving.

Mrs. James R. Spears (Gayle Reid)

Curried Tomatoes
"A great color dish."

Easy
Serve Immediately

Serves: 6
Bake: 15 minutes at 425°

6 ripe tomatoes, skinned and stems removed	4 tablespoons grated sharp cheddar cheese
1 cup tomato sauce	3 tablespoons fresh breadcrumbs
2 teaspoons curry powder	6 slices bacon, cooked crisp
2 tablespoons currant jelly	

♦ Preheat oven to 425°.
♦ Place tomatoes in shallow, buttered baking dish.
♦ Combine tomato sauce, jelly and curry powder in a sauce pan.
♦ Heat five minutes and pour over tomatoes.
♦ Sprinkle with breadcrumbs and cheese.
♦ Bake 15 minutes.
♦ Garnish with bacon and serve hot.

Mrs. Van Noy Thornhill (Jane Lucas)

Tomatoes Supreme

Easy
May Prepare Ahead

Serves: 6-8
Bake: 30 minutes at 350°

6 medium tomatoes, sliced
1 small onion, thinly sliced
1 cup seasoned croutons
¼ cup grated Parmesan cheese

1½ teaspoons basil
1 teaspoon salt
¼ teaspoon pepper
3 tablespoons butter

♦ Layer tomatoes, onions and croutons in shallow buttered casserole dish.
♦ Sprinkle with cheese, basil and seasonings.
♦ Dot with butter.
♦ Bake uncovered at 350° for 30 minutes.

Mrs. Thomas W. Alexander (Patricia Cochrane)

Zucchini Tomato Vegetable Casserole
"A lowcountry favorite."

Easy
May Prepare Ahead

Serves: 6
Bake: 40 minutes at 300°

3 medium zucchini squash, sliced
5 fresh tomatoes, sliced
2 medium onions, sliced
   basil
   seasoning salt

   pepper
6 ounces mozzarella or cheddar
   cheese, grated
3 slices bacon

♦ Place ½ of zucchini in bottom of pyrex dish.
♦ Layer 2½ tomatoes and one onion on top of zucchini.
♦ Sprinkle with basil, salt and pepper.
♦ Sprinkle with ½ cheese.
♦ Repeat layers and seasonings.
♦ Top with the raw bacon.
♦ Cover with foil and bake at 300° for 40 minutes.
♦ The last 5 minutes, cook uncovered.

Mrs. Barnaby Henderson (Sue Allen)

Zucchini-Corn Pudding

Easy
Partial Prepare Ahead

Serves: 8
Bake: 45 minutes at 350°

1½ pounds zucchini, thinly sliced
1 medium onion, thinly sliced
1 green pepper, minced
1 or 2 cloves of garlic, minced
¼ teaspoon rosemary

¼ cup salad oil
1 No. 2 can cream style corn
½ - 1 cup grated cheese
3 eggs, well beaten
salt and pepper to taste

♦ Cook zucchini in boiling salted water until tender.
♦ Drain - squeeze out all liquid.
♦ Sauté onion, green pepper, garlic and rosemary in oil until tender.
♦ Add zucchini, corn, cheese, eggs, salt and pepper. Mix.
♦ Turn into a greased 2 quart casserole.
♦ Bake 45 minutes at 350° or until firm.

* This can be put together ahead except for eggs. Add these to mixture just before baking.

Mrs. Lawrence Walker (Phyllis Corson)

Sautéed Zucchini And Tomatoes
"Very simple, yet delicious."

Easy
Serve Immediately

Serves: 6
Bake: 30 minutes

3 tablespoons butter, melted
3 medium zucchini, sliced
3 medium fresh tomatoes, chopped

1 tablespoon Cavender's Greek seasoning
Parmesan cheese

♦ Melt butter.
♦ Add zucchini and tomatoes.
♦ Cook for 30 minutes.
♦ Add Cavender's Greek seasoning.
♦ When ready to serve, sprinkle with Parmesan cheese.

* Cavender's Greek seasoning is in the gourmet section.

Mrs. Alton Blue Currie (Nancy Smith)

Vegetable Ragout
"Great flavors."

Easy
Serve Immediately

Serves: 6
Bake: 1 hour at 350°

6   tablespoons onion, chopped
2   tablespoons butter
2   pounds green beans, strung and
    sliced diagonally
½   pound okra, sliced

1   pound tomatoes, chopped
1   bay leaf
1   teaspoon summer savory
4   tablespoons white wine
    salt and pepper to taste

♦ Fry onion in butter.
♦ Put all together in casserole and bake for 1 hour at 350°.
* Cook covered for more juices.

Mrs. Berkeley Grimball (Emily Kirkland)

Summer Vegetable Medley
"Excellent served over rice."

Easy
Serve Immediately

Serves: 4
Cook: 20 minutes

4   tablespoons oil
2   medium onions, coarsley
    chopped
1   pound fresh okra, cut in ¼ inch
    slices
2   ears corn, cut off cob

2   medium tomatoes, quartered,
    skinned
1   teaspoon basil
½   cup dry white wine
    salt and pepper

♦ Lace wok or large frying pan with oil over medium heat.
♦ Stir fry onions about 5 minutes.
♦ Add okra, corn and tomatoes and stir fry.
♦ Mix in basil and wine.
♦ Salt and pepper to taste.
♦ Cover and simmer 10-15 minutes.

Mrs. A. A. Burris, III (Anne Cogswell)

Florence's Vegetable Gumbo
"Summer delight."

Easy
May Prepare Ahead

Serves: 6-8
Simmer: 40 minutes

4   slices bacon, cut into 1 inch
    pieces
1   large onion, sliced
4   large ears corn, cut off cob (or
    1 16-ounce can shoe peg corn)
3   large very ripe tomatoes, cut in
    wedges (or 1 16-ounce can
    tomatoes and juice)

½   cup water, if you use fresh
    tomatoes
1   teaspoon salt
1   teaspoon sugar
1   pound okra, cut into 1 inch
    pieces

♦ Fry bacon in heavy skillet.
♦ Add onion and sauté lightly.
♦ Add corn and tomatoes - simmer 10 minutes.
♦ Add salt, sugar and okra - simmer 30 minutes.
♦ DO NOT OVERCOOK.

Mrs. Charles Lowndes Mullally (Pauline Slay)

Mediterranean Garden Medley

Easy
Serve Immediately

Serves: 4
Cook: 15 minutes

1   small eggplant, cut in small
    chunks
2   tablespoons olive oil
1   small onion, sliced
1   clove garlic, minced

1   medium zucchini, sliced
1   sweet red pepper, cut in strips
1   green pepper, cut in squares
    salt
    pepper

♦ Brown eggplant on all sides in non-stick pan or pan sprayed with non-stick
  coating.
♦ Add oil, onion, garlic, zucchini, peppers, salt and pepper.
♦ Cook, stirring constantly until vegetables begin to soften.

Jane Lucas Thornhill

Glazed Apples
"Good with breakfast!"

Average
May Prepare Ahead

Serves: 6
Simmer: 50 minutes

½ cup sugar	⅛ teaspoon cinnamon
1½ cups water	6 medium tart apples, quartered

♦ Combine sugar and water in dutch oven - boil 10 minutes, remove from heat, add cinnamon and apples, stir gently.
♦ Simmer uncovered 30 minutes, cover and simmer 20 minutes.
♦ Serve in a buttered 1 quart casserole.

Mrs. Robert H. Bowles (Elizabeth Pritchard)

Lucy's Curried Fruit Bake
"Great with ham and red rice."

Easy
Serve Immediately

Serves: 8
Bake: 40 minutes at 350°

1 No. 2½ can fruits for salad	2 tablespoons cornstarch
1 cup black cherries, pitted and halved	1 tablespoon curry powder
½ cup marachino cherries	2 large bananas, sliced
½ cup brown sugar	1 small packaged slivered almonds
	½ cup butter, melted

♦ Cut and drain the fruit, except bananas, for several hours.
♦ Combine sugar, cornstarch and curry powder.
♦ Add bananas and almonds to other fruit.
♦ Add melted butter to the fruit and sprinkle with sugar mixture.
♦ Mix fruit lightly.
♦ Turn into a buttered casserole and bake at 350° for 40 minutes.

Mrs. J. Stanley Claypoole, III (Barbara Pringle)

Escalloped Pineapple
"Perfect with ham."

Easy
May Prepare Ahead

Serves: 6
Bake: 1 hour at 350°

½ pound butter
1 cup sugar
2 eggs
1 20-ounce can chunk pineapple
with juice

½ cup milk
1 quart bread cubes, 5-6 slices

♦ Cream butter and sugar.
♦ Add eggs and beat.
♦ Add pineapple with juice, milk and bread cubes - stir by hand.
♦ Bake in 2 quart casserole dish for 1 hour at 350°.

Mrs. James Spears (Gayle Reid)

Remoulade Sauce
"This is a great gift."

Easy
May Prepare Ahead

Yield: 3-4 cups

2 cloves garlic, peeled
4 green onions, chopped
3 hard boiled eggs, grated
3 cups mayonnaise
*1 5¼-ounce Zatarain's Creole
mustard
2 tablespoons Worcestershire
sauce

1 tablespoon lemon juice
1 tablespoon vinegar
2 tablespoons anchovy paste
1 tablespoon horseradish
1 tablespoon sherry

♦ Combine garlic and onion in blender or food processor and blend.
♦ Add remaining ingredients. Process/blend until well blended.

* May substitute any coarse mustard.
Serve with fresh vegetables or any seafood.

Jane's Bechamel Sauce
"White sauce dressed up"

Easy
May Prepare Ahead

Serves: 4
Cook: 1 to 2 minutes

3   tablespoons butter
3   tablespoons flour
1   cup chicken bouillon

½   cup cream
    salt and pepper to taste
    (1-2 egg yolks-optional)

- Melt butter and stir in flour.
- Gradually stir in bouillon and cook until thickens.
- Blend in cream and seasonings.
- (Beat egg yolks well. Add gradually, stirring constantly.)
- Cook for 1 to 2 minutes.

Mrs. Joseph P. Bucknum (Jane Smith)

Blender Hollandaise
"So easy and so good"

Easy
Serve Immediately

Yield: 1 cup

3   egg yolks
½   teaspoon salt

1   tablespoon lemon juice, fresh
1   stick butter

- Put egg yolks, salt and lemon juice in blender.
- Melt butter.
- Blend butter with other ingredients at high speed until butter is absorbed (about 30 seconds).
- Serve Immediately.

Mrs. Edmund Rhett (Sally Aichele)

PASTA

Pasta Alla Carbonara

Easy
Serve Immediately

Serves: 6
Cook: 20-30 minutes

7   eggs
½   cup sour cream
½   cup grated Parmesan cheese

1   pound bacon
10   ounce package garden peas
1   pound pasta

- Beat eggs, sour cream and cheese together and set aside.
- Cut bacon crosswise into 1 inch pieces.
- Fry bacon until semi-crisp. Drain.
- Cook peas according to package directions.
- Cook pasta in boiling water for 6 to 8 minutes until it is AL DENTE.
- Drain pasta.
- Return pasta to pot, immediately coating hot pasta with egg mixture.
- Add bacon and peas.
- More Parmesan cheese may be added if desired.

* Can substitute chicken or pork and vegetables for bacon and peas.

Barbara Dunbar Lyles

Frank's Birthday Dinner Pasta
"Great as a first course."

Easy
Serve Immediately

Serves: 6-7
Cook: 20 minutes

1   bunch fresh broccoli
1   1½ pounds homemade or
     purchased pasta (prefer flat
     thick noodles)
2   cups fresh Parmesan cheese,
     finely grated

1   stick butter, cut into 4 pieces
     salt
     white pepper

- Clean and cut broccoli so that flower tops are in bite-size pieces.
- Steam flower tops, discarding stems.
- Boil pasta according to directions.
- Warm serving bowls by letting them stand with hot water for a few minutes.
- Put pasta, broccoli and butter into serving bowl.
- Toss. Add Parmesan. Toss.
- Salt and pepper to taste. Toss.
- Serve in hot bowls.

Mrs. Raphael MacDawson Jones (Anne Holcombe)

Linguine With Artichokes
"Add a garden salad and a hearty bread."

Easy
Partial Prepare Ahead

Serves: 4
Cook: 20 minutes

6	tablespoons olive oil	8	artichoke hearts, cooked and
5	tablespoons stick butter		drained
1	teaspoon flour	3	tablespoons fresh grated
1	cup chicken stock or broth		Parmesan cheese
1	clove garlic, crushed	1	teaspoon drained capers
2	teaspoons lemon juice	1	pound linguine
1	teaspoon minced parsley	2	tablespoons olive oil
	salt and pepper to taste	½	teaspoon salt

- In a large heavy skillet, heat 4 tablespoons olive oil over moderately low heat.
- Add 4 tablespoons butter, and after melted, add 1 teaspoon flour. Cook, stirring for 3 minutes.
- Stir in heated chicken stock. Increase heat to moderately high. Cook sauce for 1 minute. Add garlic, lemon juice, parsley, and salt and pepper.
- Cook over moderately low heat for 5 minutes, stirring occasionally.
- Add artichoke hearts, 2 tablespoons Parmesan cheese, capers. Cover sauce, basting hearts several times, and cook 8 minutes.
- Cook linguine in 6 quarts salted water al dente. Drain in colander.
- In another pot, combine 2 tablespoons olive oil, 1 tablespoon Parmesan cheese, 1 tablespoon butter, ½ teaspoon salt.
- Return linguine to pot and toss with artichoke mixture.
- Top with sauce.

Mrs. Paul Keene (Edith Potter)

Spaghetti Salad

Easy
Prepare Ahead

Serves: 8
Chill: 24 hours

1	package 8-ounce spaghetti noodles	2	slices pimento, chopped
2	cups cheddar cheese, grated	1	cup mayonnaise
3	stalks celery, chopped	½	teaspoon salt
1	medium bell pepper, chopped	3	tablespoons lemon juice
½	small onion, chopped		dash red pepper
			pinch oregano

- Cook noodles, rinse with cold water, drain, and cut with scissors into 5-inch pieces.
- Combine rest of ingredients and toss with noodles.
- Best when refrigerated for 24 hours.

Mrs. F. Avery Burns (Susan Crabtree)

Pastichio

"Baked macaroni with cream sauce and meat sauce"

Complicated
May Prepare Ahead

Serves: 12
Bake: 40 minutes at 350°

4	tablespoons butter	2	teaspoons salt
1	large onion, chopped	¼	teaspoon pepper
1	clove garlic, minced	½	teaspoon oregano
2½	pounds ground beef	½	teaspoon basil
8	ounces tomato sauce	1	bay leaf
14½	ounces tomatoes, chopped	1	teaspoon fresh mint, chopped
		1	pound macaroni (ready-cut)

Sauce

4	tablespoons butter	1	cup Romano cheese, grated
6	tablespoons butter	5	eggs beaten
6	tablespoons flour	4	ounces cheddar cheese, grated
3	cups milk	½	teaspoon nutmeg

- Melt 4 tablespoons butter, and sauté onions until transparent.
- Add garlic and ground beef and brown well.
- Add tomato sauce, tomatoes, salt, pepper, oregano, basil, bay leaf and mint.
- Simmer 30 minutes and remove bay leaf.
- Cook macaroni according to package directions, drain, and add 4 tablespoons butter to coat.
- Make cream sauce by melting 6 tablespoons butter in saucepan, then add flour slowly until well blended. Add milk gradually, stirring constantly until thickened. Add ½ cup Romano cheese and stir until melted. Remove from heat and slowly add beaten eggs, stirring quickly until well blended.
- Combine ⅓ cream sauce with 4 ounces cheddar cheese and macaroni.
- Grease 11 x 14 pan and spread ½ macaroni mixture on bottom.
- Spread meat mixture over macaroni and evenly top with rest of macaroni.
- Spread remaining cream sauce on top and sprinkle with remaining ½ cup Romano cheese and nutmeg.
- Bake 40 minutes at 350°.

Mrs. J. Michael Grayson (Hope Gazes)

Pasta Primavera
"Spring in Italian."

Easy
Serve Immediately

Serves: 8
Cook: 30 minutes

⅓   cup olive oil
3   medium zucchini, diced
1   large green pepper, diced
1   large red pepper, diced
1   large onion, diced
8   sprigs parsley, diced

2   large cloves garlic, diced
1   pound linguine noodles (fresh, if you can find it or make it)
   grated Parmesan cheese
   freshly ground black pepper/salt to taste

♦ Sauté all vegetables in oil until fairly soft and blended (6-8 minutes).
♦ Boil linguine in salted water until "Al dente".
♦ Drain linguine.
♦ Toss vegetable mixture with linguine and transfer to heated serving dish.
♦ Sprinkle with Parmesan and freshly ground black pepper.

* Use a large frying pan. Can substitute almost any vegetable.

Mrs. James F. Chandler (Kay Haselden)

Mother's Tomato Mac

Average
May Prepare Ahead

Serves: 8
Bake: 30 minutes at 350°

2   tablespoons vegetable oil
½   cup onions, chopped
½   cup bell pepper, chopped
½   cup celery, chopped
1   8-ounce can tomato pureé

½   cup water
   salt and pepper to taste
1   8-ounce box elbow macaroni
8 - 10 ounces grated medium cheddar cheese

♦ Sauté onion, bell pepper and celery in oil, until glossy.
♦ Add tomato puree, water, salt and pepper.
♦ Cook until it bubbles.
♦ Cook noodles according to package directions. Drain.
♦ Combine macaroni with tomato mixture.
♦ Add half grated cheese.
♦ Stir until cheese is melted.
♦ Transfer into baking dish.
♦ Top with remaining cheese.
♦ Bake 30 minutes at 350°.

Mrs. Charles Gary Rackley (Kathleen Kennerty)

Spinach Lasagne
"Excellent"

Complicated
Partial Prepare Ahead
Freezes Well

Serves: 4-6
Bake: 35-45 minutes at 350°

1 pound fresh spinach
(remove tough stems)
2 tablespoons vegetable oil
1 medium onion, chopped
2 cloves garlic, minced
2 teaspoons oregano leaves
½ teaspoon basil
¾ teaspoon salt

3 1-pound cans tomatoes
(crushed or pieces) drained
½ pound whole wheat or other
lasagna noodles
1¼ pounds mozzarella cheese,
sliced thin
1 pound ricotta cheese
fresh grated Parmesan cheese

- Rinse spinach leaving leaves damp.
- Steam spinach (using vegetable steamer) until wilted (about 2 min.).
  Set aside.
- In saucepan, heat vegetable oil.
- Sauté onion, garlic, oregano and basil until onion is soft.
- Add salt and tomatoes.
- Cover and cook 20-30 minutes.
- Cook lasagna noodles according to package directions.
- To assemble, oil pan.
- Cover bottom of pan with tomato mixture.
- Layer in order: noodles, spinach, ricotta, mozzarella, Parmesan.
- Repeat (beginning with sauce) until all ingredients are used.
- Bake 35-45 minutes or until bubbly.
- Let stand 15 minutes before cutting.

* May substitute cottage cheese for ricotta.

Louise Evans Holcomb

Shrimp 'N Shells

Easy
May Prepare Ahead

Serves: 6-8
Cook: 20-30 minutes

8   ounce package seashell pasta
1   tablespoon olive oil
4   tablespoons butter
2   tablespoons Worcestershire sauce
1   quart (1½ pounds) raw shrimp, peeled
1   teaspoon garlic salt

1   bunch fresh broccoli, cut into bitesize florets
2   tablespoons Parmesan cheese
2   tablespoons fresh parsley, chopped
2   tablespoons Vidalia onion, chopped
    salt and pepper to taste

♦ Cook pasta according to package directions.
♦ Drain pasta and toss with olive oil.
♦ Set aside.
♦ Melt butter in skillet.
♦ Add Worcestershire sauce and sauté raw shrimp. Save butter.
♦ In separate saucepan, steam broccoli until tender. Drain.
♦ Toss shrimp and broccoli into pasta.
♦ Add one half remaining butter/Worcestershire liquid.
♦ Add Parmesan cheese, parsley, onion and garlic salt.
♦ Serve at room temperature. Salt and pepper to taste.

Mrs. David H. Maybank (Ann English)

Shrimp and Pasta Marinade

Easy
Prepare Ahead

Serves: 10-12
Chill: 3 hours

1   pound shrimp
1   cup shell or twist pasta
1   can pitted black olives, drained
1   teaspoon butter
8   ounces fresh mushrooms
1   small onion, thinly sliced

¼   cup olive oil
½   cup red wine vinegar
½   tablespoon garlic salt
1½ tablespoons sugar
1   package dry Italian dressing mix
    salt and pepper to taste

♦ Boil shrimp, peel, and reserve liquid.
♦ Boil pasta in shrimp liquid according to directions.
♦ Sauté mushrooms in small amount of butter. Drain.
♦ Mix oil, vinegar, and seasonings together, correcting seasoning with salt and pepper.
♦ Pour over shrimp, pasta, olives, mushrooms, and onions, stirring gently.
♦ Refrigerate several hours.
♦ Serve with toothpicks or on a bed of lettuce.
* Keeps several days.

Mrs. James Alden Huggins (Marshall Hemphill)

O.M.'s Pesto
"Use the bumper crop of basil."

Easy   **Yield:** 1½-2 cups
Prepare Ahead

1   cup fresh basil leaves, tightly   ¼   cup pine nuts
     packed (only use fresh basil)   2   cloves garlic, peeled
½   cup parsley   ¼   teaspoon salt
½   cup grated Parmesan cheese   ⅓   cup oil or less

♦ Place all ingredients except oil in blender or food processor.
♦ Blend/process until everything is finely chopped.
♦ Add oil gradually to desired consistency. Less oil can be used.
♦ Refrigerate or freeze.
♦ Toss with hot spaghetti or fettucini.

* Almonds may be substituted for pine nuts.

Mrs. David Knott (Marian C. Greely)

Creamy Pesto Dressing
"Delicious on pasta salad or cold broccoli"

Easy   **Yields:** 1½ cups
May Prepare Ahead   **Chill:** until serving time

3   cloves garlic   ¼   cup fresh parsley, chopped
1   tablespoon dried basil   ½   teaspoon salt
1   tablespoon red wine vinegar   ¼   teaspoon pepper
½   cup Pine nuts   1   cup mayonnaise or olive oil
¼   cup Parmesan, grated

♦ Combine garlic, basil, and vinegar in processor and process.
♦ Add nuts, Parmesan, parsley, salt and pepper and mayonnaise.
♦ Process, scraping down sides.
♦ If using olive oil, pour in a slow, steady stream into running processor.
♦ Refrigerate until ready to serve.

Mrs Ronald B. Shealy (Sharon Amos)

RICE

Red Rice
*"A favorite from **Charleston Receipts**."*

Average
May Prepare Ahead

Serves: 6-8
Cook: about 1½ hours

4 strips bacon, cubed	2-3 teaspoons sugar
2 onions, chopped fine	½ teaspoon pepper
1 small can tomato paste	2 cups raw rice
1½ -2 cans water	8 tablespoons bacon grease,
3 teaspoons salt	optional

♦ Fry bacon, remove from pan.
♦ Sauté onions in grease.
♦ Add tomato paste, water, salt, sugar and pepper.
♦ Cook uncovered slowly (about 10 minutes) until it measures about 2 cups.
♦ Pour into the top of the steamer with the rice.
♦ Add the extra bacon grease.
♦ Steam for 30 minutes then add crumbled bacon and stir with a fork.
♦ Cook 30-45 minutes longer.

Mrs. Charles Gibbs (Wilmot Welch)

Chicken Pilaf
"Side dish for chicken"

Easy
Serve Immediately

Serves: 4
Cook: 20 minutes

½ cup spaghetti, broken and uncooked	2 tablespoons margarine
½ medium sized onion, chopped (optional)	1 10½-ounce can chicken broth
½ cup mushrooms, sliced (optional)	⅓ cup water
	½ cup raw rice

♦ Brown noodles, onion and mushrooms in butter, stirring often.
♦ Add remaining ingredients, bringing to a boil.
♦ Simmer 20 minutes covered, or until liquid is absorbed, stirring often.

Mrs. Charles T. Cole, Jr. (Joanne Gilmer)

Cinnamon-Curried Rice
"A great dish for chicken or seafood."

Easy
May Prepare Ahead

Serves: 8
Cook: 45 minutes

2½ cups raw rice
3 cups chicken broth
1½ teaspoons curry powder, or
    more to taste

1 teaspoon cinnamon

♦ Steam in top of steamer.

✻ Adjust the amount of liquid, if you do not have a steamer.

Mrs. D. William Wallace (Sally Benson)

Kerry's Green Chili Rice

Easy
May Prepare Ahead
Serve Immediately

Serves: 8
Bake: 30 minutes at 350°

1 cup rice, cooked and cooled
2 cups sour cream
8 ounces sharp cheddar cheese,
    grated

2 cans chopped green chilies,
    drained
    butter
    Parmesan cheese

♦ Mix rice and sour cream.
♦ Place one half of mixture in lightly greased casserole dish.
♦ Sprinkle one half cheddar cheese over mixture.
♦ Spread all of chilies, then top with other half of cheese.
♦ Add remaining rice mixture and dot with butter.
♦ Sprinkle with Parmesan cheese.
♦ Bake at 350° for 30 minutes.

Mrs. John Ball Howard (Eleanor Vest)

Stir Fried Rice With Pea Pods

Average
Serve Immediately

Serves: 8
Cook: 30 minutes

2 tablespoons oil
1 package frozen Chinese pea pods, defrosted
1 bunch spring onions, sliced
2 ribs celery, sliced
1 large green pepper, sliced in strips

1 can water chestnuts, sliced
5 cups cooked white rice
2 tablespoons teriyaki sauce
½ teaspoon garlic powder
fresh ground pepper/salt to taste

♦ Sauté all vegetables in hot oil, using either large frying pan or wok.
♦ Cook until sizzling, but still crunchy.
♦ Add cooked rice and seasonings.
♦ Stir until well mixed, about 3 to 5 minutes.
♦ Serve immediately.

Mrs. James F. Chandler (Kay Haselden)

Rice Casserole

Easy
Serve Immediately

Serves: 6-8
Bake: 1 hour at 300°

1 stick margarine
1 large onion, chopped
1 package slivered almonds
2 stalks celery, chopped

1½ cups long grained rice
2 cans beef bouillon
6 medium fresh mushrooms, sliced

♦ Sauté onions, celery and almonds in margarine for 3 minutes.
♦ Add mushrooms, then rice and bouillon, and cook for 1 minute.
♦ Pour mixture into casserole dish and cover.
♦ Cook for 1 hour or until all liquid is absorbed.

* Can substitute an 8-ounce can of whole mushrooms with juice.

Mrs. Douglas Purcell (Pauline Watkins)

Savory Fried Rice
"Great with barbequed chicken."

Average
Serve Immediately

Serves: 4-6
Cook: 45-60 minutes

2 medium onions, chopped
3 tablespoons butter
1 cup raw rice
1 teaspoon marjoram, crushed

1 teaspoon summer savory, crushed
1 teaspoon rosemary, crushed
3 cups chicken bouillon

♦ Sauté onion in butter in large frying pan for 5 minutes.
♦ Add rice, marjoram, summer savory and rosemary to mixture.
♦ Cook until rice begins to brown, stirring frequently.
♦ Add chicken bouillon.
♦ Cover and simmer until juice is gone (about 45 minutes to 1 hour).

Mrs. Fred Anderson, Jr. (Kay)

Wild Rice
"A perfect accompaniment."

Easy
Serve Immediately

Serves: 6-8
Bake: 1 hour at 350°

1 medium onion, chopped
1 package slivered almonds or pecans
1 stick butter
1 cup wild rice

1 cup brown rice
1 can mushrooms
2 cups bouillon (2 cubes dissolved in 2 cups water)

♦ Sauté onions and nuts in butter in a casserole dish.
♦ Add rice, mushrooms and bouillon; bring to a boil.
♦ Cover and bake in a 350° oven for 1 hour.
♦ Stir and serve.

Mr. J. Conrad Zimmerman, Jr.

Baked Hominy
"Great with fish, crab or shrimp."

Easy
May Prepare Ahead

Serves: 6-8
Bake: 30 minutes at 400°

1 quart milk	1 teaspoon salt
½ cup butter	1 teaspoon pepper
⅓ cup butter	1 cup grated gruyere cheese
1 cup plain grits	⅓ cup grated Parmesan cheese

- Combine milk, grits, and ½ cup butter in saucepan.
- Cook until smooth, then add salt and pepper.
- Beat five minutes with electric mixer.
- Pour into 13 x 9 casserole and cool.
- Cut into rectangular pieces and arrange in buttered casserole.
- Sprinkle with ⅓ cup butter and cheeses.
- Bake 30-35 minutes at 400°.

Rachel C. MacRae

DESSERTS

Summertime weekends mean regattas, and regattas mean wiry seven-year-olds stonily staring down their competition and seasoned salts skillfully maneuvering their crafts through the throng of boats.

The contests are spirited and so is the partying after the classes are over when boats raft up and sailors share stories, cold beers and picnics.

During these multi-level sailboat races, the harbor is filled with color — flags flapping, spinnakers sailing and boats darting in and out.

DESSERTS

Charlotte Russe

*"A favorite from **Charleston Receipts** that deserves repeating."*

Average
Prepare Ahead

Serves: 6
Chill: 2-3 hours

1	pint whipping cream	¼	cup cold milk
1	teaspoon vanilla	¼	cup warm milk
½	cup sugar	5	egg whites
¼-	½ cup sherry (more if you wish)		lady fingers, split
½	tablespoon gelatin		

♦ Whip cream with vanilla, sugar and sherry until stiff.
♦ Soften gelatin in cold milk, then dissolve in warm milk.
♦ Cool, then add to whipped cream, beating continuously.
♦ Whip egg whites, then add to whipped cream mixture.
♦ Pour in bowl or dessert glasses lined with lady fingers.
♦ Chill until ready to serve.

Mrs. J. Stanyarne Stevens (Caroline Simonds)

Chocolate Mousse Annabelle

"A rich, but light conclusion to a special dinner."

Complicated
Prepare Ahead
Freezes Well

Serves: 10-12
Bake: 28 minutes at 350°

9	large egg yolks	1	tablespoon + 2 teaspoons
1	cup sugar		orange liqueur
	zest of ½ orange	9	large egg whites
3	packages (4 ounces each) sweet		pinch of salt
	cooking chocolate	1	pint whipping cream
¾	cup butter, sizzling hot	¼	cup confectioner's sugar

♦ Butter spring-form pan.
♦ Process yolks and sugar 1 minute. Remove from bowl.
♦ Process zest and chocolate. Pour in hot butter and process 10 seconds. Add yolk/sugar and 1 tablespoon orange liqueur. Process 5 seconds.
♦ Beat egg whites until frothy. Add salt. Whites should be firm and shiny, not dry.
♦ Spoon out ¼ of whites into chocolate and process 4 times. Put chocolate into egg whites. Spread half of mixture in pan and bake 28 minutes.
♦ Cool 20 minutes.
♦ Process ½ pint cream 15 seconds until thickened. Add 2 teaspoons liqueur and 2 tablespoons confectioner's sugar. Process until thick.
♦ Fold into remaining chocolate mixture. Spread over cooled shell and freeze.
♦ Thaw 2-3 hours in ice box before serving.
♦ Garnish with whipped cream sweetened with remaining confectioner's sugar.

Mrs. G. Simms McDowell III (Elsa Freeman)

Lemon Mousse "Eggs" with Raspberry Sauce
"A colorful finish."

Average   **Serves:** 6
Prepare Ahead   **Chill:** 2-3 hours

Mousse

2½ teaspoons unflavored gelatin   1   teaspoon grated lemon rind
¾   cup sugar   3   egg whites
¼   cup fresh lemon juice   pinch cream of tartar

♦ In large bowl, sprinkle gelatin over ¼ cup cold water and let set 10 minutes until softened.
♦ Add 1 cup boiling water and ¾ cup sugar, stirring until sugar dissolves.
♦ Stir in lemon juice and rind.
♦ Chill mixture for 1 hour or until just begins to set.
♦ Beat with electric mixer until light and frothy.
♦ In separate bowl, beat egg whites until stiff with a pinch of cream of tartar until they will hold soft peaks.
♦ Stir meringue gently into lemon mixture and chill mousse covered 1 hour or until set.

Sauce

3   10-ounce packages frozen   3   tablespoons heavy cream
    raspberries, thawed and   fresh raspberries or mint for
    drained   garnish
1½ tablespoons sugar

♦ Pureé in food processor raspberries, sugar, and cream.
♦ Force mixture through sieve into bowl.
♦ Divide sauce among 6 chilled plates, using a soup spoon to make 3 "eggs" on each plate.
♦ Add garnish.

Mrs. Thomas F. Stevenson III (Irven Myer)

Ouma's Mousse in Minutes
"Ouma is South African for Grandmother."

Easy   **Serves:** 4-6
Prepare Ahead   **Freeze:** 6 hours
Freezes Well

1   box frozen raspberries or   ½   cup sugar
    strawberries   1   teaspoon lemon juice
1   pint sour cream

♦ Mix all ingredients in electric blender or mixer until smooth.
♦ Put in shallow dish in freezer for a couple of hours.
♦ Stir and return to freezer to refreeze before serving.

Mrs. Norman Howard Bell (Ledlie Dinsmore)

Amaretto Mousse

Average
Prepare Ahead

Serves: 16
Chill: 4 hours

4 egg yolks
2 envelopes unflavored gelatin
1 cup sugar

1 cup Amaretto
1 quart whipping cream, whipped
2 tablespoons water

♦ Dissolve gelatin in water as on package directions. Stir over boiling water.
♦ Beat egg yolks until very light in color, with 2 tablespoons water.
♦ Cook eggs over double boiler and whisk until it resembles pudding. (Do not cook too long or over too high heat because eggs will cook too much.)
♦ Add gelatin to eggs after they have cooled slightly.
♦ Add sugar, Amaretto, and whipped cream and fold with a spatula.
♦ Pour into 2 quart soufflé pan and refrigerate 4 hours or overnight.

* Soufflé pan should have a collar. Use aluminum foil and measure it to fit around the pan. Do the same with saran wrap. Place aluminum foil on top of saran wrap and fold in half — with saran wrap on outside. Wrap around sides and crimp the ends.

Mrs. Gregory A. Jones (Betsy Fant)

Quick Chocolate Mousse

Easy
Prepare Ahead

Serves: 6
Chill: overnight

1 cup heavy cream
½ cup sugar
¼ cup water
2 eggs

1 6-ounce package semi-sweet chocolate morsels
1 teaspoon instant coffee
4 tablespoons brandy

♦ Whip cream until soft peaks forms.
♦ Heat sugar and water in small saucepan until sugar dissolves. Simmer for 2 minutes.
♦ Mix eggs and chocolate in food processor or blender. Add coffee and sugar mixture while machine is running. Mix for 2 minutes.
♦ Add brandy and mix for 30 seconds more.
♦ Fold chocolate mixture into whipped cream.
♦ Pour into a 1-quart casserole or individual dessert cups and refrigerate overnight.

Mrs. William T. Tamsberg (Merle Sparkman)

Peach Crisp

"Will keep several days in the refrigerator."

Easy
May Prepare Ahead

Serves: 6
Bake: 30 minutes at 350°

2	pounds firm fresh peaches (8-10 medium sized)
1	tablespoon sugar
1	tablespoon lemon juice
¾	cup quick-cooking rolled oats

½	cup brown sugar
½	cup all-purpose flour
6	tablespoons butter, softened
	vanilla ice cream

♦ Preheat oven to 350°.
♦ Peel and slice peaches.
♦ Place in 8-inch pie pan and sprinkle with sugar and lemon juice.
♦ Cream brown sugar and butter and add flour and oats. Mix well.
♦ Spread mixture over peaches.
♦ Bake for 30 minutes until top is brown and crisp.
♦ Serve warm with ice cream.

* When fresh peaches are not available, use 29 ounce size canned peaches, and omit white sugar and lemon juice.

Mrs. Wade Hampton Logan, Jr. (Virginia Watson)

Fly Dessert

Easy
Prepare Ahead

Serves: 8
Chill: 12 hours

1	15-ounce can sweetened condensed milk
¼	cup fresh lemon juice
¼	teaspoon lemon extract

2	cups fresh blueberries
2	egg whites, stiffly beaten
24	vanilla wafers

♦ Blend together sweetened condensed milk, lemon juice, and extract.
♦ Add blueberries.
♦ Beat egg whites until stiff and fold into mixture.
♦ Line 1½-2 quart casserole with waxed paper.
♦ Cover bottom with filling.
♦ Add layer of whole vanilla wafers, alternating this way until all filling is used finishing with a layer of whole wafers.
♦ Chill in refrigerator, uncovered, 12 hours or longer.
♦ To serve, turn out on small platter, carefully remove waxed paper.
♦ Cut in slices and serve plain or with whipped cream.

Polly Eells

Sherried Custard
"Relatively low calorie dessert."

Average
Prepare Ahead

Serves: 6
Bake: 45 minutes at 325°

2 whole eggs	¼ cup sherry
2 egg yolks	½ teaspoon vanilla
¼ cup sugar	¼ teaspoon almond extract
½ teaspoon salt	pinch of nutmeg
1¾ cup milk	

- Preheat oven to 325°.
- Beat eggs and yolks until well blended.
- Add sugar and salt and stir until dissolved.
- Stir in milk, sherry, vanilla, and almond extract.
- Pour into 6 custard cups and place in a pan of water 1 inch deep and bake 45 minutes.

Mrs. Bachman S. Smith III (Ann Bell)

Boiled Custard
"Our version of an old favorite"

Easy
May Prepare Ahead

Serves: 4
Cook: 15 minutes

2 eggs	2 cups milk
pinch of salt	1 teaspoon vanilla
4 tablespoons sugar	

- Beat eggs.
- Add salt and sugar and continue to beat until mixed well.
- Add milk and mix.
- Cook in double boiler over medium heat until it coats spoon.
- Stir constantly and do not allow to boil.
- Let cool.
- Add vanilla.

Mrs. J. Palmer Gaillard (Henrietta Freeman)

Easy Baklova
"It takes more time, but divine."

Complicated
Prepare Ahead

Serves: 24
Bake: 1 hour and 25 minutes at 300°

4 cups California walnuts (1 16-ounce package), finely chopped	1 teaspoon ground cinnamon
½ cup granulated sugar	1 pound phyllo (strudel leaves)
	1 cup butter or margarine, melted
	1 12-ounce jar honey

♦ Preheat oven to 300°F.
♦ Grease 13 x 9 baking dish.
♦ Mix in large bowl chopped nuts, sugar and cinnamon.
♦ Cut phyllo in 13 x 9 rectangles. Place 1 sheet on dish and brush with butter. Repeat to make five more layers of phyllo.
♦ Sprinkle with 1 cup walnut mixture.
♦ Place 1 sheet phyllo on walnut mixture and brush with butter. Repeat to make 6 more layers of phyllo.
♦ Sprinkle with 1 cup walnut mixture.
♦ Repeat layering 2 more times placing remaining phyllo on top of last walnut layer and brush with butter.
♦ With a sharp knife, cut just halfway through layers in triangular pattern making 24 servings.
♦ Bake 1 hour and 25 minutes or until top is golden brown. While baking heat honey in small sauce pan to hot but not boiling.
♦ Spoon hot honey over Baklava while hot.
♦ Cool on wire rack at least 1 hour, then cover and leave at room temperature until served.

* Keep dough under a moist towel to prevent drying while working.

Mrs. J. Stanley Claypoole (Barbara Pringle)

Steamed Chocolate Pudding with Sauce

Average
Serve Immediately

Serves: 6-8
Steam: 2 hours

2 cups sifted flour	½ cup sugar
2 teaspoons baking powder	1 egg, beaten well
½ teaspoon soda	3 squares unsweetened chocolate, melted
¼ teaspoon salt	1 cup milk
⅓ cup butter	

♦ For pudding, mix ingredients in order, mixing well between each addition.
♦ Turn into greased mold. (If mold does not have a cover, cover with tin foil tightly. A tin can may be used also covered with foil.)
♦ Steam for 2 hours.

Sauce

¼ cup brown sugar, sifted
1 egg yolk
  dash of salt

1 egg white
¼ cup cream, whipped
½ teaspoon vanilla

♦ Add ½ of the sugar and ½ teaspoon vanilla to egg yolk and beat until light.
♦ Add salt to egg white and beat until foamy.
♦ Combine remaining sugar with whipped cream.
♦ Mix these 3 mixtures together.
♦ Serve over hot pudding.

Mrs. Thomas W. Alexander (Patricia Cochrane)

Fruit Pizza

Easy
Prepare Ahead

Serves: 8
Cook: 10-12 minutes

Pizza

1 package refrigerator sugar
  cookie dough
1 8-ounce package cream
  cheese, softened

1 cup powdered sugar
3 tablespoons lemon juice

Combination of fresh and/or canned drained fruit, enough to cover pizza 1-2 inches high. May choose 1 fruit (i.e. strawberries) or combination (i.e. strawberries, blueberries, grapes, bananas, kiwi fruit, pineapple and peaches). If you choose 1 fruit you will need 3-4 cups. If you choose the above combination you will need about ½-¾ cups each.

Glaze

1 cup orange juice
½ cup lemon juice
½ cup hot water

3 tablespoons cornstarch
1 cup sugar

♦ Cook and stir glaze ingredients until it boils for 30 seconds, then cool.
♦ Slice cookie dough and spread over 12-inch pizza pan to cover pan.
♦ Cook as directed on cookie dough package. About 450° 10-12 minutes. It will look like one giant golden brown cookie.
♦ Mix cream cheese, powdered sugar, and lemon juice. Beat until creamy.
♦ Spread cream cheese over cookie.
♦ Cut up fruit and arrange fruit on top of pizza.
♦ Pour cooled glaze over fruit pizza.
♦ Refrigerate and serve when firm and thoroughly cooled.

Mrs. Douglas McAdams (Allison Murray)

Baked Fudge Dessert

Easy
May Prepare Ahead

Serves: 6-8
Bake: 45 minutes at 300°

2 cups sugar	½ pound real butter, melted
½ cup flour	2 teaspoons vanilla
½ cup cocoa	1 cup chopped pecans
4 eggs well beaten	whipped cream

- Preheat oven to 300°.
- Mix sugar, flour, and cocoa. Add to beaten eggs and mix thoroughly.
- Add butter, vanilla, and nuts.
- Pour into 9 x 9 pan or glass baking dish and place in a pan of hot water.
- Bake for 45 minutes or a little longer. Check by inserting a silver knife. It will have the consistency of custard but will not be stiff. As it cools it will become firmer.
- Cut into squares and serve with fresh whipped cream.

Kelly Warner

Easy Baked Alaska

Easy
Prepare Ahead

Serves: 10-12
Bake: 8-10 minutes at 350°
Freeze: overnight

Crust

1¼ cups vanilla wafer crumbs	⅓ cup melted butter
¼ cup finely chopped walnuts	

Pie

1 pint coffee ice cream, softened	5 egg whites
1 pint chocolate ice cream, softened	⅓ teaspoon cream of tartar
	6 tablespoons sugar

- The day before serving, prepare crust by combining all ingredients and press into 9-inch springform pan.
- Bake at 350° for 8-10 minutes.
- Cool thoroughly.
- Spread coffee and chocolate ice cream into two separate layers.
- Cover and freeze until firm.
- Mix egg whites and cream of tartar until stiff peaks form.
- Gradually add sugar until stiff and glossy.
- Pile meringue on pie and freeze overnight.
- 10 minutes before serving put on cookie sheet and bake at 450° for 5 minutes or until meringue tips brown.
- Serve immediately.

Mrs. G. Simms McDowell, III (Elsa Freeman)

English Trifle – My Version
"Beautiful and Delicious"

Easy
Prepare Ahead

Serves: 6-8
Chill: 4 hours

2   packages lady fingers
2   packages frozen raspberries, thawed
    amaretto, enough to saturate, about 1 cup
2   3¾-ounce packages sliced almonds, lightly toasted

2   3¾-ounce packages instant vanilla pudding
½   pint whipping cream, whipped
    nutmeg

♦ Drain raspberries and save juice.
♦ Prepare instant pudding according to package directions.
♦ In trifle bowl, layer the ingredients as follows: lady fingers, amaretto, sliced almonds, raspberry juice, raspberries, and vanilla pudding. Make as many layers as you desire.
♦ Cover with plastic and let stand in refrigerator to blend flavors.
♦ Top with whipped cream and a dash of nutmeg.

Mrs Robert H. Moore II (Barbara Black)

Grape Sundae

Easy
Prepare Ahead

Serves: 4
Chill: 2-5 hours

1   pound green seedless grapes
¼   cup cognac (or brandy of your preference)
¼   cup honey
½   teaspoon lemon juice (optional)

1   8-ounce sour cream (plain yogurt or whipping cream, whipped)
½   cup dark brown sugar

♦ Rinse grapes; drain.
♦ Mix cognac, honey, and lemon juice in separate container.
♦ Pour liquid over grapes to marinate 2-5 hours or overnight.
♦ Prior to serving, mix sour cream and brown sugar, allowing sugar to melt in sour cream.
♦ Divide grapes into 4 dessert dishes or goblets and spoon sour cream mixture over grapes.

* Can also be served as fruit and dip at a Cocktail Party!

Emma McLain

Celia's Chocolate Bread Pudding

Average
Serve Immediately

Serves: 6-8
Bake: 1 hour at 350°

2 cups white bread (day old bread, not good if fresh)
3 cups milk
1 cup sugar
4 eggs

1 teaspoon vanilla
4 squares Baker's unsweetened chocolate
heavy cream (optional)

- Preheat oven to 350°.
- Cut crusts off bread and crumble bread up into little pieces.
- Add sugar to 2 cups milk and pour over bread to soak thoroughly.
- Mash and beat bread so that it doesn't show lumps in pudding.
- Melt chocolate in a small pan with 1 cup milk. Set aside.
- Beat eggs in with bread. Add vanilla.
- Add melted chocolate to mixture and stir.
- Pour into 4½-5 cup soufflé dish. While baking it will rise like a soufflé.
- Serve immediately in individual bowls and pass the cream in a pitcher.
- Also good served with ice cream.

Mrs. Thomas Waring (Janice Duffie)
Mrs. Robert Berretta (Randolph Waring)

French Cream Dessert
"Pretty served in stemmed glasses."

Easy
Prepare Ahead

Serves: 6-8
Chill: 3 hours

1 pint whipping cream
1½ cups sugar
1 ¼-ounce package unflavored gelatin
1 pint sour cream

1 teaspoon vanilla extract
1 cup cold water
1 10-ounce package frozen raspberries, thawed

- In top of double broiler, heat together whipping cream and sugar.
- Soften gelatin in one cup cold water in small bowl for 5 minutes.
- Add gelatin to cream mixture and heat.
- Chill for several hours until thickened.
- Add sour cream and vanilla extract.
- To serve, spoon desired amount into stemmed glass and garnish with raspberries.

Mrs. Morgan Millis (Joanna Morgan)

Heavenly Chocolate Roll
"A great presentation."

Average
Prepare Ahead

Serves: 12-14
Bake: 15 minutes at 350°
Chill: 3 hours

6 eggs, separated and at room temperature
¾ cup sugar
6 squares semi-sweet chocolate
3 tablespoons strong cold coffee

pinch of salt
cocoa
1¼ cups heavy cream
2 tablespoons confectioner's sugar
½ teaspoon vanilla

- Preheat oven to 350°.
- Beat eggs yolks until creamy; gradually beat in sugar until mixture is very thick and light in color.
- Place the chocolate and coffee in double boiler over hot but not boiling water, to melt.
- Stir the melted chocolate into the yolk mixture.
- Beat egg whites with salt until stiff, but not dry.
- Carefully fold whites into the yolk mixture.
- Turn mixture into 10 x 15 jelly roll pan that has been greased, lined with wax paper, and greased again. Spread mixture evenly with spatula.
- Bake 15 minutes.
- Cool on rack, covering the top of cake with damp dish towel for at least 1 hour.
- Sift a layer of cocoa evenly over a piece of wax paper that is slightly larger than jelly roll pan. Invert cake on this cocoa and carefully remove top wax paper.
- Beat heavy cream with confectioner's sugar and vanilla until thick.
- Spread over chocolate roll and roll like a jelly roll placing seam on platter.
- Chill several hours.
- Cut 12-14 slices.

* Also delicious with softened ice cream, but must be frozen, not chilled.

Mrs. William McCullough (Betty Davis)

Cheese Filled Pears

Easy
Partial Prepare Ahead

Serves: 4
Bake: 30 minutes at 350°

4   pears, halfed, peeled and cored
1   8-ounce package of
     cream cheese, softened

¼   cup honey
¼   cup vanilla wafer crumbs

- Combine cream cheese and honey.
- Beat until well blended.
- Fill pear halves with mixture.
- Place in shallow baking pan.
- Sprinkle with crumbs.
- Bake 30 minutes at 350° or until tender.

* Crushed pecans may be added to mixture.

Margaret M. Meynardie

Cheese Cake

Average
Prepare Ahead
Freezes Well

Serves: 10
Bake: 50 minutes at 350°
Chill: 5 hours

Crust

⅓   pound graham crackers, crushed
¼   cup sugar

½   cup butter, melted

Cake

24   ounces cream cheese,
      softened
4   eggs

1½ cups sugar
4   teaspoons vanilla
2   teaspoons lemon juice

Topping

1   cup sour cream
3½ tablespoons sugar

1   teaspoon vanilla

- Mix the crust ingredients together and press on bottom of ungreased 12-inch springform pan.
- Beat cream cheese in bowl, then add eggs, sugar, vanilla, and lemon juice.
- Transfer mixture into springform pan.
- Bake 30 minutes. Cover with aluminum foil and bake 10 minutes more.
- Take from oven and cool 5 minutes. While cake is cooling mix the topping ingredients.
- Spread topping evenly over cake.
- Bake 10 minutes longer.
- Let cool and then refrigerate for at least 5 hours or overnight.

Sara Turpin

Chocolate Torte

Average
May Prepare Ahead

Serves: 10 to 12
Cook: 10 to 20 minutes
Chill: 3 hours

12 ounces semi-sweet chocolate pieces
14 ounces Eagle brand condensed milk
½ cup butter
2 tablespoons water

2 tablespoons Kirsch
2 dozen lady fingers, split
1 cup heavy cream
1 tablespoon confectioner's sugar
1 teaspoon vanilla

- In a double boiler, over hot water, combine chocolate, milk, butter, and water. Heat until smooth.
- Remove from heat and stir in Kirsch.
- Line 9 x 5 x 3 pan with foil. Then line bottom and sides with 27 lady finger halves.
- Pour ⅓ of chocolate mixture over bottom layer.
- Use 7 lady finger halves to make another layer. Cover with chocolate.
- Repeat layers 2 more times ending with lady finger layer.
- Chill at least 3 hours.
- Just before serving, whip cream with sugar and vanilla.
- To serve, lift foil from pan, slice thinly and dollop with whipped cream.

Mrs. Philip W. Cotton (Ann Copenhaver)

Ice Cream Cake
"Light dessert for summer evenings."

Easy
Prepare Ahead

Serves: 12
Freeze: 2 hours

1 large packaged angel food cake
½ gallon vanilla ice cream
1 6½-ounce package thin mints, chopped

1 cup pecans, chopped
1 teaspoon peppermint extract

- Slice cake into 3 layers.
- In a large mixing bowl, combine rest of the ingredients.
- Place 1 layer of cake on a serving plate and ice with ice cream mix. Top with next layer and continue adding ice cream, ending up with ice cream on top.
- Freeze immediately for at least 2 hours.
- If you make more than a day ahead, wrap tightly after the ice cream hardens.
- For ease in cutting, use a wet knife.

Mrs. Robert H. Hood (Bernie Burnham)

Meringue Ice Cream Torte

Average
May Prepare Ahead

Serves: 12
Bake: 2 to 3 hours at 225°
Freeze: until ready to serve

3	egg whites, room temperature	1	cup sugar
1	teaspoon vanilla	½	gallon coffee ice cream
1	teaspoon vinegar	1	jar fudge topping
1	teaspoon water	1	pint whipping cream
⅛	teaspoon salt	¼	cup powdered sugar

- Combine egg whites, vanilla, vinegar, water, and salt.
- Beat until peaks form, gradually add sugar, and continue beating until whites are very stiff.
- Draw 8-inch circles on 3 pieces of waxed paper.
- Spread meringue in circles to form 3 layers.
- Bake at 225° for 2-3 hours or until dry.
- Cool and store in plastic bags for up to 3 days.
- Slightly soften ice cream and spread on 2 of the meringue layers, topping each layer with fudge sauce. Top with the 3rd meringue layer.
- Whip cream, add powdered sugar, and use this mixture to ice torte, piping extra whipped cream around top.
- Freeze until ready to serve.

Mrs. William C. Cleveland (Anne Walker)

Blue Ribbon Cheese Cake Torte
"Not for the weak of heart!"

Easy
May Prepare Ahead

Serves: 8 to 10
Bake: 25 minutes at 350°
Chill: 2 hours

24	ounces cream cheese	1	teaspoon vanilla
4	egg whites	⅔	cup zweiback crumbs (8 slices)
1	cup sugar		

Topping:

2	cups thick sour cream	⅓	cup almonds, toasted, shaved,
½	teaspoon vanilla		blanched
2	tablespoons sugar		

- Cream cheese until soft.

- Beat egg whites until stiff, then blend in 1 cup sugar. Combine the eggs with the cheese and add vanilla. Beat well.
- Pour into 8-inch spring pan 3-inch deep, buttered and dusted with zwieback.
- Bake at 350° for 25 minutes.
- Mix together sour cream, sugar, and vanilla. Spread over top of cake.
- Sprinkle with almonds.
- Bake 5 minutes longer at 475°.
- Chill 2 hours. Unmold.

* If desired, garnish with fresh fruits or dessert fruit topping (cherry, strawberry).

Mrs. William M. Lemmon (Jane Reimer)

Chocolate Chip Tortoni

Average
Prepare Ahead

Serves: 8
Freeze: 4 hours

1	egg white	½	cup semi-sweet chocolate chips
4	tablespoons sugar	1	teaspoon margarine
1	cup whipping cream	¼	cup toasted almonds, finely
2	teaspoons vanilla		chopped

- Set control of freezer at coldest point.
- Beat egg white until stiff, but not dry. Gradually add 2 tablespoons of sugar and beat until stiff and satiny.
- Whip cream, remaining sugar, and vanilla until stiff.
- Fold cream mixture into egg white mixture.
- Pour into freezing tray and chill until the mixture has frozen ½ inch from sides of tray.
- Melt chocolate chips and shortening over hot water (not boiling).
- Stir frozen mixture until smooth, but not melted. Fold in melted chocolate as you drizzle it slowly over cream mixture. This "chips" the chocolate.
- Pour into 8 2-ounce paper cups placed in a muffin tin. Sprinkle with almonds.
- Continue to freeze until firm.
- For a different flavor, substitute strong coffee or creme de menthe for the vanilla flavoring...or experiment with other flavors!

Mrs. William M. Lemmon (Jane Reimer)

Apple Bavarian Torte

Average
May Prepare Ahead

Serves: 8
Bake: 30 minutes at 450°/400°

Crust

½ cup softened butter
⅓ cup sugar

½ teaspoon vanilla extract
1 cup all purpose flour

Filling

2 8-ounce cream cheese, softened
½ cup sugar

2 eggs
1 tablespoon vanilla

Topping

4 cups peeled, cored and thinly sliced golden delicious apples
⅓ cup sugar

½ teaspoon cinnamon
½ cup chopped walnuts or pecans

- Preheat oven to 450°.
- For crust, cream butter and sugar, stir in vanilla.
- Add flour and mix well.
- Spread in bottom and up 2 inches on side of 9-inch greased springform pan.
- For filling, combine cream cheese and sugar.
- Beat in eggs and vanilla. Mix well.
- For topping, place apples in mixing bowl. Mix with sugar, cinnamon, and nuts.
- Pour cream cheese mixture into crust.
- Arrange apples in concentric circles on top.
- Bake in preheated oven 450° for 5 minutes.
- Reduced heat to 400° and bake 25 minutes.
- Cool in pan before serving.

Mrs. Henry West (Sally Izard)

CAKES

Orange Date Cake

Average
May Prepare Ahead

Yields: 1 tube cake
Bake: 45 minutes to 1 hour at 325°

Cake

½ cup butter
1 cups sugar
2 eggs
2 cups all-purpose flour
¼ teaspoon salt

1 teaspoon baking soda
⅔ cup buttermilk
1 8-ounce package dates, chopped
1 cup chopped pecans
1 teaspoon grated orange rind

Orange Glaze

¾ cup orange juice
1 cup sugar

1 teaspoon grated orange rind

- Preheat oven to 325°.
- Cream butter; gradually add sugar, beating well.
- Add eggs, one at a time, beating well between each one.
- Dissolve soda in buttermilk.
- Add salt to flour, stirring thoroughly.
- Coat dates and nuts with small amount of flour. Set aside.
- Add flour to creamed mixture, alternating with buttermilk, ending with flour.
- Add dates, nuts, and orange rind to mixture. Stir until just moistened.
- Spoon batter in greased tube pan.
- Bake 45 minutes to 1 hour.
- For orange glaze, mix all ingredients and bring to boil, stirring constantly until sugar dissolves.
- While cake is still hot, prick surface and pour orange glaze over cake in pan and cool 10 minutes before removing from pan.

Catherine T. Brooks

Fulton Plantation Apricot Pound Cake

Average
May Prepare Ahead

Yields: 1 2½-quart bundt cake
Bake: 1 hour at 325°

Cake

2	sticks of unsalted butter, softened	1	teaspoon vanilla
3	cups sugar	1	teaspoon orange extract
6	large eggs	1½	teaspoons rum
1	cup sour cream	3	cups sifted all-purpose flour
⅔	cup apricot brandy	½	teaspoon salt
		¼	teaspoon baking soda

Topping

2	dozen Turkish apricots	1	tablespoon cornstarch
½	cup unsalted butter	½	cup apricot brandy
½	cup light brown sugar	¼	cup rum
2	teaspoons milk		

- Preheat oven to 325°.
- In a large bowl, cream the butter, adding sugar a little at a time. Beat until light and fluffy.
- Add eggs while beating, one at a time.
- Add sour cream, brandy, vanilla, orange extract, and rum.
- Sift together flour, salt, and baking soda in separate bowl.
- Add dry ingredients to butter mixture and stir.
- Transfer batter to well-buttered and floured 2½-quart bundt pan.
- Bake one hour or until cake tester inserted in center comes out clean.
- Let cool in pan on rack for one hour.
- For topping, mince 16 apricots in food processor with metal blade.
- Soak these apricots in the brandy and rum for at least 4 hours.
- After marinating, combine all ingredients in small sauce pan over low heat and stir constantly until thickened.
- Spoon slightly cooled mixture over cake and decorate with remaining 8 apricots.

Mr. John H. Bennett

The Best Apple Cake

"Absolutely The Best!"

Average
May Prepare Ahead

Yields: 1 9-inch tube cake
Bake: 1½ hours at 350°

Cake

2	sticks unsalted butter	½	teaspoon mace
2	cups sugar	1¾	teaspoons baking soda
3	cups flour	1	cup raisins
2	cups chunky applesauce	1	cup chopped pecans
1	teaspoon cinnamon	1	teaspoon vanilla
1	teaspoon nutmeg		

Frosting

2	cups light brown sugar	1	teaspoon vanilla
6	tablespoons heavy cream	1	cup sifted powdered sugar
½	stick butter		

- Preheat oven to 350°.
- Cream butter and sugar thoroughly.
- Fold in applesauce.
- Sift together flour, spices, and baking soda.
- Take ¼ cup of dry ingredients to dredge the raisins and nuts.
- Fold flour mixture into butter-sugar mixture.
- Add vanilla, nuts, and raisins.
- Pour in well-buttered and floured 9-inch tube pan.
- Bake in oven 1½ hours. Cool in pan.
- For frosting, put all ingredients, except powdered sugar and vanilla, in a heavy bottomed pan.
- Slowly bring to rolling boil, stirring constantly.
- Remove from heat and beat in powdered sugar and vanilla.
- Pour over top and sides of cake. The frosting is a hard setting one, so don't spread with a spatula.

Mrs. Henry C. West (Sally Izard)

Heavenly Hash Cake

Average
May Prepare Ahead

Yields: 1 9 x 13 cake
Bake: 20 to 25 minutes at 350°

Cake

4	eggs	4	tablespoons cocoa
2	cups sugar	1	or 2 cups chopped nuts
2	sticks soft butter or margarine	2	teaspoons vanilla
1½	cups self-rising flour	1	small bag marshmallows

Icing

1	box confectioner's sugar	½	cup evaporated milk
4	tablespoons cocoa	4	tablespoons melted butter

- Preheat oven to 350°.
- Mix by hand the eggs, sugar, and butter.
- In a separate bowl, mix flour, cocoa, chopped nuts, and vanilla. Add this to the egg mixture.
- Bake in well-greased and floured pan for 20-25 minutes.
- When done, cut large marshmallows in half and place on cake while hot. Return to oven for a few minutes more.
- Combine all icing ingredients and stir until smooth.
- Pour icing over hot cake and marshmallows.

Grandmother's Applesauce Cupcakes

Average
May Prepare Ahead
Freezes Well

Yields: 15 to 18 cupcakes
Bake: 20 to 25 minutes

½	cup shortening	1	teaspoon allspice
1	cup granulated sugar	½	teaspoon cloves
2	teaspoons baking powder	½	teaspoon nutmeg
1	teaspoon baking soda	1	cup soaked raisins
2	cups all-purpose white flour	1	cup chopped pecans
½	teaspoon salt	1	egg, well-beaten
½	teaspoon cinnamon	1	16-ounce can applesauce

- Preheat oven to 350-375°.
- In a large mixing bowl, cream butter and sugar until light and fluffy.
- Add beaten egg and mix well.
- Add applesauce and mix.
- Mix together all dry ingredients. Slowly add to cream mixture.
- Next add raisins and nuts, to blend.
- Place batter in lined cupcake tins and bake 20-25 minutes.

Mrs. William R. Lomax (Nadine Nielsen)

Traveling Cupcakes

Average
May Prepare Ahead

Yields: 1 dozen
Bake: 25 minutes at 350°

4 squares semi-sweet baking chocolate	1¾ cups sugar
1 cup butter, no substitutes	1 cup unsifted flour
1¾ cups broken nut meats	4 large eggs, beaten
	1 teaspoon vanilla

♦ Melt chocolate and butter in double boiler.
♦ Add nuts and stir until well coated.
♦ Combine sugar, flour, eggs, and vanilla. Do not beat.
♦ Add chocolate/nut mixture and mix carefully, again not beating.
♦ Turn into paper cups ⅔ full.
♦ Bake 350° for 25 minutes.

Mrs. Ritchie H. Belser (Gale Johnson)

Apple Nut Cake

Easy
May Prepare Ahead
Freezes Well

Yields: 1 bundt cake
Bake: 1 hour at 350°

2 cups sugar	4 eggs
2 cups self-rising flour	2 tablespoons vanilla
4 tablespoons cinnamon	3 large apples, peeled and diced
1 cup vegetable oil	1 cup chopped pecans

♦ Preheat oven to 350°.
♦ Grease and flour bundt pan.
♦ Combine all ingredients in order listed; mix together.
♦ Transfer to bundt pan and bake for 1 hour.

Mrs. Robert K. Sadler (Frances Adele Allen)

Pineapple Cake
"Moist and delicious"

Easy
May Prepare Ahead

Yields: 1 3-layer cake
Bake: 25-30 minutes at 350°

3 cups self-rising flour (sift then measure)
2 cups sugar

4 eggs
2 sticks butter
1 cup buttermilk

- Mix the first 5 ingredients. Reserve 1 cup of batter.
- Pour remaining batter in 3 9-inch cake pans.
- Bake 25-30 minutes at 350°.

Glaze

1 cup batter
1 stick butter

1 cup sugar
1 medium size can crushed pineapple

- Combine glaze ingredients in the top of a double boiler.
- Cook until thick and glossy.
- Spread between layers, on top and sides of cake.

Mrs. William W. Boles, III (Elizabeth Brown)

Pumpkin Cake

Average
May Prepare Ahead

Yields: 1 tube cake
Bake: 1 hour at 350°

2 cups sugar
2 cups flour
1 teaspoon salt
2 teaspoons soda
2 teaspoons cinnamon
4 eggs

1½ cups salad oil
1½ cups pumpkin
½ pound powdered sugar
½ stick butter
1 8-ounce package cream cheese
½ cup crushed pecans

- Preheat oven to 350°.
- Sift dry ingredients together.
- Beat eggs, oil, and pumpkin until well mixed and smooth.
- Add dry ingredients and mix until smooth.
- Pour into well-greased tube pan and bake for 1 hour.
- For icing, mix together butter and cream cheese.
- Add powdered sugar.
- Stir in nuts and spread on cake.

Mrs. William W. Boles III (Elizabeth Brown)

Charleston Chocolate Cake

Average
May Prepare Ahead

Yields: 1 cake
Bake: 25 minutes at 350°

Cake

2	cups all purpose flour	1	cup water
2	cups sugar	4	tablespoons cocoa
½	teaspoon salt	½	cup sour cream
1	teaspoon soda	2	eggs, slightly beaten
2	sticks butter		

Frosting

1	stick butter	1	box powdered sugar
6	tablespoons milk	1	teaspoon vanilla
4	tablespoons cocoa	1	cup chopped nuts

♦ Preheat oven to 350°.
♦ In a large mixing bowl, sift flour, sugar, salt, and soda together and set aside.
♦ Melt butter in saucepan; then add cocoa and water.
♦ Remove from heat and pour over dry ingredients. Mix thoroughly.
♦ Add sour cream and eggs.
♦ Transfer to lightly greased and floured pan (15 x 10 x 2).
♦ Bake 25 minutes. Frost while warm, still in pan.
♦ For frosting, melt butter in saucepan and add milk and cocoa.
♦ Cook over medium heat until it comes to a boil. Remove.
♦ Add powdered sugar, vanilla, and nuts. Beat with mixer.

Barbara Dunbar Lyles

Gateau Chocolat Au Rhum

Easy
Prepare Ahead

Yields: 1 10-inch tube cake
Bake: according to directions
Refrigerate: 2 hours or overnight

1	box devil's food cake mix	1	pint whipping cream
¾	cup white corn syrup	2	tablespoons white sugar
¾	cup white rum		

♦ Bake cake according to package instructions in 10-inch tube pan.
♦ Cool cake in pan for 15 minutes.
♦ Combine corn syrup with rum and pour ¾ cup over cake while in the pan.
♦ When cake is completely cool invert on plate and baste with remaining mixture.
♦ Refrigerate at least 2 hours or overnight.
♦ Shortly before serving whip cream with sugar and spoon on top of cake.

* Chocolate curls or toasted almonds make pretty garnish.

Mrs. John L. Paul (Gaylord Beebe)

White Chocolate Cake

Average
May Prepare Ahead
Freezes Well

Yields: 2 - 9-inch layer pans or
1 large tube pan
Bake: 30 minutes at 350° for layers
and 70 minutes for tube

¼ pound white chocolate	2½ cups cake flour
1 cup butter	1 teaspoon baking powder
2 cups sugar	1 cup buttermilk
4 eggs	1 cup chopped pecans
1 teaspoon vanilla	1 cup coconut
dash of salt	

- Preheat oven to 350°.
- Grease and flour 2 9-inch layer pans or 1 large tube pan.
- Melt chocolate over double boiler.
- Cream butter and eggs and add chocolate.
- Add eggs one at a time, mixing well between additions.
- Add vanilla.
- Sift all dry ingredients together and slowly add to creamed mixture, alternating with buttermilk.
- Stir in nuts and coconut.
- Bake 30 minutes for layers and 70 minutes for a tube.

Mrs. James J. Ravenel (Denie Peeler)

Valentine Cake

Average
May Prepare Ahead

Serves: 12
Bake: 20 to 25 minutes at 375°

Cake

2⅓ cups sifted cake flour	¼ cup maraschino cherry juice
3½ teaspoons baking powder	1 teaspoon vanilla extract
1 teaspoon salt	2 teaspoons almond extract
1½ cups sugar	4 egg whites, unbeaten
½ cup shortening	18 maraschino cherries, chopped
¾ cup milk	½ cup walnuts, chopped

Icing

2 tablespoons shortening	4 cups confectioner's sugar
2 tablespoons butter	6 tablespoons evaporated milk,
1 teaspoon vanilla	scalded
½ teaspoon almond extract	red food coloring
½ teaspoon salt	

- Preheat oven to 375°.

- Sift together all dry ingredients and cream together with shortening.
- Combine milk, juice and extracts.
- Add ¾ cup of the liquid to dry ingredients and mix well.
- Add remaining liquid and egg whites and beat at low speed.
- Add cherries and walnuts and mix well.
- Bake 20-25 minutes and cool.
- For icing, combine all ingredients and beat until smooth.

Mrs. Whitemarsh Seabrook Smith (Anne Frampton)

Chocolate Fudge Cake

Average
May Prepare Ahead

Serves: 15 to 20
Bake: 30 minutes at 350°

Cake

1	stick butter		pinch salt
1	cup sugar	1	16-ounce can Hershey's
4	eggs, separated		chocolate syrup
1	cup flour	1	teaspoon vanilla
1	teaspoon baking powder		

- Cream butter and sugar.
- Separate eggs and add yolks 1 at a time.
- Sift all dry ingredients and add, alternating with chocolate syrup.
- Add vanilla and mix well.
- Beat egg whites until stiff, then fold in.
- Pour into 2 greased and floured 8 x 8 or 8-inch round cake pans.
- Bake 350° oven for 30 minutes.

Frosting

½	stick butter	½	cup semi-sweet chocolate
1	cup sugar		morsels
½	small can evaporated milk		

- Mix and boil butter, sugar, and milk for about 2 minutes.
- Remove and add chocolate morsels.
- Pour on hot cake while frosting is hot.

Mrs. Sam Howell (Lavinia Maybank Grimball)

Angel Bavarian Cake

Average
Prepare Ahead

Serves: 15 to 18
Cook: approximately 20 to 30 minutes
Chill: 4 hours or overnight

4	egg yolks, saving egg whites		1	package gelatin (plain)
1	pint milk		½	cup water
1	tablespoon flour		½	pint whipping cream
1	cup sugar		1	large angel cake loaf
1	pinch salt		1	fresh coconut
1	teaspoon almond flavoring			

- Cook first 5 ingredients until consistency of a thick custard.
- Dissolve gelatin in cold water and add to hot mixture.
- Add flavoring.
- Whip egg whites until stiff. Fold into mixture.
- Slice angel food cake into 4 ½-inch slices.
- Line 9 x 14 pan with 2 of the cake slices.
- Pour half the custard mixture over the cake slices.
- Put another layer of cake and then another layer of custard.
- Let stand 4 hours or overnight.
- Before serving, whip ½ pint cream, add a little sugar to cream, and spread over top.
- Sprinkle generously with fresh grated coconut.
- Cut into squares and serve.

Mrs. Robert W. Keesler (Jeannie Nissen)

Fruit Temptation
"Good over pound cake, ice cream, or alone."

Easy
May Prepare Ahead

Serves: 4

2	oranges, peeled		cinnamon
2	apples, preferably Granny Smith	2	teaspoons poppy seeds
1	lemon		(optional)
1	cup raisins	½	cup sweet vermouth

- Dice apples and peeled oranges from which the seeds have been removed.
- Squeeze juice of lemon over mixture.
- Add raisins.
- Sprinkle generously to taste.
- Mix in remaining ingredients.
- Chill or serve immediately.

* May substitute sherry for vermouth.

Deborah L. Cochelin

CANDIES

Chocolate Amaretto Truffles
"A Christmas favorite"

Average
Prepare Ahead

Yields: 2-3 dozen
Cook: 5 minutes
Chill: about 1 hour

8   ounces sweet baking chocolate
¼   cup Amaretto
2   tablespoons strong coffee
⅓   cup sugar
1   stick butter, cut in pieces

¼   cup ground hazelnuts or pecans
½   cup cookie crumbs (vanilla
     wafers or butter cookies)
½   cup powdered cocoa
¼   cup powdered sugar

♦ Melt chocolate with Amaretto, strong coffee and sugar in top of double boiler over simmering water.
♦ Remove from heat after about 5 minutes. Stir until smooth.
♦ Add butter and mix until melted.
♦ Add ground nuts and cookie crumbs.
♦ Pour mixture into wax paper lined square baking dish.
♦ Refrigerate until firm.
♦ Cut into squares and roll each square into a ball.
♦ Roll each ball in mixture of cocoa and sugar.
♦ Cover and store in refrigerator or freezer.

Catherine T. Brooks

Mexican Fudge
"A different kind of fudge"

Average
May Prepare Ahead

Yields: 3 dozen pieces
Cook: until firm ball stage

3 cups white sugar	1 pound pecans (halved)
1 pint whipping cream	1 teaspoon vanilla
1 cup light syrup	dash salt

♦ Combine sugar, cream and syrup.
♦ Cook over medium heat until a firm ball forms when dropped in water.
♦ Add nuts, vanilla and salt.
♦ Let stand for 5 minutes.
♦ Beat until firm.
♦ Pour into a buttered 8 x 10 pan and cool.

Margaret McI. Meynardie

St. George Chocolate Fudge
"Sure to please any sweet tooth"

Average
May Prepare Ahead

Yields: 64 small pieces
Cook: until soft ball stage

4 cups sugar	1 egg yolk
1 large can evaporated milk	1 teaspoon vanilla
3 tablespoons cocoa	1-2 cups nuts chopped
½ stick margarine	

♦ Mix sugar, milk and cocoa in a saucepan.
♦ Cook on medium heat using candy thermometer.
♦ After mixture bubbles, add margarine.
♦ When thermometer registers one degree below soft boil, add egg yolk by mixing yolk with a small amount of chocolate mix from the saucepan.
♦ Cook until thermometer shows soft ball stage.
♦ Remove pan from heat and put in sink filled with cold water. Beat until cool.
♦ Add vanilla and nuts.
♦ Pour into greased 12 x 8 pan.
♦ Cut into squares when cooled.

Mrs. C. Fletcher Carter III (Bosie Westbury)

Caramel Candy
"Wonderful!"

Average
May Prepare Ahead

Yields: 2 pounds
Cook: until hard ball stage –
45 minutes

1½ cups light corn syrup
1 can (13-ounces) canned milk
(divided in half)
3 cups sugar

½ pound margarine
1 tablespoon vanilla
1 cup pecans, chopped

♦ In a heavy saucepan, combine syrup, ½ can milk, sugar, and margarine.
♦ Cook over medium heat, stirring constantly.
♦ When boiling begins, slowly add the other half can of milk. Boiling should not stop.
♦ Cook until hard ball forms, stirring constantly, about 45 minutes (about 250-260 on candy thermometer).
♦ Cool. Stir in vanilla and nuts.
♦ Pour into a buttered 10 x 12 pan.
♦ Cool completely and cut into squares.
♦ Wrap pieces in waxed paper.

Mrs. Berkeley Grimball (Emily Kirkland)

Almond Bark
"A Treat for all Ages"

Easy
May Prepare Ahead

Yields: 3 to 4 dozen pieces
Microwave: 15 minutes

1½ pounds Hershey bars with
almonds
½ cup chunky peanut butter

1 cup dry roasted peanuts
1½ cups Rice Krispies
1 cup miniature marshmallows

♦ Melt chocolate in microwave.
♦ Add peanut butter and mix until smooth.
♦ Combine cereal and nuts in a large bowl.
♦ Pour chocolate mixture over cereal mixture and mix.
♦ Add marshmallows and mix.
♦ Drop, by teaspoon, onto waxed paper lined cookie sheets.
♦ Put in refrigerator to cool.

Mrs. B. Lee Webb (Ashley)

Tut's Toffee
"Easy and Quick!"

Easy
May Prepare Ahead

Serves: 10 to 12
Bake: 20 minutes at 350°
Chill: 30 minutes

35 saltine crackers	1 12-ounce package of semi-sweet
2 sticks butter	chocolate chips
1 cup brown sugar	1 cup pecans, chopped

- ♦ Preheat oven to 350°.
- ♦ Line 10 x 15 jelly roll pan with aluminum foil.
- ♦ Place saltines (7 down, 5 across) in pan.
- ♦ Combine brown sugar and butter in glass bowl or microwave container.
- ♦ Cook in microwave on high for 4 minutes.
- ♦ Stir thoroughly and pour over crackers.
- ♦ Bake at 350° for 20 minutes.
- ♦ Remove from oven and cover with chocolate chips. When chips melt, smooth over with spatula.
- ♦ Sprinkle with chopped nuts.
- ♦ Chill for ½ hour.
- ♦ Break into bite-sized pieces.

Mrs. Joab Dowling (Tut)

Better Peanut Butter Batter Balls
"A great party treat"

Easy
May Prepare Ahead

Yields: 3 to 4 dozen pieces
No Cooking Required

1 cup crunchy peanut butter	¼ teaspoon almond or vanilla
½ cup dry milk powder	extract
1 cup coconut, shredded	1 cup dates, chopped
	¼ cup sesame seeds

- ♦ Combine peanut butter and dry milk powder in mixing bowl.
- ♦ Stir in coconut, extract and dates. Blend thoroughly.
- ♦ Roll mixture into bite-size balls.
- ♦ Coat with sesame seeds.
- ♦ Store balls in refrigerator.

Mrs. John Skudlarick (Linda)

Minted Nuts
"With a holiday taste"

Average
May Prepare Ahead

Yields: 2 to 4 dozen pieces
Cook: until soft ball stage

1	cup sugar	6	large marshmallows
½	cup water	½	teaspoon peppermint extract or
1	tablespoon light corn syrup		2 drops peppermint oil
⅛	teaspoon salt	3	cups pecan halves

- Combine sugar, water, corn syrup, and salt.
- Cook over medium heat until soft ball stage.
- Remove from heat and stir in marshmallows.
- Add peppermint and nuts.
- Stir until all nuts are coated.
- Cool on aluminum foil.
- Break apart when completely cooled.
- Store in an airtight container.

Mrs. Berkeley Grimball (Emily Kirkland)

Nut Snackers
"Great gift"

Easy
May Prepare Ahead
Freezes Well

Yields: 3 dozen pieces
Bake: 1 hour at 250°

1	egg white	½	teaspoon vanilla
¾	cup brown sugar	1¼	cups pecan halves
2	tablespoons self-rising flour		

- Preheat oven to 250°
- Beat egg white until stiff.
- Mix in sugar, flour and vanilla.
- Fold in pecans.
- Place well-coated pecans, one at a time, on cookie sheets covered with waxed paper.
- Bake 30 minutes.
- Turn off oven and leave nuts in oven for another 30 minutes.
- Remove from paper and store in airtight containers.

Mrs. H. Parker Jones (Josephine Neil)

Date Loaf Candy
"Great for Christmas gifts"

Average
Prepare Ahead

Yields: 3 to 5 dozen pieces
Cook: until firm ball stage

2 cups white sugar
1 small (5.3-ounces) can
  evaporated milk

1 box (8-ounce) dates, chopped
1½ teaspoons dark rum
1 cup nuts, chopped

- Combine sugar, milk and dates.
- Cook over medium heat until mixture forms a firm ball when dropped in water.
- Remove from heat.
- Stir in rum.
- Beat by hand until mixture begins to get stiff and cool.
- Add nuts.
- Form into long rolls (1 to 1½ inches thick) on waxed paper.
- Roll up and refrigerate until firm.
- Next day slice thin rounds off "loaves" and put in tight containers.

Mrs. Edgar S. Jaycocks, Jr. (Lucia Harrison)

COOKIES

Toffee Shortbread

Average
May Prepare Ahead

Serves: 8 to 10
Bake: 20 to 30 minutes at 350°

⅔ cup butter, softened
½ cup sugar
2 cups flour
½ teaspoon salt
½ cup butter
2 tablespoons light corn syrup

½ cup Eagle Brand sweetened condensed milk
½ cup sugar
1 teaspoon vanilla
1 cup semi-sweet chocolate chips

+ Preheat oven to 350°.
+ For crust, beat together butter and sugar.
+ Sift together flour and salt.
+ Combine these mixtures using fingertips or food processor.
+ Press firmly into greased 10-inch springform pan.
+ Bake 20-30 minutes until light brown.
+ Cool.
+ For filling, combine remaining butter, sugar, syrup, milk, and vanilla in a heavy saucepan.
+ Boil for 4 minutes, stirring constantly.
+ Cool until still barely warm.
+ Pour this mixture on cooled shortbread, leaving about ¼-inch around edges.
+ For topping, melt chocolate chips.
+ When toffee is cool, spread chocolate on top.
+ Cut into wedges when chocolate is set.

Mrs. Henry West (Sally Izard)

Butter Cookies
"Great for the holidays"

Easy
May Prepare Ahead

Yields: 4 to 5 dozen
Bake: 10 minutes at 350°

2 sticks butter
1 cup sugar
1 egg

1 tablespoon bourbon
3 cups flour, sifted

+ Preheat oven to 350°.
+ Cream butter and sugar.
+ Add egg and bourbon.
+ Gradually add flour until thoroughly mixed.
+ Put dough in cookie gun and press onto cookie sheets.
+ Bake for 10 minutes.

Mrs. Winston M. Eaddy (Janet Raggio)

Johanna's Cookies
"Excellent item for the church bazaar."

Average
May Prepare Ahead
Freezes Well

Yields: 100 +
Bake: 12 to 13 minutes at 350°

½ cup butter	3½ cups plain flour, sifted
½ cup Crisco	1 teaspoon soda
1 cup sugar	1 teaspoon salt
1 cup brown sugar, firmly packed	1 cup rolled oats
1 egg	1 cup Rice Krispies
1 cup salad oil	½ cup shredded coconut
1 teaspoon vanilla	½ cup nuts, chopped

♦ Preheat oven to 350°.
♦ Cream together butter, Crisco and sugars until fluffy.
♦ Add egg, salad oil and vanilla, mixing well.
♦ Add remaining ingredients.
♦ Form into balls the size of walnuts.
♦ Place on ungreased cookie sheets and flatten with a fork dipped in water.
♦ Bake for 12-13 minutes.
♦ Allow to cool on cookie sheets for a few minutes before removing.

Mrs. George G. Spaulding (Dorie Voss)

Sybil's Cream Cheese Cookies
"Oooh, so good!"

Average
May Prepare Ahead

Yields: 2 dozen
Bake: 15 minutes at 350°

1 stick butter	2 cups sugar
1 stick oleo	2 cups plain flour
1 eight ounce package cream cheese	2 teaspoons vanilla
	½-1 cup nuts, chopped

♦ Preheat oven to 350°.
♦ Cream together butter and oleo.
♦ Add the rest of the ingredients, beating after each addition.
♦ Stir in nuts.
♦ Drop by half teaspoon on cookie sheet sprayed with Baker's Secret or lined with tin foil.
♦ Bake until edges are brown, approximately 15 minutes.
♦ Watch carefully, as they burn easily.

Mrs. Richard M. Kline (Sybil Singleton)

Oatmeal Lace Cookies
"Nice for an afternoon tea."

Average
May Prepare Ahead
Freezes Well

Yields: 200 cookies
Bake: 8 to 10 minutes at 350°

2	cups quick oats	½	teaspoon salt
2	cups sugar	1	teaspoon vanilla
1	cup butter, melted	2	eggs
6	tablespoons flour	½	teaspoon baking powder

♦ Preheat oven to 350°.
♦ Mix ingredients in order listed.
♦ Line cookie sheets with tin foil.
♦ Drop ½ teaspoon batter on cookie sheet, spacing two inches between.
♦ Bake 8-10 minutes.
♦ Cool on foil on cake racks.
♦ Peel from foil when cooled.

Mrs. Claron A. Robertson, III (Martha Ann Monroe)

Christmas Tea Cookies

Average
May Prepare Ahead

Yields: 2½ to 3 dozen
Bake: 45 to 60 minutes at 275°

1	cup butter, softened	2	cups plain flour, sifted
1	cup sugar	1	teaspoon cinnamon
1	egg yolk	1	teaspoon sugar
1	egg white, beaten slightly	1	cup pecans, finely chopped

♦ Preheat oven to 275°.
♦ Cream butter and sugar.
♦ Add egg yolk and beat well.
♦ Blend in flour.
♦ Press dough onto a large cookie sheet, leaving about 2 inches around the sides, because dough will spread during baking.
♦ Brush on slightly beaten egg white and sprinkle with cinnamon and sugar.
♦ Top with finely chopped nuts and gently press into dough.
♦ Bake at 275° for 45 minutes - 1 hour.
♦ Remove from oven and cut into 2-inch squares while still hot. Remove from pan when cooled.

Mrs. E.L. Query (Carolyn Rivers)

Mama's Ice Box Cookies
"Our own slice 'n bakes!"

Average
May Prepare Ahead

Yields: 5 to 6 dozen
Bake: 10 to 12 minutes at 400°

1 cup butter	½ teaspoon salt
2 cups brown sugar, firmly packed	1 teaspoon soda
2 eggs	2 cups pecans, chopped
3½ cups plain flour	

- Preheat oven to 400°.
- Cream butter and brown sugar.
- Add eggs, one at a time, beating well after each.
- Sift flour, soda, and salt together three times.
- Add nuts to flour mixture.
- Combine butter and flour mixtures. This will be very stiff and may need to be mixed be hand.
- Divide dough into two parts. Roll each into a long roll in waxed paper.
- Place in refrigerator overnight or freeze.
- To bake, cut in thin slices and cook 10-12 minutes at 400° until golden.
- Store in an airtight container.

Mrs. William Charles Hood (Barbara Gaines)

Sis' Meringues
"Excellent"

Easy
May Prepare Ahead

Yields: 10 dozen small cookies
Bake: 15 to 20 minutes at 300°

4 egg whites	1½ cups sugar
½ teaspoon cream of tartar	10 ounces of mini chocolate chips
1 teaspoon vanilla	

- Preheat oven to 300°.
- Beat egg whites until they almost stand in peaks.
- Add cream of tartar and vanilla.
- Gradually beat in sugar.
- Beat until stiff.
- Fold in chips.
- Drop by teaspoons onto foil lined cookie sheet.
- Bake at 300° for 15-20 minutes.

Mrs. Floyd I. Dovell, III (Elizabeth Simons)

Brownies

*"A favorite from **Charleston Receipts** that can not be improved."*

Easy
Prepare Ahead

Yield: about 30
Bake: 30 minutes at 350°

¼ pound butter	1 cup flour
2-3 squares unsweetened chocolate	1 cup nuts, chopped
2 cups sugar	1 teaspoon vanilla
2 eggs, beaten	

♦ Melt butter and chocolate over low heat.
♦ Pour over sugar and mix.
♦ Add eggs, flour, vanilla and chopped nuts.
♦ Pour in a greased pan (about 7 x 10).
♦ Bake 30 minutes at 350°.
♦ Cut in squares when hot, then let cool before removing from pan.

* They seem underdone when you cut them.

Mrs. Gustave P. Richards (Lizetta Wagener)

Brownies

"For a special treat, top with ice cream and serve while warm."

Average
May Prepare Ahead
Freezes Well

Yields: 12 large
Bake: 20 minutes at 350°

½ cup butter, softened	½ cup flour
1 cup sugar	¼ teaspoon salt
2 squares unsweetened chocolate, melted	2 teaspoons vanilla
	¼ teaspoon baking powder
2 eggs	1 cup pecans, chopped

♦ Preheat oven to 350°.
♦ Cream butter and sugar.
♦ Melt chocolate and add to above mixture.
♦ Add the rest of the ingredients.
♦ Pour into greased 8 x 8 pan.
♦ Bake for 20 minutes at 350°.

Rachel C. MacRae

Miss Tillie Finley's Fudge Brownies

Average
May Prepare Ahead

Serves: 24
Bake: 20 minutes at 375°

1	8-ounce box unsweetened chocolate squares
½	pound real butter
4	cups sugar

2	cups plain flour, sifted
4	eggs, room temperature
2	cups pecans, broken

- Preheat oven to 375°.
- Melt chocolate and butter in top of double broiler.
- Cool slightly.
- Add sugar, stir, and then add unbeaten eggs.
- Sift in flour.
- Add pecans.
- Pour mixture into 2 greased pans, approximately 9 x 15.
- Bake for 20 minutes at 375°.
- Cut in squares and cool 20 minutes before removing from pan.

Mr. Craig M. Bennett

Peanut Butter Brownies

"Delicious combination of peanut butter and chocolate."

Average
May Prepare Ahead

Yields: 2 dozen
Bake: 20-25 minutes at 350°

½	cup butter
½	cup white sugar
½	cup brown sugar
1	egg
⅓	cup peanut butter

½	teaspoon soda
¼	teaspoon salt
½	teaspoon vanilla
1	cup flour
1	cup oatmeal

Frosting:

1	cup powdered sugar
2	teaspoons cocoa, generous

2-4 tablespoons milk

- Preheat oven to 350°.
- Cream together butter and sugars.
- Blend in egg, peanut butter, soda, salt, and vanilla.
- Stir in flour and oatmeal.
- Spread in greased 8 x 10 pan.
- Cook for 20-25 minutes in a 350° oven.
- For frosting, beat all ingredients until smooth.
- Frost while still warm.

Mrs. Clarence M. Glenn (Ferne Fulton)

Cathy's Chess Squares
"Too easy to be so good!"

Easy
May Prepare Ahead
Freezes Well

Yields: 30 squares
Bake: 55 to 60 minutes at 325°

1 box Duncan Hines butter cake mix (yellow or chocolate)
1 stick butter, melted
1 egg, beaten

1 box 4x confectioner's sugar
1 8-ounce cream cheese, softened
3 eggs

No

- Preheat oven to 325°.
- Mix cake mix, butter and egg.
- Press mixture into 13 x 9 pan.
- Combine sugar, cream cheese and 3 eggs.
- Mix thoroughly and spread over first mixture.
- Bake for 55-60 minutes.
- Cut into squares when cool.

Mrs. Charles E. Bennett (Fran Seabrook)

Pecan Bars
"Mmmm"

Average
May Prepare Ahead

Yields: 24 bars
Bake: 30 minutes at 350°

1 package yellow cake mix (reserve ⅔ cup)
½ cup butter, melted
4 eggs

1½ cups dark corn syrup
½ cup dark brown sugar
1 teaspoon vanilla
1 cup pecans, chopped

- Preheat oven to 350°.
- For crust, mix butter, 1 egg, and cake mix (reserve ⅔ cup).
- Press mixture into a jelly roll pan.
- Bake for 20 minutes at 350°.
- Next, mix remaining ingredients.
- Pour over baked crust.
- Bake for 30 minutes.
- Cut into 1½ x 3-inch bars.
* Can serve with a scoop of ice cream on top.

Mrs. Bachman S. Smith III (Ann Bell)

Brambles

Easy
Serve Immediately

Serves: 24
Bake: 30 minutes at 350°

1   15-ounce package seedless
     raisins
1½ cups sugar
3   eggs, beaten

juice from 2 lemons and grated
rind from 1 lemon
2   packages pie crust mix – enough
     for double crust

♦ Preheat oven to 350°.
♦ Cook all ingredients in double boiler for 15 minutes. Cool.
♦ Roll enough pie crust (a little over half) for bottom and sides of 13 x 9 pan.
♦ Spread raisin mixture over crust.
♦ Roll out rest of mixture for top crust. Fold tightly together all around edges.
♦ Prick all over top of crust with fork.
♦ Bake 30 minutes.
♦ Cut into 2-inch squares while still warm.

Mrs. James Spears (Gayle Reed)

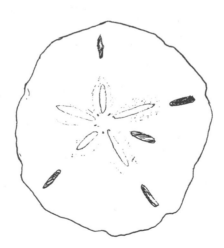

ICE CREAMS

James' Homemade Chocolate Ice Cream

Average
May Prepare Ahead

Yields: 1 gallon
Freeze

5   almond Hershey bars
1   pound can Hershey's chocolate
    syrup
1   cup sugar

1   pinch salt
1   pint whipping cream
1   quart half and half
1   quart milk

♦ Grate candy bars.
♦ Mix all ingredients (except milk) in a large bowl and then pour into churn.
♦ Add milk.
♦ Churn according to churn directions.

Mrs. William R. Gideon (Ann Weaver)

Homemade Ice Cream
"No Cooking"

Average
May Prepare Ahead

Yields: 1 gallon
Freeze:

2   cups fruit (cherries, peaches,
    strawberries, bananas, etc.)
    mashed
½   cup sugar
5   eggs

1   cup sugar
1   can condensed milk (14-ounce)
1   can evaporated milk (13-ounce)
1   tablespoon vanilla
    plain milk

♦ Mash fruit by hand, in blender or processor.
♦ Add ½ cup sugar to fruit and set aside.
♦ Beat eggs until frothy.
♦ Add 1 cup sugar and beat well.
♦ Blend together fruit, egg mixture and canned milks.
♦ Pour into a 1-gallon churn.
♦ Add plain milk to fill line on churn.
♦ Freeze until firm according to freezer directions.
♦ Let ripen about 1 hour.

Mrs. William J. Bates (Cheryl Dangerfield)

Dot Bonham's Coconut Ice Cream
"Wonderful summer treat."

Average
Prepare Ahead

Serves: 8
Chill: 3 days

1 fresh coconut	1 can (5-ounce) evaporated milk
3 cups whipping cream	1½ cups sugar
2 cups half and half	

♦ Crack open coconut, drain milk and reserve.
♦ Peel coconut and grate meat.
♦ Scald cream and half and half. Cool completely.
♦ Add evaporated milk, sugar, and grated coconut.
♦ Refrigerate for 3 days stirring occasionally.
♦ Churn according to churn directions.

Mrs. J. Palmer Gaillard, III (Henrietta Freeman)

Frozen Fruit Ice
"A child's delight."

Average
May Prepare Ahead

Serves: 6 to 8
Freeze

1 egg	juice of one lemon
1 cup sugar	1 8½-ounce can crushed
1 cup water	pineapple, drained
pinch salt	1 banana, mashed
1 cup orange juice	

♦ Mix all ingredients and freeze.
♦ Serve with vanilla ice cream in parfait glasses with cherries on top or serve by itself.

Mrs. David Latimer (Kate Wolfe)

Lime Ice

Average
Prepare Ahead

Serves: 4 to 6
Freeze

1 3¾-ounce lime jello	1 lemon
1 cup sugar	3 cups milk
1 cup boiling water	

♦ Dissolve jello and sugar in boiling water.
♦ Grate lemon rind and squeeze juice from lemon.
♦ Add lemon, rind, and milk to jello.
♦ Stir.
♦ Freeze.

Mrs. Edward J. Reynolds (May Robertson)

Hot Fudge Sauce

Average
May Prepare Ahead

Yields: 1 to 2 cups
Cook: 3 to 5 minutes

2   squares bitter chocolate
1   tablespoon butter˙
⅓   cup half and half
1   cup sugar

⅛   teaspoon salt
2   tablespoons corn syrup
2   tablespoons vanilla

♦ Melt chocolate with butter over low heat.
♦ Gradually stir in half and half and then add sugar, salt and corn syrup.
♦ Bring to a boil for 2-3 minutes.
♦ Remove from heat and add vanilla.
♦ Store in a jar in the refrigerator and reheat to serve over ice cream.

Mrs. Carolyn Hutson (Carolyn Wetherford)

Sherry Syrup For Ice Cream

Easy
May Prepare Ahead

Yields: 1 quart
Cook: 10 minutes

2   eggs, beaten
1   box light brown sugar

1½ cups sherry

♦ Combine ingredients in saucepan.
♦ Cook over low heat, uncovered, for 10 minutes.
♦ Stir constantly.
♦ Serve over ice cream.
♦ Lasts indefinitely in refrigerator.

Elizabeth L. Cleveland

Fudge Sauce
"Heavenly"

Easy
May Prepare Ahead

Yields: 1½ pints
Cook: 30 minutes

½ cup butter
2¼ cup confectioner's sugar
⅔ cup evaporated milk

5 squares bitter chocolate
1 teaspoon vanilla

- Combine butter and sugar in top of a double boiler.
- Heat until butter is melted and mixture is creamy.
- Add chocolate and milk and continue to cook over hot water for 30 minutes, but do not stir while cooking.
- Remove from heat, add vanilla, and beat with spoon.
- Serve over ice cream while still warm.
- Store leftovers in refrigerator and reheat as needed.

Allison Porcher Murray

Easy Almond Amaretto Cream
"Excellent on fruit."

Easy
May Prepare Ahead

Yields: 1 cup
Chill: 1 hour

1 cup sour cream
3 tablespoons confectioner's sugar

½ teaspoon almond extract
3 tablespoons Amaretto liqueur

- Mix all together.
- Use as a dip for fresh strawberries or on top of other fresh fruit.

Mrs. Berkeley Grimball (Emily Kirkland)

PIES

Cottage Apple Pie
"S-o-o-o yummy"

Average
May Prepare Ahead

Serves: 6 to 8
Bake: 30 minutes at 425°

1 prepared pie crust, unbaked	1 tablespoon lemon juice
1½ cups sugar	10 apples, peeled and sliced
1 teaspoon cinnamon	2 tablespoons butter
¼ teaspoon nutmeg	1 cup sour cream
¼ teaspoon allspice	1 tablespoon sugar
1 cup water	dash nutmeg
1 tablespoon cornstarch	

- Preheat oven to 425°.
- Combine sugar, spices, and water.
- Cover and cook over low heat until sugar dissolves, then bring to a boil for 5 minutes.
- Stir in cornstarch and lemon juice.
- Continue cooking and stirring until syrup thickens.
- Add apple slices and cook until apples are tender, stirring carefully and frequently.
- Spoon into pie shell and dot with butter.
- Bake at 425° for 30 minutes.
- Remove from oven and spread with sour cream mixed with sugar.
- Sprinkle with nutmeg and return to oven for 5 minutes.

Mrs. William Strunk (Carol Ann Koeller)

Blueberry Cream Pie
"What a treat!"

Easy
May Prepare Ahead

Serves: 6
Chill: 1 hour

1 prepared Graham Cracker crumb pie shell	1 tablespoon lemon juice
8 ounces cream cheese, softened	1 teaspoon vanilla
½ cup sugar	1 cup whipping cream, whipped
	1 pint blueberries, washed

- Beat cream cheese until light and fluffy.
- Blend in sugar, lemon juice, and vanilla.
- Carefully fold in whipped cream and berries.
- Spoon into crust and refrigerate for at least 1 hour.

Mrs. John Chrisman Hawk, III (Fran Solley)

My Mom's Cherry Ice Box Pie

Easy
May Prepare Ahead

Serves: 8
Chill: 2 to 3 hours

1   prepared 10-inch Graham
   Cracker crust
1   can sweetened condensed milk
¼   cup lemon juice
¼   teaspoon almond flavoring

   a few drops red food coloring
1   No. 2 can of cherries, red, sour,
   pitted
½   pint whipping cream

♦ Mix milk, lemon juice, and almond flavoring.
♦ Add red food coloring to suit.
♦ Drain cherries and add to mixture.
♦ Fill pie crust and chill.
♦ Top with whipped cream.

Mrs. Robert W. Kessler (Jeannie Nisson)

Light Pineapple Pie

Average
May Prepare Ahead

Serves: 6 to 8
Bake: 30 minutes at 350°

20   saltines, crushed
1¼   teaspoons baking powder
4   egg whites
1⅓   cups sugar
1   teaspoon vanilla

1   cup pecans, chopped
1   large container of Cool Whip
1   20-ounce container of crushed
   pineapple, drained

♦ Preheat oven to 350°.
♦ Mix saltines and baking powder.
♦ Beat egg whites until almost stiff, gradually add sugar and continue to beat until mixture forms stiff peaks.
♦ Fold in cracker crumbs, vanilla, and pecans.
♦ Pour into well-buttered 9-inch pie pan.
♦ Hollow out middle to make a place for filling.
♦ Bake at 350° for 30 minutes. Cool.
♦ Mix Cool Whip and pineapple.
♦ Fill pie shell and chill.

* Fresh fruit may be substituted for pineapple.

Mrs. Robert K. Sadler (Frances Adele Allen)

Strawberry Pie I

Average
May Prepare Ahead

Serves: 6 to 8
Chill: 3 to 4 hours

1   9-inch pie shell, baked and
    cooled
1   cup sugar
3   tablespoons cornstarch
1   cup water

dash salt
1   3-ounce strawberry jello (delete
    1 tablespoon)
1   pint strawberries, hulled
    whipped cream

- In a saucepan combine sugar, cornstarch, water, and salt.
- Cook over medium heat, stirring constantly, until thick and clear.
- Add strawberry jello.
- Pour half of mixture into pie shell.
- Arrange strawberries in jello mixture.
- Pour remaining mixture over strawberries.
- Refrigerate until congealed.
- Serve with whipped cream.

Mrs. Laney R. Mills (Nonie Gillmore)

Strawberry Pie II

Average
May Prepare Ahead

Serves: 6 to 8
Chill: 3 to 4 hours

1   9-inch pie shell, baked and
    cooled
1   pint fresh strawberries
1   envelope unflavored gelatin
½   cup sugar

2   eggs, separated
½   cup milk
1   cup strawberry yogurt
1   teaspoon lemon juice

- Puree enough strawberries in blender to equal ¾ cup. Reserve remaining berries for garnish.
- In a medium sauce pan, combine gelatin, ¼ cup sugar, and egg yolks beaten with milk.
- Let stand for 1 minute.
- Stir over low heat until gelatin dissolves (about 5 minutes).
- Using a wire whisk, blend in pureed strawberries, yogurt and lemon juice.
- Chill, stirring occasionally until mixture mounds when dropped from spoon.
- Beat egg whites, adding remaining sugar, until stiff.
- Fold egg whites into gelatin mixture.
- Pour into prepared crust and chill.
- Garnish with reserved strawberries.

* Can substitute fresh peaches and peach yogurt for strawberries.

Mrs. Thomas A. Kirkland, Jr. (Patricia Trotter)

Pear and Custard Tart

Average
May Prepare Ahead

Serves: 6 to 8
Chill: 3 to 4 hours

1 pie shell, baked (deep dish)	1 teaspoon vanilla
½ cup sugar	1 cup sugar
¼ cup cornstarch	1 cup water
dash salt	1 cup orange juice
3 cups milk	2 pears, pared and eighthed
2 eggs, beaten	1 tablespoon cornstarch
2 tablespoons butter	toasted almond slices

♦ In a saucepan combine sugar, cornstarch and salt.
♦ Slowly whisk in milk and eggs.
♦ Cook over medium heat until mixture begins to thicken, about 15 minutes. Watch mixture carefully and stir constantly.
♦ Boil one minute, then remove from heat.
♦ Stir in butter and vanilla.
♦ When mixture has cooled, pour into pie shell and chill.
♦ In a saucepan, combine sugar, water, orange juice.
♦ Bring to a boil, add pears, and simmer 15 minutes or until tender.
♦ Drain pears and reserve one cup of liquid.
♦ Arrange pears on chilled custard.
♦ Slowly add cornstarch to reserved liquid and cook until thickened.
♦ When liquid has cooled, pour over pears to glaze.
♦ Garnish outer rims with almonds.
♦ Chill.

Mrs. E.L. Query (Carolyn Rivers)

Peach Polka-Dot Pie

Average
May Prepare Ahead

Serves: 6 to 8
Bake: 45 minutes at 325°

1 9-inch pie shell, unbaked	½ teaspoon cinnamon
4 large peaches, peeled, pitted and halved	¼ teaspoon salt
½ cup blueberries	1 cup whipping cream, unwhipped
¾ cup sugar	¼ cup slivered almonds
¼ cup flour	

♦ Preheat oven to 325°.
♦ Place peaches cut side down in pierced pie shell.
♦ Sprinkle blueberries over peaches.
♦ Combine sugar, flour, cinnamon, and salt, mixing with a spoon.
♦ Stir in cream and pour over fruit.
♦ Sprinkle almonds over top and bake at 325-350° for about 45 minutes.

Mrs. William J. Bates (Cheryl Dangerfield)

Blender Lemon Pie

Easy
May Prepare Ahead

Serves: 6
Bake: 30 minutes at 350°

1 prepared 9-inch pie shell, baked and cooled
1½ lemons
½ cup water
1½ cups sugar

3 tablespoons plain flour
dash salt
2 eggs
½ stick margarine, melted

- Preheat oven to 350°.
- Wash lemons thoroughly. Quarter and remove the seeds.
- Cut each piece again and put in blender with water.
- Blend well and add sugar. Blend again.
- Add flour, salt, eggs, and margarine. Blend again.
- Pour in pie shell and bake for 30 minutes at 350°.
- When cool, garnish with whipped cream and a sprig of mint.

Elizabeth W. Cannon

Mrs. Calhoun's Pecan Pie

"Nothing tastes better than pecan pie a la mode."

Easy
May Prepare Ahead

Serves: 6 to 8
Bake: 40 minutes at 375°

1 prepared pie shell, unbaked
3 tablespoons butter
1 cup light brown sugar
3 eggs, well beaten

1 cup light corn syrup
1 teaspoon vanilla
dash salt
1 cup pecans (whole or chopped)

- Preheat oven to 375°.
- Cream butter and sugar.
- Add eggs, syrup, salt, and vanilla.
- Add pecans.
- Pour into unbaked pie shell.
- Bake at 375° for approximately 40 minutes.

Mrs. Thomas A. Kirkland, Jr. (Patricia Trotter)

Mocha Frozen Cheese Pie

Easy
Prepare Ahead
Freezes Well

Serves: 10-12
Freeze: 6 hours

1½ cup chocolate wafer cookies, crushed
¼ cup sugar
¼ cup butter or margarine, melted
1 8-ounce package cream cheese, softened
1 14-ounce can Eagle Brand condensed milk

⅔ cup chocolate flavored syrup
2 tablespoons instant coffee in dry state
1 teaspoon hot water
½ pint whipping cream, whipped

- Combine cookie crumbs, butter and sugar, and press into 9-inch springform pan or 13 x 9 baking dish to cover bottom and sides.
- Chill.
- Beat cheese until fluffy, add milk and syrup.
- Dissolve coffee in water and add.
- Mix well and fold in whipped cream.
- Garnish with a sprinkling of wafer crumbs around outer edge.
- Freeze.
- Remove 10 minutes before serving for easier cutting.

Mrs. E.L. Query (Carolyn Rivers)

Kiss Pie

"A mixmaster is a must for this light dessert."

Easy
Prepare Ahead

Serves: 6-8
Bake: 45 minutes at 225°

3 egg whites
1¼ cups sugar
3 tablespoons water
dash of salt
1 teaspoon vanilla

1 teaspoon vinegar
½ pint cream
4 tablespoons confectioners sugar
2 tablespoons grated dark chocolate

- Put first six ingredients in mixmaster bowl.
- Beat constantly for 30 minutes.
- Pour into a pie plate lined with waxed paper.
- Bake 45 minutes at 225°. Not over this temperature!
- Cool for 1 hour.
- Whip cream sweetened with confectioners sugar.
- Fill pie with whipped cream and top with grated chocolate.

Mrs. Joseph Rutledge Young (Elizabeth Jenkins)

Edisto Island Mud Pie
"Irresistible"

Average
Prepare Ahead

Serves: 4 to 6
Freeze

18   oreo cookies
⅓   cup milk
⅓   cup butter, melted
½ - 1 pint vanilla ice cream
½ - 1 pint coffee ice cream

2   squares unsweetened chocolate
½   cup sugar
⅔   cup evaporated milk
1   tablespoon butter
    add nuts if desired

♦ Scrape centers out of oreos and discard or freeze.
♦ Crush cookies and blend with milk and butter.
♦ Shape mixture into crust in a pie pan.
♦ Freeze.
♦ Spread softened vanilla ice cream into frozen crust.
♦ Freeze.
♦ Spread softened coffee ice cream over layer of vanilla.
♦ Freeze.
♦ Blend chocolate, sugar, evaporated milk, and butter in top of double boiler until thickened.
♦ Cool chocolate sauce and pour over ice cream.
♦ Sprinkle with chopped nuts if desired.
♦ Keep frozen.

Mrs. J. Conrad Zimmerman (Barbara Hubbard)

Moncks Corner Chocolate Pie

Average
May Prepare Ahead

Serves: 6 to 8
Bake: 3 to 5 minutes at 350°

1   prepared pie shell, baked
1   cup sugar
¼   cup cocoa
2   tablespoons plain flour
    pinch salt
3   eggs, separated

1½ cups milk
2   tablespoons butter
1   teaspoon vanilla
3   tablespoons sugar
½   teaspoon vanilla

♦ In a saucepan combine sugar, cocoa, flour, and salt.
♦ Add egg yolks and milk.
♦ Cook until thickened. Remove from heat and add butter and 1 teaspoon vanilla.
♦ Cool and pour into pie shell.
♦ Beat egg whites until stiff.
♦ Add sugar and ½ teaspoon vanilla to egg whites.
♦ Top chocolate filling with egg white mixture.
♦ Bake at 350° until golden brown on top.

Mrs. Raymond Lockwood Murphy (Nancy Jane Dennis)

Daiquiri Pie

Average
May Prepare Ahead

Serves: 6 to 8
Cook: 3 to 5 minutes
Chill: 1 hour

Filling:

1   9-inch pie shell, baked
1   envelope unflavored gelatin
½   cup sugar
¼   teaspoon salt
5   egg yolks
½   cup lime juice

¼   cup frozen orange juice
     concentrate, thawed
1   ounce light rum
5   egg whites
½   cup sugar

Topping

1   cup whipping cream
3   tablespoons confectioner's sugar

1   ounce light rum
1   teaspoon grated lime peel

♦ In a saucepan, combine gelatin, sugar, salt, egg yolks, lime juice, and orange juice.
♦ Cook until mixture begins to boil.
♦ Remove from heat and stir in 1 ounce of rum.
♦ Chill mixture until it mounds when spooned.
♦ Beat egg whites until stiff, gradually adding ½ cup sugar.
♦ Fold egg whites into chilled gelatin mixture.
♦ Pour into pie shell and chill until firm.
♦ To serve, whip cream and blend in confectioner's sugar and 1 ounce rum.
♦ Before serving, top pie with cream mixture and sprinkle with grated lime peel.

Mrs. Harold Michaelis (Norma Dewey)

Coffee Velvet Pie
"Excellent"

Complicated
Prepare Ahead

Serves: 6 to 8
Chill: 3 hours

1¾ cups sweet cookie crumbs
4 tablespoons butter, softened
1 envelope unflavored gelatin
¼ cup cold water
3 eggs, separated
6 tablespoons sugar

4 level teaspoons instant coffee
2 tablespoons sugar
1 cup heavy cream
¼ teaspoon cinnamon
1 teaspoon sugar

- Preheat oven to 300°.
- Roll cookies with a rolling pin to make crumbs uniform but not too small.
- Combine crumbs and butter and press into 9-inch pie pan. Reserve ¼ cup of crumbs for topping.
- Bake 10 minutes or until slightly brown.
- Dissolve gelatin in water.
- In a double boiler, combine egg yolks, 6 tablespoons sugar, and instant coffee.
- Beat with spoon until foamy.
- Place over hot water, and when mixture is hot add softened gelatin.
- Stir continuously until custard coats spoon well. Caution – mixture sets quickly; watch closely.
- Remove from heat and cool slightly.
- Beat egg whites with 2 tablespoons sugar until stiff.
- Whip cream until stiff.
- Combine custard, egg whites, and whipped cream.
- Pour into pie shell and top with mixture of reserved crumbs, cinnamon and sugar.
- Chill 3 hours.

Mrs. Rutledge R. Webb (Mary Louis Stevens)

My Version of Charleston Rum Pie

Average
May Prepare Ahead
Freezes Well

Serves: 6 to 8
Cook: 5 to 10 minutes
Chill: 1 hour

1	9-inch pie shell, baked
1	tablespoon gelatin
¼	cup cold water
2	cups heavy cream
2	eggs, separated
¼	cup sugar

6	tablespoons sugar
6	tablespoons golden rum
1	teaspoon vanilla
1	square bitter unsweetened chocolate

- Soak gelatin in water for 5 minutes.
- Scald cream in a double boiler.
- Beat egg yolks with fork and slowly add ¼ cup sugar.
- Combine cream and eggs, stirring constantly.
- Place over boiling water and stir until mixture is smooth and begins to thicken.
- Remove from heat and add gelatin.
- Stir until gelatin is completely dissolved.
- Refrigerate until quite firm.
- Beat egg whites with 6 tablespoons sugar until stiff.
- Whip gelatin mixture until light and fluffy, adding rum and vanilla.
- Fold in egg whites to gelatin mixture.
- Pour into baked pie shell. Refrigerate 1 hour.
- Top with shaved chocolate before serving.

Mrs. Jordan T. Jack (Bennett Pierrepont)

When holidays come, entertaining is elegant and formal. There is an air of gentility and refinement that pervades the season.

But there is nothing stilted about Charleston. Parties have the warmth of being welcomed into friends' houses, of familiar traditions and of festive decorations.

The holidays are a good time for enjoying delectable desserts and for baking sinful sweets to share with friends.

PRESERVES

Charlotte Lide's Peach Conserve

Average
Prepare Ahead

Yield: 7 half-pints
Cook: about 45 minutes

18 firm peaches
5   oranges (use rind of 3 of
    these oranges)
3   lemons (use juice and rind of
    these lemons)

1½ cups sugar to 1 cup fruit
1   cup maraschino cherries, cut
    and drained

- Wash and pit peaches. Do not peel.
- Seed oranges and lemons.
- Combine peaches, oranges and lemons and put through meat grinder.
- Measure fruit and juice.
- Add 1½ cups sugar to each 1 cup fruit.
- Boil mixture until it lips.
- Add cherries and boil one more minute.
- Pour into jars.
- Let cool, then cover with paraffin.

Mrs. John McCrady (Charlotte Lide)

Pear Honey
"Make lots - it will go fast."

Average
Prepare Ahead

Yields: 4-5 pints
Cook: about 1 hour

1   peck of hard cooking pears
5   cups of sugar
2   16-ounce cans of crushed
    pineapple

1   bottle of Marischino cherries
    (if desired)

- Peel and grind pears.
- To 8 cups of pears, add 5 cups of sugar.
- Cook in a large pot, stirring until it comes to a boil.
- Let simmer about 30 minutes.
- Add pineapple and chopped cherries.
- Continue simmering 15 minutes.
- Spoon into hot sterilized jars and seal.

Mrs. Bachman S. Smith, Jr. (Eunice Green)

Fig Marmalade

Easy
Prepare Ahead

Yield: 6 cups
Cook: 30 minutes

2   lemons, thinly sliced
2   pounds fresh sugar figs, washed and blemish free

2   oranges, grated rind and juice
2   pounds sugar

- In small saucepan, simmmer lemon slices in water until tender. Drain.
- Chop figs.
- Combine figs, juice and rind of oranges and sugar in large pot.
- Bring to a boil and cook over low heat for 15 minutes, stirring occasionally.
- Add drained lemons.
- Continue to cook slowly until thick.
- Seal in hot sterile jars.

Mrs. Blaine Ewing, III (Phyllis Walker)

Peach Marmalade
"Delicious"

Average
Prepare Ahead

Yield: 7 half-pints
Cook: about 1 hour

1   orange
1   lemon
1   cup water
2   pounds fresh peaches

5½ cups sugar
1   (1¾-ounce) powdered fruit pectin

- Quarter orange and lemon. Remove seeds and chop fine in food processor.
- Simmer chopped fruit with water for about 20 minutes.
- Remove pits from peaches, cut in chucks and grind in processor. Do not peel peaches.
- Add enough peaches to orange-lemon mixture to make 4 cups.
- Measure sugar and set aside.
- Stir fruit pectin into peach mixture in a heavy 6-8 quart pot.
- Stir over high heat until mixture comes to a full, rolling boil.
- Cook gently for 1 minute.
- Immediately add all the sugar.
- Bring again to a full, rolling boil. Boil for 1 minute, stirring constantly.
- Remove from heat, skim off foam with a metal spoon.
- Stir and skim for 5 minutes to cool slightly and prevent floating fruit.
- Spoon into sterilized jars and seal at once.

Mrs. John L. Paul (Gaylord Beebe)

Granny's Pear Chutney

Average
Prepare Ahead

Yield: 6-8 pints
Cook: 1 hour

8	cups diced pears	3	cups sugar
2	cups seeded raisins	1	tablespoon celery seed
½	cup onions, chopped	1	tablespoon salt
3	cups vinegar	½	teaspoon cayenne pepper

- Combine all ingredients in large sauce pan.
- Cook together for 1 hour, stirring constantly, until thick.
- Pour into sterilized jars and seal.

Susan C. Clarkson

Cranberry Chutney
"A Perfect Holiday Gift."

Average
Prepare Ahead

Yield: 5 half-pints
Cook: about 45 minutes

1	pound (4 cups) fresh cranberries	¼	cup snipped candied ginger
2¼	cups brown sugar	¼	cup lemon juice
1	cup white raisins	2	teaspoons salt
1	cup water	1	teaspoon grated onion
½	cup coarsley chopped toasted almonds	¼	teaspoon ground cloves

- Combine all ingredients in a 5 quart sauce pan.
- Bring to a boil, stirring constantly.
- Reduce heat. Simmer uncovered for 15 minutes; stir occasionally.
- Seal in sterilized jars.

Mr. Eugene Frost Lesesne

Miracle Chutney
"Just don't tell a soul how easy it is!"

Easy
Prepare Ahead

Yield: 6 half-pints
Cook: 30 minutes

1　29-ounce can of fruit cocktail
1　cup light brown sugar
1　cup vinegar
1　clove garlic, crushed
¼　teaspoon crushed dried red
　　pepper

½　teaspoon ground ginger
½　teaspoon salt
1　18-ounce package chopped
　　dates
½　cup apricot jam
½　cup raisins

♦ Drain fruit cocktail.
♦ Boil fruit cocktail with sugar and vinegar for 10 minutes.
♦ Add garlic, pepper, ginger and salt.
♦ Cook 10 minutes more.
♦ Add rest of ingredients and simmer until thick.
♦ Seal in sterilized jars.

Mrs. Nathaniel Ingraham Ball, III (Jane Brooks)

Brandied Cranberries
"An easy Christmas gift."

Easy
Prepare Ahead

Yield: 5 half-pints
Bake: 1 hour at 300°

1　pound cranberries
2¼ cups sugar

4　tablespoons (or more) brandy

♦ Wash and spread cranberries out in a flat pan.
♦ Sprinkle with 2¼ cups sugar.
♦ Cover tightly with foil.
♦ Bake in 300° oven for 1 hour.
♦ Remove from oven and cool slightly.
♦ Put cranberries in a bowl and sprinkle with brandy.
♦ Pour into jars.

Mrs. Kenneth E. Pritchett (Jennifer Boozer)

Lydie's Chow Chow

Average
Prepare Ahead

Yield: 12 pints
Cook: about 1 hour

4 quarts cabbage, shredded (6-8 pounds)	½ dozen bell peppers, green
2 quarts green tomatoes, sliced thin	½ dozen bell peppers, red
	1 quart onions, sliced thin (2 pounds)

Sauce:

1 cup plain flour	1½ quarts vinegar
2 tablespoons salt	1 tablespoon celery seed
2 tablespoons dry mustard	2 pounds sugar (4 cups), brown or white
2 tablespoons tumeric	

- Measure and prepare vegetables and set aside.
- Combine sauce ingredients in large saucepan and bring to full boil.
- Cook for 15 minutes to thicken, stirring carefully. Do not burn.
- Pour cooked sauce over prepared vegetables.
- Cook almost to boil, mixing completely, and careful not to let it stick.
- Seal in sterilized jars.

Mrs. Nathaniel Ingraham Ball, III (Jane Brooks)

Pickled Okra
"A lowcountry favorite"

Easy
Prepare Ahead

Yield: 4-5 pints
Cook: about 15 minutes

3½ pounds small okra	1 pint white vinegar
3 small hot peppers garlic (optional)	1 quart water
2 tablespoons dill seed	⅓ cup salt

- Pack okra in hot jars.
- Put in small pieces of pepper (about ¼ of pepper), small clove of garlic and divide the dill seed among jars.
- Mix vinegar, water and salt and bring to a boil.
- Fill jars and put on lids.
- Place in hot water bath and simmer 10 minutes at 180°—190°.

Margaret M. Meynardie

Chopped Artichoke Pickle
*"A variation of a **Charleston Receipts** favorite"*

Average
Prepare Ahead

Yields: 16-20 pints
Soak: 24 hours
Cook: about 1½ hours

6½ pounds Jerusalem artichokes
 (6 quarts)
4 pounds onions
2 large cauliflowers

12 green peppers
2 gallons water
2 pints salt

♦ Slice vegetables in a food processor.
♦ Mix all together and cover with salt and water.
♦ Let stand 24 hours.
♦ Drain well.

Sauce

2 cups flour
3 small tins dry mustard or 12
 tablespoons

2 tablespoons tumeric
1 gallon vinegar
1 5 pound bag sugar

♦ Mix sauce ingredients in a large pot and boil until it thickens, stirring constantly.
♦ Add vegetables, bring to a boil and seal in jars while hot.

Mrs. Wade H. Logan III (Eunice Smith)

Icebox Cucumber Pickles

Easy
Prepare Ahead

Yield: 1 gallon
Refrigerate

1½ cups water
1½ cups cider vinegar
1½ cups sugar
1½ tablespoons diced onion
¾ teaspoon salt

¾ teaspoon celery seed
½ teaspoon garlic salt
½ teaspoon onion salt
½ teaspoon celery salt
10-12 cucumbers

♦ Put water, vinegar and sugar in blender and mix until sugar is dissolved.
♦ Add remaining seasonings and mix.
♦ Pour over washed and sliced cucumbers.
♦ Cover and refrigerate. This will keep for a month.
♦ When cucumbers get low - just add more to the liquid.

Mrs. William R. Lomax (Nadine Nielson)

"No-Work" Pickles

Easy
Prepare Ahead

Yield: 1 gallon

1   gallon kosher dill pickles, processed (processed must be on jar)

5   pounds sugar
1   ¾-ounce box of stick cinnamon
1   glove garlic, chopped

♦ Drain pickles, discarding juice.
♦ Cut pickles into ⅛ inch slices.
♦ Place in large enamel pot.
♦ Add sugar gradually, stirring until all sugar is dissolved.
♦ Add cinnamon sticks and garlic.
♦ Stir to mix.
♦ Let stand, stirring 3 times a day for 3 days.
♦ Store in large glass containers.

Mrs. W. Dale Blessing (Rosy Hay)

Tomato Relish
"Great on hamburgers."

Average
Prepare Ahead

Yield: 7-8 pints
Cook: about 1 hour

1   peck firm, ripe tomatoes
8   small onions
6   bell peppers, red or green
1   teaspoon salt
1   cup sugar

1   teaspoon cinnamon
1   teaspoon ginger
1   teaspoon cloves
1½ cups vinegar

♦ Peel and grind together tomatoes, onions and peppers.
♦ Add salt, sugar, spices and vinegar to this mixture.
♦ Cook slowly over medium heat for 1 hour.
♦ Pour into pint jars and seal.

Mrs. James J. Ravenel, III (Denie Parker)

Sallie's Tomato Catsup

"Wonderful in homemade soup or on roast pork."

Average
Prepare Ahead

Yield: 2 quarts
Cook: 3 hours over low heat

1	peck of tomatoes
3	tablespoons salt
½	tablespoon cloves
½	tablespoon mace
1	tablespoon allspice
1	tablespoon cinnamon

3	tablespoons black pepper
3	tablespoons dry mustard
3	tablespoons sugar
1	tablespoon red pepper
½	gallon vinegar

♦ Peel tomatoes, scald and pass through sieve or blender.
♦ Add remaining ingredients.
♦ Simmer 3 hours. Let cool.
♦ Bottle when cold.

Mrs. Fred J. Martschink, Jr. (Pauline Califf)

RESTAURANTS

Janson 1985

82 Queen Street
The Baker's Café
Café Picollo
The Colony House
The Common Ground
The Cotton Exchange
East Bay Trading Company
Ferantés
The Francis Marion Hotel
Garibaldi's
The Island House at Wild Dunes
Jilich's
Joe's Pilot House
Joe's Seafood Emporium
The Lodge Alley Inn
The Mills House Hotel
Papillon
Perdita's
Reuben's Delicatessan
Robert's of Charleston
Shem Creek Bar and Grill
Skoogie's
Supper at Seven at the Guild's Inn
The Wine Cellar
The Upper Crust

RESTAURANTS

Robert's of Charleston
Duckling Oriental With Sweet And Sour Sauce

Average
Partial Prepare Ahead

Serves: 4 to 6
Cook: 1 hour 15 minutes

Cooking the Duckling

1	4-5 pound duckling (partially defrosted)	2	carrots, chopped
1	bay leaf	2	ribs of celery, chopped
½	teaspoon thyme	1	small onion, chopped
		4	green onions, for garnish

+ Remove as much skin as possible from the entire duck.
+ Place duck in large stock pot and cover with water.
+ Add vegetables and spices and bring to boil.
+ Skim surface of stock with ladle and simmer duckling for about 1 hour or 1 hour and 15 minutes, until joints are slightly loose.
+ Pierce the knee joint to see if all blood is cooked away.
+ Let duckling cool at room temperature and remove all meat from bones. (Try to remove each breast half in its entirety.)
+ Arrange meat in even piles with thinly sliced breast pieces on top.

Sweet and Sour Sauce

1	cup raspberry preserves (seedless)	2	teaspoons Chinese hoisin sauce
10	ounces chicken broth (canned or made from chicken or duck)	¼	cup red wine
		½	teaspoon chopped garlic
2	tablespoons Japanese bean paste (Miso Paste)		pinch of Chinese Four Spice seasoning (optional)
1	tablespoon soy sauce	1	tablespoon cornstarch diluted with ¼ cup additional wine
1	tablespoon lemon juice		

+ Place all ingredients in pan except cornstarch mixture.
+ Bring to a slow boil.
+ Add cornstarch mixture and stir with wire whip until a boil starts again.
+ Simmer 3 minutes.
+ Strain through a fine sieve and serve over duck.
+ Garnish duck and sauce with thinly sliced green onions.

Robert's of Charleston

325

Robert's Of Charleston
Chocolate Grand Marnier Gateau
"Worth every moment of your time!"

Complicated
Prepare Ahead

Serves: 12
Bake: 15 minutes at 375°
Chill: 2½ hours

Chocolate Cake

6 ounces semi-sweet chocolate	6 egg yolks
½ cup granulated sugar	6 egg whites, stiffly beaten
¼ cup water	1 tablespoon strong coffee

♦ Preheat oven to 375°
♦ Melt chocolate in double boiler.
♦ Mix sugar and water in a saucepan and bring to a boil. Cook for 2 minutes over medium heat.
♦ Place egg yolks in above.
♦ Slowly pour hot sugar syrup over yolks, beating vigorously with whisk for 5 minutes, until it is light, smooth, and pale in color.
♦ Mix in chocolate and coffee.
♦ Add ⅓ of the egg whites to chocolate mixture and mix with a whisk.
♦ Add remaining whites and fold with a spatula – just enough to combine. Do not overwork.
♦ Spread on a sheet pan lined with buttered wax paper, about ½-inch thick.
♦ Bake cake in 375° oven for 15 minutes until cake is springy to touch.
♦ Cool at room temperature.
♦ Cover with plastic wrap and cool for 2 hours.

Chocolate Filling

11 ounces semi-sweet chocolate	2 egg whites room temperature
4 ounces unsweetened chocolate	pinch cream of tarter
3½ cups heavy cream	3 tablespoons grand marnier liquer

♦ Melt chocolate over simmering water.
♦ Let rest on table for 10 minutes.
♦ Beat egg whites with cream of tarter.
♦ Fold into chocolate and add grand marnier.
♦ Whip cream until stiff and fold into above mixture.
♦ Chill in refrigerator for at least ½ hour.
♦ Line a loaf pan wtih wax paper bottom and sides.
♦ Cover with chocolate cake, cut a long piece first to fit the bottom of the loaf pan. Cut pieces to stand up in the sides.
♦ Fill with chocolate filling to the top edge of the cake.
♦ Cover the entire length with the remaining cake.
♦ Chill for two hours. Remove from pan, discard wax paper and slice into about 1-inch pieces.
♦ Serve with a plain vanilla sauce.

Robert's of Charleston

The Colony House
Privateer Low Country Crabcakes

Average
May Prepare Ahead

Yields: 8 cakes
Pan Fry: 3 to 5 minutes

1	pound jumbo lump blue crabmeat	1	tablespoon red pepper, diced
8	slices white bread, crusts removed and diced	1	tablespoon parsley, chopped
		½	teaspoon tarragon, chopped
1	egg	¼	teaspoon dry mustard
2	tablespoons green pepper, diced		pinch ground mace
			mayonnaise – enough to bind

♦ In a large ceramic or stainless steel bowl, combine all ingredients.
♦ Do not overmix so the crabmeat doesn't break up.
♦ Let sit in refrigerator for at least 30 minutes to give the bread time to absorb any moisture and bind effectively.
♦ Prepare crabcakes and panfry in butter until an even brown color on both sides.
♦ May be served with sauce remoulade.

* Buy jumbo lump crab if possible, as this grade has little or no shell.

The Colony House & The Wine Cellar
Oysters And Shrimp 'Colony House'

Average
May Prepare Ahead

Serves: 4
Cook: 15 to 20 minutes

2	ounces butter	4	ounces mushrooms, sliced
6-8	ounces shrimp, small, peeled and deveined	1	cup fish stock
2	ounces scallions, diced	8	oysters, shucked

Seasoning:

½ teaspoon parsley, chopped
¼ teaspoon garlic, chopped
salt and pepper to taste

1/10 teaspoon each of black pepper, white pepper, basil leaves, thyme leaves and cayenne pepper

♦ Melt butter in large skillet.
♦ Sauté shrimp, scallions, mushrooms.
♦ Add seasonings and cook for 5 minutes until shrimp turn pink.
♦ Add fish stock and let simmer for an additional 5 minutes.
♦ Add oysters and taste for seasoning.
♦ Serve over a bed of hot rice.

* After adding oysters, do not let simmer long as oysters tend to shrink.

Pingle Reddy, Executive Chef

327

The Cotton Exchange
Stuffed Baby Salmon

Average
Partial Prepare Ahead

Serves: 4 to 6
Bake: 10 minutes at 450°

Grouper Mushroom "Farci" Stuffing

½	pound grouper/any leftover fish	1	egg
½	cup canned mushrooms	1	cup bread crumbs
1	cup heavy whipping cream	1	tablespoon of fish stock
½	cup shallots	1	teaspoon Worcestershire sauce

♦ Blend all ingredients in a blender or food processer to a firm "doughy" consistency.

4-6 baby salmon

♦ Butterfly (lay open) the salmon and squeeze stuffing through a pastry bag on one side of fish using an "S-like" motion.
♦ Fold other side back over stuffing.
♦ Lay fish in a shallow baking dish/poaching pan with 1 cup dry white wine and a "bouquet garni" (½ onion with 2 bay leaves and 2 cloves stuck to it).
♦ Bake at 450° for 10 minutes.
♦ Trim dorsal fin and tail.
♦ Serve with wine sauce.

White Wine Sauce

½	gallon milk		pinch of white pepper
1	cup fish stock		salt to taste
1	cup roux (flour and butter browned in a pan)	1	tablespoon aromat seafood seasoning
1	teaspoon Old Bay Seasoning	2	cups of white wine

♦ Simmer all ingredients over medium heat for 20-25 minutes whisking frequently until sauce thickens to consistency of heavy cream.
♦ Spoon sauce over fish and sprinkle with parsley.
♦ Serve with rice or boiled potatoes.

The Cotton Exchange

Ferante's
Roasted Grouper

Easy
Serve Immediately

Serves: 6 to 8
Bake: 30 minutes at 375°

1 large whole fish (about 4 pounds) (striped bass, spotted grouper or gray mullet)	salt to taste
	freshly ground pepper, to taste
3 cloves garlic	5 tablespoons olive oil
1 tablespoon rosemary leaves	juice of one lemon
	lemon wedges

♦ Clean fish very well, removing the scales but not the head.
♦ Cut off the lower half of the tail.
♦ Make 2 or 3 short slits in the skin of the fish.
♦ Cut the garlic cloves into quarters and put inside each slit and inside the fish's cavity along with rosemary, salt and pepper.
♦ Preheat oven to 375°.
♦ Place 4 tablespoons of olive oil in roasting pan.
♦ Place fish on oil and sprinkle remaining oil and a little salt on the fish.
♦ Bake for 30 minutes.
♦ Remove from oven and sprinkle with lemon juice.
♦ Garnish with lemon wedges.

* A roasted fish retains its full flavor if left whole, with head and tail on.

Shahram Aghapour, Executive Chef

Garibaldi's
Sword Fish Madagascar

Average
Serve Immediately

Serves: 2
Bake: 5 to 8 minutes at 450°

3 tablespoons butter, melted	parsley, to taste
½ cup plain flour	1 tablespoon green peppercorn, crushed
1 pound sword fish, two slices	
1 clove garlic, finely chopped	½ teaspoon salt
4 tablespoons white wine	paprika, to taste
juice from one lemon	

♦ Preheat oven to 450°.
♦ Lightly flour two pieces of sword fish.
♦ Place in skillet with melted butter and brown on one side for two minutes.
♦ Turn and add garlic to skillet.
♦ When garlic turns light brown, add white wine, lemon juice, parsley, peppercorn, salt and sprinkle of paprika.
♦ Bake in 450° oven for 5-8 minutes.

Garibaldi's

Island House at Wild Dunes
King Mackerel Marinated In Mustard, Basil And Citrus

Easy
Serve Immediately

Serves: 4
Grill or Broil

4   7-ounce king mackerel fillets   salt

Marinade:

3   oranges, juiced
2   lemons, juiced
1   cup olive oil
3   tablespoons dijon mustard

1   cup diced onion
1   teaspoon minced garlic
2   cups fresh basil, chopped
¼   teaspoon cayenne

- Combine all ingredients of marinade and marinate fish at least 2 hours.
- Grill over hot coal or broil, basting frequently. Do not overcook.
- Garnish with hot marinade and finely chopped basil.

Island House at Wild Dunes

Francis Marion Hotel
Chicken Mandarine

Average
Serve Immediately

Serves: 4
Cook: 25 to 30 minutes

3   pounds chicken parts
¼   cup oil
¼   cup orange liqueur
1   cup orange juice concentrate
1   small can mandarin oranges
     (save a few for garnish)

1   cup sour cream
¼   cup slivered almonds (save a few
     for garnish)

- In large skillet, brown chicken in oil.
- Drain fat.
- Deglaze skillet with orange liqueur.
- Add orange juice concentrate and mandarin oranges.
- Cook until hot.
- Mix in sour cream.
- Return chicken and cook until done.
- Add almonds.
- Put portions on serving dish - garnish with oranges and almonds.

Francis Marion Hotel

Skoogie's
Skoogie's Homemade Chili

Average
May Prepare Ahead

Yields: 2 quarts
Cook: 1½ hours

2   jumbo onions ground into pulp with juice
5   pounds very lean ground beef
1   No. 10 whole, peeled plum tomatoes with juice
4   ounces simple syrup (bar syrup)

2   tablespoons garlic powder
6   ounces dark chili powder
2   tablespoons black pepper
½   cup salt
2   quarts soft boiled pinto beans (dried)

♦ Simmer ground onions.
♦ Add beef and stir till done.
♦ Add the other ingredients and cook for 1½ hours.
♦ Serve with slice of Swiss cheese and onions.

Mr. Jerry Swhwimmer
Skoogies

Reuben's Delicatessen
Chicken Soup

Average
May Prepare Ahead

Yields: 5 gallons
Cook: 45 to 60 minutes

    the meat of 5 chickens, cooked
2   onions, chopped
3   pounds mushrooms, sliced
4-5 pounds carrots, peeled and sliced
2   stalks celery, cut into bite size pieces
6   potatoes, peeled and sliced into bite size pieces

1   pound green beans, snapped into small pieces
3-4 zucchini, sliced
3-4 yellow squash, sliced
1   head cabbage, chopped
6-8 ounces Legout special chicken base

♦ Put water in soup pot and add vegetables.
♦ Boil until vegetables are done.
♦ Add chicken and cook until warmed through.

Judy Kaplan, Chef
Reuben's Delicatessen

Café Picollo
Quailo Picollo

Complicated
May Prepare Ahead

Serves: 4
Broil: 20 to 30 minutes

4 small, boned quail, split in half
3 tablespoons butter, melted
1 tablespoon bourbon
¾ cup molasses
1 tablespoon white pepper
1 tablespoon ginger
1 egg yolk
  pinch of salt
4 tablespoons sugar
8 squares French bread, cut 2 x 2
  sautéed in garlic and butter (the
  croutons)

8 tarts of puff pastry (vol-au-vent
  by Pepperidge Farm - OK),
  baked according to package
  directions
16 baby carrots, steamed until
  tender, green caps left on to
  1 inch in length - Keep warm

♦ Broil quail for 15 minutes, and baste with mixture of butter and bourbon the first 5 minutes.
♦ Baste quail until done with mixture of heated molasses, white pepper, ginger, egg yolk, salt and sugar.
♦ Place cooked crouton in bottom of baked vol-au-vent.
♦ Place ½ of quail in pastry shell and arrange two baby carrots to peek out of pastry shell.
♦ Paint quail with remainder of molasses baste and run a pepper mill with black pepper corns over the quail.

Café Picollo - Joanne Yeager

The Common Ground
Hot Crab

Easy
Partial Prepare Ahead

Serves: 6
Bake: 3 to 5 minutes at 350°

1 pound crabmeat
6 tablespoons mayonnaise
1 teaspoon dijon mustard
4 dashes Worcestershire sauce
2 dashes tabasco

¼ teaspoon granulated garlic
6 English muffins, split and
  lightly toasted
12 slices cheddar cheese
12 slices ripe tomato

♦ Mix first 6 ingredients together.
♦ Spread over English muffin halves.
♦ Top with tomato slices and cheese slices.
♦ Bake 350° until cheese melts and is bubbly.

The Common Ground

Café Picollo
Chicken Breasts Stuffed With Pineapple Gourmandise Cheese And Pecans

Easy
Partial Prepare Ahead

Serves: 6
Bake: 15 minutes at 350°

6   chicken breasts, boned
12 tablespoons pineapple
    gourmandise cheese or kirsch
    gourmandise

6   tablespoons pecan, ground
    butter
    opal basil, chopped (may
    substitute basil)

- Pound breasts with flat end of cleaver or mallet. (Breasts should be approximately the size of a bread plate.)
- Place 2 tablespoons pineapple gourmandise on center of each breast.
- Sprinkle ground pecans on top of cheese.
- Tuck in ends of meat and roll up. Fasten with a toothpick.
- Sauté in butter with basil. Cook until lightly colored.
- Transfer to baking pan and bake 15 minutes or less at 350°.
- Top with basil and drizzle with more butter.
- Serve with yellow wax beans and summer salad.

Café Picollo

Shem Creek Bar and Grill
Grilled Shrimp And Sausage

Easy
May Prepare Ahead

Serves: 4
Cook: until shrimp are pink

1   pound peeled shrimp
1   pound smoked sausage, cut in
    ½ inch slices

1   stick margarine, melted
1   lemon, juiced

Spice Mix:

1   teaspoon black pepper
1   teaspoon red pepper
1   teaspoon oregano

1   teaspoon paprika
1   teaspoon salt
1   teaspoon granulated garlic

- Combine all ingredients in spice mix.
- Heat in large cast iron skillet until very hot.
- Add melted margarine, sausage and shrimp.
- Sprinkle with spice mix and lemon juice.
- Cook until shrimp are just pink.

Shem Creek Bar and Grill

82 Queen
Oysters Elizabeth

Average
May Prepare Ahead

Yields: 12 oysters on the half shell
Bake: 5 to 7 minutes at 350°

12 oysters on the half shell

Mix:

1 cup cooked chopped spinach (fresh)
½ cup white crabmeat
¼ cup sautéed onion, finely chopped
¼ cup cracker meal

3 teaspoons mayonnaise
½ teaspoon dry mustard
1 teaspoon Worcestershire
1 teaspoon lemon juice
salt and pepper to taste
dash tabasco

- Blanch spinach in boiling water for 10 seconds.
- Drain and chop.
- Add all other ingredients.
- Toss gently.
- Stuff oysters.
- Top with melted butter.
- Cook in hot oven 5-7 minutes.

* Optional: Top with white wine sauce or bacon.

82 Queen Restaurant

Jilich's
Mushroom Consommé

Easy
May Prepare Ahead

Serves: 6
Cook: 20 minutes

1 pound mushrooms, sliced thin
2 large shallots, diced
1 piece 1x2 inches ginger, sliced and peeled
6 cups chicken stock

2 tablespoons (approx.) soy sauce
salt
1 lime, juiced
1 tablespoon cilantro (coriander leaves), chopped

- Reserve ⅓ mushrooms.
- Combine the rest in food processor with shallots, ginger and 2 cups of stock.
- Process until finely chopped.
- Add mixture to remaining stock and simmer 20 minutes.
- Strain through cheesecloth.
- Add to both remaining mushrooms.
- Add lime juice, soy sauce, and cilantro to taste.
- Garnish with springs of cilantro and lime slice.

Jilich's

82 Queen
Strawberry Banana Pie

Easy
May Prepare Ahead

Yields: 2 pies
Bake: 10 minutes at 325°

Crust

2⅓ cups graham cracker crumbs
½ cup sugar

1⅓ sticks butter, melted

Filling

1   8-ounce package cream cheese
⅔ box powdered sugar
2   cups chopped walnuts

2   medium size bananas, sliced
1   quart strawberries, sliced
1   8-ounce container Cool Whip

♦ To prepare crust, mix crumbs, sugar, and butter together and press in 2 deep dish 9-inch pie pans.
♦ Bake at 325° for 10 minutes.
♦ For filling, mix with beater cream cheese and powdered sugar. Divide between the 2 crusts evenly and spread along bottom.
♦ Sprinkle on top of the cream cheese layer a layer of chopped walnuts.
♦ Next layer of sliced bananas and then a layer of sliced strawberries.
♦ Divide Cool Whip and spread evenly over the pies.
♦ Top with another layer of chopped walnuts.

82 Queen

Jilich's
Shrimp Awendaw

Average
Serve Immediately

Serves: 2
Sauté: 1½ minutes
Cook: 3 to 5 minutes

2   tablespoons olive oil
12 large shrimp, peeled
2   tablespoons flour
3   slices salt cured country ham
2   shallots, chopped fine

½   teaspoon dried red chili
2   kiwi fruits, peeled and chopped
½   cup dry white wine
    salt to taste

♦ Heat oil.
♦ Toss shrimp in flour and sauté for 30 seconds.
♦ Add ham, shallots, and chili.
♦ Sauté another 30 seconds.
♦ Add kiwi fruit and sauté another 30 seconds.
♦ Add wine and reduce to half.
♦ Season to taste.

Jilich's

Joe's Seafood Emporium
Grouper Florentine

Average　　　　　　　　　　　　　　**Serves:** 2
Partial Prepare Ahead

6 ounces grouper, cut in ¾-inch cubes	½ ounce clarified butter
5 ounces Florentine sauce	1 sprig parsley
¾ ounce Parmesan cheese, grated	1 lemon wedge

- ◆ Place grouper chunks in shell casserole.
- ◆ Top with Florentine sauce.
- ◆ Just before cooking, top with cheese and drizzle with clarified butter.
- ◆ Cook in hot oven for 15 minutes or until grouper is flaky.
- ◆ Garnish with parsley and lemon wedge.

Florentine Sauce

½ cup milk	½ cup cooked spinach, chopped
1 ounce roux (equal amounts of melted butter and flour)	season with granulated garlic, salt and pepper

- ◆ In a saucepan, bring milk to scalding.
- ◆ Stir in roux with wire whisk and reduce heat to simmer and cook 3-5 minutes, stirring frequently.
- ◆ Remove from heat and add spinach and season.

Joe's Pilot House
Shrimp Burger

Average　　　　　　　　　　　　　　**Serves:** 1
Serve Immediately　　　　　　　　　**Grill:** 2 to 3 minutes per side

3 ounces shrimp, peeled and deveined	1 onion roll
1½ ounces hush puppy mix	1 ounce remoulade sauce
1 ounce clarified butter	1 lemon wedge

Remoulade Sauce:

½ cup Hellmann's mayonnaise	½ teaspoon Worcestershire sauce
1 teaspoon sweet green relish	½ teaspoon lemon juice
2 teaspoons chopped capers	salt and pepper for season
1 teaspoon onions, chopped fine	

- ◆ Mix shrimp and hush puppy mix together.
- ◆ Butter grill and place shrimp mixture on grill in a four inch circle.
- ◆ Cook approximately 2-3 minutes on each side or until shrimp is cooked.
- ◆ Split and butter onion roll, grill until toasted.
- ◆ Serve open face and garnish with remoulade sauce and lemon wedge.

Joe's Pilot House

Papillon
Fettucini With Shrimp And Bechamel Sauce

Average
Partial Prepare Ahead

Serves: 4
Cook: 30 minutes

1 pound peeled and deveined medium shrimp	¼ pound fresh mushrooms, sliced thin
1 pound fettucini	1 recipe of Bechamel sauce

- Prepare Bechamel sauce and bring to a simmer.
- Add shrimp and mushrooms to sauce.
- Simmer, uncovered for 15 minutes.
- Season to taste.
- Cook fettucini al dente, drain, and place in hot bowl.
- Pour ½ sauce over fettucini.
- Toss well with wooden forks.
- Serve with remaining sauce spooned atop.

Bechamel Sauce:

6 tablespoons butter	black pepper
4 tablespoons flour	2½ cups milk, warmed
1 teaspoon salt	pinch of grated nutmeg

- In double boiler, melt butter.
- Add flour and stir.
- Sprinkle in salt and pepper.
- When mixture is golden and velvety, slowly stir in milk.
- Stir constantly for 15 minutes, until sauce is thickened and smooth.
- Taste for flavour.
- Stir in nutmeg.

Makes 2½ cups sauce.

Mr. Ali Rahanmoon, Executive Chef
Papillon

Supper At Seven

Guilds Inn Chicken Breast Wellington With Bacon Horseradish Sauce

Complicated
May Prepare Ahead

Serves: 4
Bake: 25 to 30 minutes at 400°

4	4-5 ounce chicken breasts
4	1-ounce slices of preferred paté
1	sheet frozen puff pastries
4	large mushrooms, washed and sliced
1	green onion, washed and chopped

½	ounce butter
1	egg, beaten with ½ teaspoon water
1	tablespoon dried thyme
	salt and white pepper

- Lightly pound chicken breast with a mallot to flatten.
- Briefly sauté mushrooms and onions in butter with thyme, salt, and pepper.
- Cool.
- Lay out chicken breasts and season.
- Cut a slice of paté and place in chicken wtih a portion of mushroom and green onion mixture.
- Roll the breast up tucking in the ends to hold the filling.
- Lay out the puff pastry and cut a square 1-inch wider than the chicken.
- Beat the egg and water and brush the edges of the pastry lightly.
- Fold in opposite corners of pastry and press together well.
- Turn pastry over and place on parchment paper on a sheet pan.
- Egg wash the entire surface.
- Preheat oven to 400° and bake 5 minutes.
- Lower heat to 350° and bake 20-25 minutes until pastry is golden brown.

Sauce

3	slices diced bacon
1	shallot, minced
2	tablespoons fresh horseradish root or 1 tablespoon prepared horseradish

1	tablespoon white vinegar
1	tablespoon dijon mustard
1	pint whipping cream
1	tablespoon unsalted butter
	salt and pepper to taste

- Fry bacon in a heavy bottomed saucepan until brown.
- Add shallot and sauté until tender.
- Add horseradish, vinegar and mustard and blend.
- Add the whipping cream and simmer until thick and shiny.
- Blend in butter off the heat and check seasoning.
- To serve: Ladle a pool of sauce onto plate and place a chicken breast on sauce.

The Guilds Inn

Supper At Seven
Honey Pecan Dressing
"Wonderful with Spinach Salad"

Average
May Prepare Ahead

Serves: 4
Cook: to a simmer
Cool: 1 hour

1 cup pecans, chopped	1 cup red wine vinegar
2 cups salad oil	1 tablespoon sesame seeds
12 ounces honey	spinach – 1 bag for 4 people

- Heat pecans and oil on stove to a simmer and cut heat off completely.
- Allow to cool to room temperature for 1 hour and blend in honey and red wine vinegar.
- As the honey melts, it will start to thicken the dressing and blend together with the oil.
- Toast sesame seeds and set aside to cool.
- Wash and pick stems from spinach.
- Shake off excess moisture and toss with sesame seeds and enough dressing to coat leaves.   *The Guilds Inn*

Supper at Seven
Cream Of Mushroom, Onion And Garlic Soup

Average
May Prepare Ahead

Serves: 8 to 10
Cook: 20 to 25 minutes

1 large yellow onion, diced	$\frac{1}{2}$ teaspoon thyme
$1\frac{1}{2}$ pounds mushrooms, thoroughly washed, chopped	1 bay leaf
	$\frac{1}{2}$ teaspoon chicken base or bouillon cube
3 cloves garlic, chopped	
4 ounces flour	1 pint heavy cream or half and half
2 tablespoons white wine	salt and pepper to taste
1 pint chicken stock	sliced green onions for garnish
1 pint milk	$\frac{1}{4}$ pound butter

- Melt 1 ounce butter in a pot.
- Sauté onion in butter until translucent.
- Add garlic and sauté briefly.
- Add one pound of the mushrooms and sauté.
- Melt remainder of butter and blend flour in to make a roux; cook 5 minutes.
- Add white wine to mushrooms and stir in.
- Add chicken stock, milk, thyme, bay leaf and chicken base.
- Heat to a simmer and blend in roux and simmer again for 15 minutes.
- Add remaining mushrooms to soup.
- Remove from heat and add cream.
- Adjust seasoning, stir thoroughly and garnish with green onions.

Guilds Inn, Supper at Seven - Mount Pleasant, S.C.

Lodge Alley Inn
Lobster Souffle With Americaine Sauce

Complicated
Prepare Ahead

Serves: 4
Bake: 10 tp 15 minutes at 450°

4	ounces pureéd lobster meat	4	tablespoons butter, melted
1	pound puff paste	½	cup fine bread crumbs
2	ounces liquid sherry		whites of 4 eggs
1	tablespoon salt		pinch of cream of tarter
	dash cayenne pepper	1	cup Americaine sauce

- Preheat oven to 450°.
- Combine the lobster pureé, puff paste, sherry, salt and cayenne pepper.
- Mix until smooth.
- In 4 8-ounce souffle cups, put the melted butter and coat the whole interior.
- Put in the bread crumbs and coat well.
- Whip the egg whites in a bowl with the cream of tartar until they hold soft peaks.
- Fold in the lobster mixture and combine well, but do not beat.
- Pour into souffle cups and place in oven.
- Bake for 10-15 minutes and serve with Americaine sauce.

Puff Paste

1	cup water	¼	pound all-purpose flour
¼	pound butter	7	ounces whole eggs

- Bring the water and butter to a boil.
- Sprinkle in the flour and mix well with a wooden spoon.
- Mix until smooth over a low flame.
- Cool 5 minutes.
- Add eggs, one at a time, allow one minute in between each, stirring constantly.
- When all eggs have been added, mix for 5 more minutes.

Américaine Sauce

the shells of one lobster (cut
into small pieces)
5 tablespoons butter
½ cup each; carrots, leeks, celery
and onion, diced
½ teaspoon garlic, chopped
6 tablespoons flour
1 cup brandy

2 cups white wine
3 tablespoons tomato paste
1 quart fish stock
1 teaspoon thyme
1 bay leaf
½ tablespoon tarragon
salt and pepper to taste

- In a sauce pan, sauté the shells in butter until the butter turns a reddish-brown.
- Add the vegetables and sauté until soft.
- Add the garlic and sauté 1 more minute.
- Stir in the flour.
- Place all other ingredients into the shells and vegetables and simmer for 1 hour.
- Strain through a fine sieve.
- Season with salt and pepper and reserve.

Lodge Alley Inn

Lodge Alley Inn
Veal With Morels

Average
Serve Immediately

Serves: 4
Sauté: 3 to 4 minutes
Cook: 7 to 10 minutes

8 2-ounce slices of veal
salt and white pepper, to taste
flour
4 tablespoons butter

1 cup madeira
2 cups heavy cream
½ cup morels (soaked in water
to cover)

- Pound the veal out until very thin.
- Season with salt and pepper.
- Lightly coat with flour and sauté in butter.
- Put onto a serving platter.
- Add madeira to the pan and reduce to one half.
- Add the cream and water from morels.
- Reduce until the consistency is thick and add the morels.
- Season with salt and pepper to taste.
- Pour the sauce over the veal slices.

Perdita's
Baked Crabmeat Remick

Average
May Prepare Ahead
Freezes Well

Serves: 6
Broil: 3 to 4 minutes

3	pounds white crabmeat	1	teaspoon tarragon vinegar
6	slices bacon, cooked and crumbled	1	teaspoon dry mustard
		½	teaspoon paprika
1¾	cups mayonnaise	¼	teaspoon celery salt
½	cup chili sauce	¼	teaspoon tabasco (or to taste)

♦ Drain crabmeat and remove boney tissue.
♦ Place in individual baking dishes and sprinkle with bacon. Heat in moderate oven (350°) while preparing sauce.
♦ Blend remaining ingredients in small bowl.
♦ Spoon over hot crabmeat and bacon.
♦ Broil close to flame until hot and bubbly (3-4 minutes).

* If freezing, bake at 350° until thawed, then brown under broiler.

Perdita's
Saint Honoré Pie

Average
May Prepare Ahead

Serves: 6 to 8
Chill: 3 to 4 hours

1	envelope gelatin	1	teaspoon vanilla
1½	cups milk, divided	2	tablespoons brandy or rum
3	eggs, divided	⅛	teaspoon salt
⅓	cup raisins, chopped	⅓	cup sugar
2	tablespoons almonds, ground	1	pie shell, baked
1	cup macaroon crumbs	1	cup strawberries, sliced
½	cup marrous (chestnuts) and syrup, chopped fine	2	cups whipped cream pecan halves

♦ Soften gelatin in ¼ cup milk.
♦ Scald remaining milk in a double boiler.
♦ Beat egg yolks and add to scalded milk, stirring constantly.
♦ Cook until mixture coats wooden spoon.
♦ Add raisins, almonds, macaroon crumbs, marrous and syrup, vanilla, brandy, and salt to gelatin mixture.
♦ Chill until cream mixture begins to set.
♦ Beat egg whites with sugar until stiff and fold into mixture.
♦ Pour into baked pie shell and chill until firm.
♦ Garnish with a layer of sliced strawberries and a layer of whipped cream.
♦ Top with pecan halves.

Mrs. G. W. Bennett

East Bay Trading Company
Paëlla

Average

Serves: 4
Bake: 10 minutes at 450°

½ tablespoon butter
½ tablespoon oil
6 oz. chicken breast, quartered
1 precooked mild Italian sausage, quartered
1 white fish fillet (preferably snapper), quartered

4 raw scallops
4 raw shrimp, peeled and deveined
4 medium clams in shell
4 mussels in shell
1 cup clam juice
1 box rice pilaf, prepared

♦ In a large skillet, melt butter and oil - do not brown.
♦ Add next 7 ingredients.
♦ Sauté mixture over medium heat - 5 minutes.
♦ Cover with clam juice.
♦ Place pan in 450° oven.
♦ Cook 10 minutes or until chicken and fish are thoroughly cooked.
♦ Place cooked rice pilaf in bottom of casserole dish.
♦ Pour paëlla mixture over rice.

* May add: precooked broccoli, whole mushroom caps or cherry tomatoes.

Rice Pilaf With Saffron:

½ tablespoon butter
½ cup rice
1 cup chicken stock

1 tablespoon onion
½ teaspoon saffron

♦ Bring ingredients to a boil.
♦ Cover and simmer until rice is tender and liquid is reduced.

East Bay Trading Company

343

The Baker's Cafe
Almond Scones (or English Tea Biscuits)

Average
May Prepare Ahead

Yields: 12
Bake: 15 minutes at 450°

1¾ cups sifted all-purpose flour
2¼ teaspoons double acting baking powder

1-2 tablespoons sugar
½ teaspoon salt
1 cup sliced, blanched almonds

- Combine these ingredients in bowl and mix.
- Work ¼ cup solid butter until blended within flour.

In Separate Bowl:

2 eggs
⅓ cup cream

2 tablespoons almond extract

- Make a pocket in flour mixture and pour liquid ingredients in middle.
- With a few swift strokes mix the two until combined. (Do not work dough too much.)
- Place on a floured surface and pat until ¾-inch thick.
- Cut with knife or cookie cutter.
- Brush with a little cream.
- Sprinkle with a little sugar.
- Bake at 450° for approximately 15 minutes.

The Upper Crust
Sour Cream Apple Pie

Average
May Prepare Ahead

Yields: 1 pie
Bake: 45 minutes at 400°

Pie

1 cup sour cream
½ cup plain flour
1 egg
2 teaspoons vanilla
½ teaspoon salt

1 cup sugar
8 granny smith apples, peeled, cored, and sliced
1 deep dish pie shell, pre-baked

Topping

1½ cups walnut pieces
⅓ cup plain flour
½ cup brown sugar

½ cup granulated sugar
1 tablespoon cinnamon
½ cup butter pieces, chopped

- Blend all ingredients, except apples, until smooth.
- Add apples and pour into pie shell.
- Bake for 45 minutes at 400° or until apples are tender.
- Mix all ingredients in the topping.
- Evenly top the pie with topping and continue baking for 15 minutes.

The Mills House Hotel
Shrimp And Chicken Edisto

Average
May Prepare Ahead

Serves: 8 to 10
Cook: per instructions

½   stick butter, melted
2   cups mushrooms, sliced
2   cups onions, diced
1½ pounds shrimp, peeled and deveined
1½ pounds chicken, boneless and skinned

1   tablespoon garlic
    salt and pepper to taste
½   cup white wine
1   cup brown sauce

- Sauté onions and mushrooms, set aside.
- Sauté chicken until half done.
- Add shrimp.
- When both are nearly cooked, add onions and mushrooms.
- Season with garlic, salt and pepper and wine.
- Add brown sauce and simmer for flavors to blend.
- Serve at once on cooked white to brown rice.

Brown Sauce (2 qts.):

¾   cup margarine
¼   cup bacon drippings
1   cup celery, chopped

1   cup onion, chopped
½   cup carrots, chopped
1¼ cup flour

- Sauté vegetables in margarine and bacon drippings for 10 minutes.
- Stir in flour until smooth.
- Cook on medium heat until flour browns - about 10 minutes.

Merv Minnich, Executive Chef
The Mills House Hotel

PLACES TO VISIT

MENUS

MENUS

Luncheons

Sherry Cooler...page 37
Cheese Bennes...page 20
Crab Corners...page 31
Curried Chicken or Shrimp...page 122
Cream Cheese Biscuits...page 69
Edisto Island Mud Pie...page 311

Cream of Broccoli Soup...page 46
Chicken Pita Sandwiches...page 53
Louise's Spinach Sandwiches...page 50
Pink Cranberry Freeze...page 91

Spiced Tea...page 37
Fabulous Chicken Salad...page 100
Orange Muffins...page 85
Chocolate Chip Tortoni...page 275

Pasta Primavera...page 252
Ambrosia Salad...page 94
Refrigerator Muffins...page 86
Brownies...page 297
Oatmeal Lace Cookies...page 295

Light Suppers

Pasta Alla Carbonara...page 249
Watercress and Orange Salad...page 92
Orange Bread...page 72
Mama's Ice Box Cookies...page 296

Cheese and White Wine Casserole...page 56
Green Bean and Mushroom Salad...page 107
or Spinach Salad...page 97
Bread Lovers Loaves...page 61
Grape Sundae...page 269

Pank's Cold Avocado Soup...page 49
Chicken Salad...page 101
English Muffin Bread I...page 64
Lime Ice...page 302

Garlic Broiled Shrimp...page 205
Baked Hominy...page 260
Tomato Aspic...page 102
Blueberry Cream Pie...page 305

Giga's Oysters, Sausage and Rice...page 197
Glazed Apples...page 246
Kiss Pie...page 310

Summer Suppers

Ham Delights on Sandwich Size Rolls...page 52
New Potato Salad...page 105
Curried Tomatoes...page 241
Congealed Asparagus Salad...page 103
Peach Crisp...page 264

Mustard Sauce...page 170
Chickaby Ham...page 151
Shrimp Pilau...page 208
Easy Eggplant...page 229
Grandmother's Spiced Beets...page 220
Meringue Ice Cream Torte...page 274

Brisket of Beef...page 140
Pasta Salad with Creamy Pesto Dressing...page 255
Green Bean and Mushroom Salad...page 107
Blueberry Muffins...page 84
Frozen Fruit Ice...page 302

Seafood Casserole...page 175
Tomato Aspic...page 102
Stir Fried Rice with Pea Pods...page 258
Eggplant and Zuccchini Oriental...page 227
Strawberry Pie...page 307

Summer Suppers, continued

Feta-Tomato Sauce with Shrimp
(Over Noodles)...page 206
Mushroom Casserole...page 229
P.A.'s Salad...page 96
Ice Box Rolls...page 80
Blender Lemon Pie....page 309

Dinners

Cold Fresh Tomato Soup...page 48
Pork Loin...page 150
Cheese Pudding *Charleston Receipts*
Missy's Green Beans...page 219
Broccoli Salad Supreme...page 104
Coffee Velvet Pie...page 313
Granny's Pear Chutney...page 317

Shrimp in Grapefruit with Sauce...page 99
Leg of Lamb...page 155
Rice *Charleston Receipts*
Sauteed Zucchini and Tomatoes...page 243
Biscuits Supreme...page 70
Lucy's Curried Fruit Bake...page 246
Lemon Mousse "Eggs" with Raspberry Sauce...page 262

Dinners, continued

Celestial Shrimp Over Rice...page 211
Eggplant and Zucchini Oriental...page 227
Tossed Garden Salad with Blue Cheese Dressing...page 110
Ladson Street Rolls...page 80
Ice Cream Cake...page 273

Flounder Fillets in Shrimp Sauce...page 190
Mediterranean Garden Medley...page 245
Vidalia Onion-Bacon Quiche...page 56
Blender Lemon Pie...page 309

Deviled Crab Supreme...page 182
Vegetable Ragout...page 244
Tomato Topped Cheese Pudding...page 55
Strawberries with Easy Almond Amaretto Cream...page 304

Congealed Asparagus Salad...page 103
Chicken Jubilee...page 132
Tomato Okra Pilau *Charleston Receipts*
Squash Casserole...page 240
Ice Box Rolls...page 80
Fly Dessert...page 264

Dinners, continued

Stuffed Shrimp...page 26
Duck Whoopee...page 163
Rice Casserole...page 258
Sweet and Sour Beans...page 219
Daiquiri Pie...page 312
Planters Duck Sauce...page 172

Fresh Stuffed Mushrooms...page 19
Pilot Duck Breasts...page 162
or Roast Wild Duck...page 164
Wild Rice...page 259
Bread Sauce...page 172
Company Carrots...page 223
Baked Vidalia Onions...page 231
Sherried Custard...page 265
Wild Game Sauce...page 172

Roast Beef...page 136
Mushroom Sauce...page 170
Potato Pears...page 234
3 Squash Casserole...page 240
Christina's Greek Beans...page 220
Blue Ribbon Cheese Cake Torte...page 274

Supper Club Fare

Rosie's Beef Burgundy...page 142
Rice Casserole...page 258
Broccoli Salad...page 104
Pat Holman's Buttermilk Whole Wheat Rolls...page 79
Charleston Chocolate Cake...page 283

Rockville Shrimp Pie...page 213
Rice *(Charleston Receipts)*
Green Salad with Nancy's Sweet and
Sour Dressing...page 109
Whispers...page 37

Party Chicken Tetrazzini...page 131
P.A.'s Salad...page 96
Olive Cheese Bread...page 65
My Version of Charleston Rum Pie...page 314

Italian Southern Oven Fried Chicken...page 116
Gratin Potatoes...page 233
Zucchini Tomatoe Vegetable Casserole...page 242
Chocolate Fudge Cake...page 285

Cocktail Party Fare

"HOLIDAY"
My Father's Egg Nog...page 39
Smithfield Ham...page 152
Pickled Oysters...page 22
Raw Vegetables with Vegetable Dip...page 33
Lavington Plantation Venison Pâté...page 7
Minted Nuts...page 291
White Chocolate Cake...page 284
Asparagus Roll-Ups...page 13
Sweet and Sour Mustard...page 171

"BAPTISM OR CONFIRMATION CELEBRATION"
Powerful Punch (for the adults)...page 40
Fruit Punch (for the children)...page 35
Chicken Curry Cheese Pie...page 8
Marinated Tenderloin in Cognac Sauce...page 12
Vinegarette Tomatoes...page 241
Longitude Lane Crab Mold with Caviar...page 30
Cathy's Chess Squares...page 299

Fresh Stuffed Mushrooms...page 19
Raw Vegetables with Embassy Dip...page 34
Pickled "Swimpee"...page 27
Beef Tenderloin or Smoked Turkey...page 135
Crunchy Cheese Sandwiches...page 50

INDEX

A composite view of "The Holy City".

INDEX

INDEX

INDEX

INDEX

364

INDEX

INDEX

INDEX

INDEX

MY FAVORITES

MY FAVORITES

NOTES

NOTES

NOTES

NOTES

NOTES

NOTES

Please send me information on ordering additional copies of **CHARLESTON RECEIPTS**, **CHARLESTON RECEIPTS REPEATS** and **PARTY RECEIPTS**, complete the form below and mail or FAX it to:

The Junior League of Charleston, Inc.
51 Folly Road
Charleston, S.C. 29407
Telephone (803) 763-5284   **Fax (803) 763-1626**

Name

Address

City   State   Zip

Phone (   )

Please send me information on ordering additional copies of **CHARLESTON RECEIPTS**, **CHARLESTON RECEIPTS REPEATS** and **PARTY RECEIPTS**, complete the form below and mail or FAX it to:

The Junior League of Charleston, Inc.
51 Folly Road
Charleston, S.C. 29407
Telephone (803) 763-5284   **Fax (803) 763-1626**

Name

Address

City   State   Zip

Phone (   )

Names and addresses of bookstores and gift shops
in your area would be appreciated:

_____

_____

_____

_____

_____

_____

_____

Names and addresses of bookstores and gift shops
in your area would be appreciated:

_____

_____

_____

_____

_____

_____

_____